OFFA'S DYKE PATH

NATIONAL TRAIL FOLLOWING THE ENGLISH–WELSH BORDER

by Mike Dunn

CICERONE

JUNIPER HOUSE, MURLEY MOSS,
OXENHOLME ROAD, KENDAL, CUMBRIA LA9 7RL
cicerone.co.uk

Second edition 2026
First edition 2016
ISBN: 978 1 78631 279 2
eISBN: 978 1 78765 269 9

Printed in China on responsibly sourced paper on behalf of Latitude Press Ltd.
A catalogue record for this book is available from the British Library.

1:100K Route mapping by Lovell Johns lovelljohns.com

Cicerone's EU representative for GPSR compliance is Easy Access System Europe, Mustamäe tee 50, 10621 Tallinn, Estonia. Email gpsr.requests@easproject.com.

Updates to this Guide

While we strive to ensure that our guidebooks are as up to date and accurate as possible, changes can occur during the lifetime of an edition. Facilities, accommodation, transport and even rights of way can change, so if you find any inaccuracies in this book or have any feedback please let us know by email at updates@cicerone.co.uk. Updates will be published on the Cicerone website (cicerone.co.uk/1279/updates), so please check before planning your trip.

To receive free updates, special offers and GPX files where available, don't forget to **register** your book at the 'My Account' tab at cicerone.co.uk.

Front cover: A view of the ruins of Castell Dinas Brân, above Llangollen, Wales (photo by Nicola, stock.adobe.com)

CONTENTS

Symbols on the route maps

route
alternative route
start point
finish point
direction of route

church/cathedral
crag/outcrop
castle
summit

Route map relief
700m
600m
500m
400m
300m
200m
100m

0 kilometres 1 2
0 miles 1
SCALE: 1:100,000

Contour lines are drawn at 50m intervals and labelled at 100m intervals.

Features on the overview map

County/Unitary boundary
National boundary
Urban area
National Park eg *BANNAU BRYCHEINIOG*
National Landscape eg *SHROPSHIRE HILLS*

Overview map relief
>800m
600m
400m
200m
75m
0m

See 1:25,000 trail map for the key to the 1:25,000 maps

GPX files for all routes can be downloaded free at cicerone.co.uk/1279/GPX.

Acknowledgements

A number of people have provided assistance and encouragement during the preparation of this book, but I would like to thank in particular Keith Ray, for so willingly sharing his expertise on the enigma of Offa's Dyke; Fiona Argyle, National Trail Officer (Powys County Council); Dave McGlade, Chairman of the Offa's Dyke Association; Helen Upson, Offa's Dyke Conservation Project (Shropshire County Council); Lucy Rogers and colleagues at Cicerone; and most of all my wife Chris, who provided transport, took many of the photographs and walked parts of the trail with me.

An obstructed stile on the path near Lower Gwarthlow (Stage 7)

IRISH SEA
LIVERPOOL
F
Prestatyn
N
ANGLESEY
Bangor
Denbigh
Clwydian
Range
Caernarfon
0
20
km
Ruthin
12
Wrexham
0
10 miles
Porthmadog
Llangollen
11
ERYRI
Oswestry
10
WALES
ENGLAND
Shrewsbury
Machynlleth
Welshpool
9
Montgomery
Shropshire
Hills
8
Aberystwyth
7
Clun
Ludlow
Knighton
6
5
Kington
4
Hay-
on-Wye
Hereford
Wye
Valley
BANNAU
BRYCHEINIOG
3
2
Gloucester
Monmouth
Abergavenny
1
SWANSEA
Chepstow
S
Newport
CARDIFF
BRISTOL CHANNEL
BRISTOL

ROUTE SUMMARY TABLE

Stage	Start	Finish	Distance km (miles)	Ascent m (ft)	Time (hr)	Page
1	Sedbury Cliffs	Agincourt Square, Monmouth	29.5 (18.3)	1025 (3360)	7–9	48
2	Agincourt Square, Monmouth	Lancaster Arms guest house, Pandy	26.2 (16.3)	535 (1755)	6–8	60
3	Lancaster Arms guest house, Pandy	Butter Market, Hay-on-Wye	26.5 (16.5)	715 (2345)	7–9	70
4	Butter Market, Hay-on-Wye	Kington Museum	23 (14.5)	680 (2230)	6–8	81
5	Kington Museum	Offa's Dyke Centre, Knighton	22.1 (13.7)	735 (2410)	6–7	91
6	Offa's Dyke Centre, Knighton	Blue Bell Inn, Brompton Bridge	24.3 (15.1)	1000 (3280)	7–9	101
7	Blue Bell Inn, Brompton Bridge	Offa's Dyke Business Park, Buttington	19 (11.8)	425 (1395)	5–6	114
8	Offa's Dyke Business Park, Buttington	Llanymynech canal bridge	17.3 (10.8)	55 (180)	4–5	124
9	Llanymynech canal bridge	Castle Mill, Chirk	22.5 (14)	725 (2380)	6–7	133
10	Castle Mill, Chirk	Llandegla church	25.9 (16.1)	775 (2540)	6–8	143
11	Llandegla church	Bodfari	28.2 (17.5)	990 (3250)	7–9	154
12	Bodfari	Prestatyn seafront	20 (12.4)	620 (2035)	5–6	165
Total			**284.5 (177)**	**8280 (27,160)**		

ROUTE PROFILE

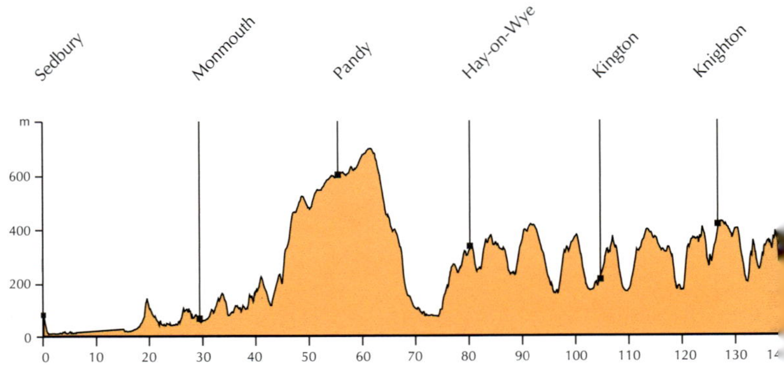

16 DAYS

Sedbury to Bigsweir	Bigsweir to Hendre	Hendre to Llangattock Lingoed	Llangattock Lingoed to Llanthony	Llanthony to Hay-on-Wye	Hay-on-Wye to Gladestry	Gladestry to Discoed	Discoed to Newcastle-on-Clun
4hr 45min	*5hr*	*4hr 30min*	*4hr*	*5hr 30min*	*4hr 45min*	*6hr 45min*	*7hr*
17.8km	*17.5km*	*16.6km*	*14.2km* *	*17.6km* *	*16.8km*	*21.6km* *	*22.8km* *

Knighton to Brompton Bridge *8hr 24.3km*

12 DAYS

Sedbury to Monmouth	Monmouth to Pandy	Pandy to Hay-on-Wye	Hay-on-Wye to Kington	Kington to Knighton
8hr	*7hr*	*8hr*	*7hr*	*6hr 30min*
29.5km	*26.2km*	*26.5km*	*23km*	*22.1km*

8 DAYS

Sedbury to Hendre	Hendre to Llanthony	Llanthony to Kington	Kington to Newcastle-on-Clun
9hr 30min	*8hr 30min*	*12hr 30min*	*10hr 15min*
35.3km	*30.8km* *	*41.8km* *	*33.9km* *

Stages marked with * are calculated to/from off-route locations. Extra distance is not represented in the main route profile above.

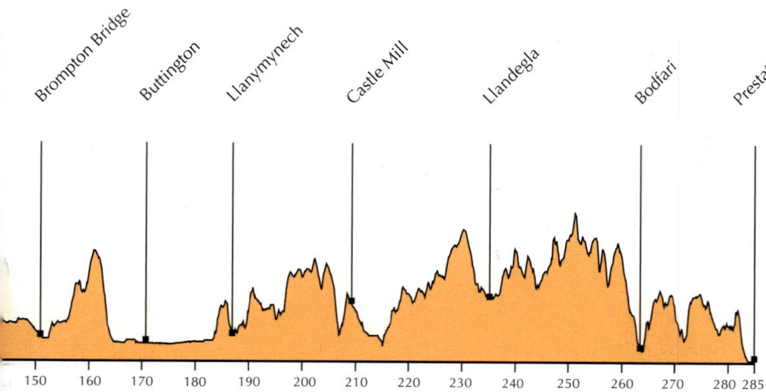

Newcastle-on-Clun to Montgomery *5hr 30min 17.6km* *

Montgomery to Buttington	Buttington to Llanymynech	Llanymynech to Castle Mill	Castle Mill to Llangollen	Llangollen to Llanarmon-yn-Ial	Llanarmon-yn-Ial to Bodfari	Bodfari to Prestatyn
5hr	*4hr 30min*	*6hr 30min*	*4hr*	*6hr 15min*	*7hr*	*5hr 30min*
17.9km	*17.3km*	*22.5km*	*14.8km*	*23.4km*	*24.7km*	*20km*
*			*	*	*	

AVERAGE DAY – 18.9km / 5hr 25min

Brompton Bridge to Buttington	Buttington to Llanymynech	Llanymynech to Castle Mill	Castle Mill to Llandegla	Llandegla to Bodfari	Bodfari to Prestatyn
5hr 30min	*4hr 30min*	*6hr 30min*	*7hr*	*8hr*	*5hr 30min*
19km	*17.3km*	*22.5km*	*25.9km*	*28.2km*	*20km*

AVERAGE DAY – 23.7km / 6hr45min

ewcastle-on-Clun to Pool Quay	Pool Quay to Castle Mill	Castle Mill to Llanferres	Llanferres to Prestatyn
10hr 30min	*10hr*	*10hr 45mins*	*11hr*
35.2km	*36.1km*	*39km*	*39.2km*
*		*	*

AVERAGE DAY – 36.4km / 10hr 20min

STAGE FACILITIES PLANNER

general accommodation · camping · refreshments · shop · ATM · info · train · bus

Stage	Place	Walking time (stage)	Distance (km)	Distance from stage start (km)	Facilities							
1	Sedbury Cliffs											
1	Chepstow	40min	2.3	2.3	accommodation		refreshments	shop	ATM	info	train	bus
1	Tidenham Chase	2hr 40min	10	12.3		camping						
1	*Tintern +15min/1km off main route*				accommodation		refreshments					bus
1	Brockweir	15min	0.7	13.0			refreshments	shop				bus
1	St Briavels Common	35min	2.7	15.7	accommodation							
1	Bigsweir	40min	2.1	17.8	accommodation							bus
1	Redbrook	1hr 40min	5.7	23.5	accommodation		refreshments	shop				bus
1	**Monmouth**	**1hr 30**	**6.0**	**29.5**	accommodation		refreshments	shop	ATM	info		bus
2	Hendre	1hr 35min	5.8	5.8	accommodation	camping						
2	Llanfihangel-Ystern-Llewern	55min	3.7	9.5	accommodation							
2	Great Treadam	1hr 45min	6.4	15.9	accommodation	camping	refreshments					
2	Llanvetherine	55min	3.4	19.3	accommodation	camping						
2	Llangattock Lingoed	50min	3.1	22.4	accommodation		refreshments					
2	**Pandy**	**1hr**	**3.8**	**26.2**	accommodation	camping	refreshments					bus
3	*Llanthony +45min/3km via allternative route*				accommodation	camping	refreshments					
3	*Longtown +45min/3km off main route*				accommodation		refreshments	shop				
3	*Llanveynoe +25min/1.5km off main route*					camping						
3	*Capel-y-Ffin +40min/2.5km off main route*				accommodation	camping						
3	Cusop	7hr 40min	25.4	25.4	accommodation							
3	**Hay-on-Wye**	**20min**	**1.1**	**26.5**	accommodation	camping	refreshments	shop	ATM	info		bus

Stage	Place	Walking time (stage)	Distance (km)	Distance from stage start (km)	Facilities							
	Rhydspence +25min/1.5km off main route				✓		✓					
	Newchurch	3hr 10min	10.9	10.9			✓					
4	Gladestry	1hr 20min	5.9	16.8	✓	✓	✓					
	Lower Hergest +30min/2km off main route				✓							
	Kington	**2hr**	**6.2**	**23**	✓	✓	✓	✓	ATM	✓		✓
	Walton +30min/2km off main route					✓						
	Discoed +25min/1km off main route					✓						
5	*Presteigne +45min/3km off main route*				✓		✓	✓	ATM			✓
	Norton +30min/2km off main route				✓							
	Knighton	**6hr 30min**	**22.1**	**22.1**	✓	✓	✓	✓	ATM	✓	✓	✓
	Llanfair Waterdine +45min/3km off main route				✓							
	Newcastle-on-Clun	3hr 50min	11.8	11.8	✓		✓					
	Clun +75min/5km off main route				✓		✓	✓	ATM			
6	Hergan	1hr 25min	4.2	16.0	✓							
	Bishop's Castle +95min/6.5km off main route				✓		✓	✓	ATM	✓		✓
	Mellington	2hr 05min	6.2	22.2	✓		✓					
	Brompton Bridge	**40min**	**2.1**	**24.3**	✓	✓						✓
	Montgomery +30min/2km off main route				✓		✓	✓	ATM			✓
7	Forden	2hr 35min	8.7	8.7	✓	✓	✓					
	Welshpool +35min/2.5km off main route				✓		✓	✓	ATM	✓	✓	✓
	Buttington	**2hr 55min**	**10.3**	**19.0**	✓	✓	✓					✓
	Pool Quay	55min	3.7	3.7	✓		✓					✓
8	Four Crosses	2hr 25min	9.0	12.7	✓	✓						✓
	Llanymynech	**1hr 10min**	**4.6**	**17.3**	✓		✓	✓	ATM			✓
9	Trefonen	2hr 45min	9.6	9.6	✓		✓	✓				
	Oswestry +60min/4km off main route				✓		✓	✓	ATM			✓

Stage	Place	Walking time (stage)	Distance (km)	Distance from stage start (km)	Facilities							
9	Candy	30min	1.7	11.3	⬆							
	Bronygarth	3hr	10.3	21.6		⛺						
	Pontfadog +60min/4km off main route				⬆		🍴					🔵
	Chirk +45min/3km off main route				⬆		🍴	🧺	ATM		🔴	🔵
	Castle Mill	**15min**	**0.9**	**22.5**								🔵
10	Froncysyllte	1h 45min	6.7	6.7			🍴					🔵
	Trevor	20min	1	7.7			🍴	🧺				🔵
	Wern Isaf	1h 20min	5	12.7		⛺						
	Llangollen +30min/2km off main route				⬆		🍴	🧺	ATM	i		🔵
	Ruthin 14km (bus) off main route				⬆		🍴	🧺	ATM			🔵
	Llandegla	**3hr 35min**	**13.2**	**25.9**		⛺	🍴	🧺				🔵
11	Llanarmon-yn-Ial *+40min/2.5km off main route*				⬆	⛺	🍴					🔵
	Llanbedr Dyffryn Clwyd *+40min/2.5km off main route*				⬆	⛺	🍴					🔵
	Llanferres +30min/2km off main route				⬆		🍴					🔵
	Llangynhafal +40min/2.5km off main route				⬆		🍴					🔵
	Bodfari	**8hr**	**28.2**	**28.2**	⬆	⛺	🍴					🔵
12	*Waen +45min/3km off main route*					⛺						
	Rhuallt	2hr 05min	7.4	7.4	⬆	⛺						
	Prestatyn	**3hr 25min**	**12.6**	**20.0**	⬆		🍴	🧺	ATM	i	🔴	🔵

The river Wye at Brockweir bridge, looking towards the Moravian chapel and Madgetts hill (Stage 1)

Offa's Dyke Path on the earthwork at the edge of Herrock Common (Stage 5)

INTRODUCTION

The view across the Monnow valley to Hatterrall Hill from above Pandy (Stage 2)

The iconic earthwork of Offa's Dyke, the longest linear earthwork in Britain, stands as a stunning testament to the determination and organisational skill of its creators, running for mile after mile as a defining landscape feature of the Welsh borders. Yet it remains an enigma: there is little documentary evidence relating to its construction, and so its purpose, extent and even its age are all the subject of vigorous dispute.

The long-distance path named after the Dyke is just as outstanding. A magnificent, long but not too difficult walk through the wonderfully diverse and at times remarkably remote countryside of the Welsh Marches, in its middle reaches it follows the Saxon earthwork unswervingly for many miles, Dyke and path together forming an intrinsic feature of the border landscape.

One of the real classics among Britain's challenge walks, the 285km (177 mile) trail offers an unforgettable journey between the Severn estuary and the North Wales coast, conquering mountain ranges, contouring above the Wye and Dee, visiting superb hillforts and Norman castles and exploring the hidden heritage of the Marches.

Both the natural and the historic landscapes of the borders are magical and inspiring. The natural landscape is one of vivid colour and extraordinary contrasts, a kaleidoscope of intimate scenery interspersed with

Offa's Dyke Path below the limestone escarpment of Eglwyseg Rocks, looking to Craig Arthur and Craig yr Adar (Stage 10)

wide-ranging and inspiring views, such as the sight of Herefordshire laid out below the Black Mountains, the Breidden hills across the Severn valley and the sands of Prestatyn and the North Wales coast from the northern end of the Clwydian hills.

The historic landscapes of the Welsh Marches weave a rich tapestry, too, reflecting the troubled past of a border region where rival tribes disputed territory and defended it with hillforts, castles on a scale unknown elsewhere in Britain, and medieval boroughs. Recent history is etched just as powerfully into the landscape, from the ruins of the industrial age in quarries, mills and blast furnaces to the evidence of early transport developments, with the Pontcysyllte Aqueduct carrying the Llangollen Canal high above the Dee valley a magnificent centrepiece, rightly acclaimed as a World Heritage Site.

Experiencing this rich heritage by walking the trail is surprisingly easy, since Offa's Dyke Path is easily accessed, the walking is only rarely arduous and the waymarking is excellent. Much of the route lies through farmed landscape, from the cider orchards of Monmouthshire to the dairy farms of the vale of Montgomery and the sheep pastures of Clun Forest. Other sections make use of old drove roads, ancient tracks and field paths, while even the moorland sections are relatively straightforward, presenting few technical challenges but providing wonderful, airy walking on high ridges.

The long trek across the Hatterrall ridge in the Black Mountains – once a notorious traverse of treacherous peat bogs – is now surprisingly easy as a result of substantial path improvements, and the heathery ridge at the heart of the Clwydian Range remains a delight. It is hardly surprising, then, that Offa's Dyke Path is widely regarded as one of the jewels in the crown of British trail walking, a journey to be savoured and long remembered.

FROM THE SEVERN TO THE IRISH SEA

Offa's Dyke Path follows the earthwork for long parts of its journey from the Severn estuary to Prestatyn on the North Wales coast, but at other times it follows a strikingly different route, seeking out the best walking experiences in the Welsh borders, including the traverse of the Black Mountains, the quintessential border country of western Herefordshire, and the outstanding Clwydian Range. The Dyke is clearly evident at its southern terminus at Sedbury Cliffs near Chepstow and the trail subsequently passes Chepstow, with the massive ramparts of its castle across the river, before tracking above the towering limestone cliffs of the lower Wye gorge to Monmouth, with dramatic lookouts high above the river at Wintour's Leap and the Devil's Pulpit.

From the fortified Monnow Bridge the way lies along the Trothy valley and past the White Castle – one of the 'Three Castles' guarding north-east Monmouthshire – and the 'holy mountain' of Skirrid Fawr. From Pandy the path climbs onto the Hatterrall ridge – the easternmost ridge of the Black Mountains. The ridge walk extends for 20km (12 miles), reaching 700m (2300ft) near Hay Bluff, with sensational views west into Wales and east across the Golden Valley and southern Herefordshire to the Malvern Hills.

The massive embankment of the Dyke, with the trail alongside, in Passage Grove above Tintern (Stage 1)

The ruins of Llanthony Priory can be seen down to the left in the Vale of Ewyas, with the ruined Norman castle of Longtown to the right.

Beyond the bookshop town of Hay-on-Wye the path skirts the River Wye for the last time before climbing a series of hills, culminating in the exhilarating traverse of the Hergest Ridge to the market town of Kington. The path is reunited with Offa's Dyke on Rushock Hill north of Kington, and follows it closely through Mid Wales and Shropshire as far as the Dee valley some 100km (60 miles) to the north.

The trail passes the ancient house of Old Burfa and the spectacular remains of the Dyke near Evenjobb before crossing the wide Lugg valley, climbing again to Hawthorn Hill and the monument to a railway pioneer, and descending into Knighton.

One really tough day and two easier ones lie ahead. First, the trail follows the Dyke across the ridges and deep valleys of Clun Forest, with superbly preserved sections of the ancient earthwork on Llanfair Hill and Edenhope Hill, before crossing the prehistoric Kerry Hill ridgeway and enjoying a downhill section to Brompton Bridge. Easier walking follows, with a lowland interlude in the Vale of Montgomery and alongside the Severn to Llanymynech, and the opportunity to divert briefly from the trail to visit quintessential border towns such as Bishop's Castle and Montgomery.

Back in the hills of the North Wales borderlands, the trail passes limeworks and tramways and then the wildlife-rich Llanymynech Rocks and Jones's Rough, skirts the Marcher

The long ridge of the Clwydian hills from the north (Stage 11)

The higher of the twin locks at Carreghofa, with the wharfinger's house beyond (Stage 8)

fortress of Chirk Castle, crosses the Dee on the Pontcysyllte Aqueduct, and runs below the serrated cliffs of Eglwyseg Rocks, with the ruined medieval stronghold of Castell Dinas Bran towering above Llangollen.

A crossing of Llandegla Moor, with its black grouse lekking sites, is a prelude to a high-level crossing of the Clwydian Range, pockmarked with Iron Age hillforts in a colourful sea of heather and bilberry. The last stage descends gently over the last of the Clwydian hills to reach the sea at Prestatyn.

For those seeking still greater challenges, the trail links with the Wales Coast Path at both Chepstow and Prestatyn, offering a 1690km (1050-mile) round-Wales challenge walk of epic proportions; while the trail also intersects with a number of other long-distance routes including the Wye Valley Walk at Chepstow and Hay, the Beacons Way near Pandy, Glyndŵr's Way at Knighton and Welshpool, and the Clwydian Way from Llangollen northwards.

The following Cicerone guides may be of use if you're planning to connect from Offa's Dyke Path to other routes:

- *The Wales Coast Path* by Paddy Dillon
- *The Wye Valley Walk* by the Wye Valley Walk Partnership
- *Glyndŵr's Way* by Paddy Dillon

The descent from Cwm-sanaham Hill to Brynorgan, with the Dyke seen climbing Llanfair Hill in the background (Stage 6)

PLANNING YOUR TRIP

Loxidge Tump from Llanthony Priory (Stage 3)

SELECTING A SCHEDULE

How long does it take? The beauty of Offa's Dyke Path is that there is no one answer to this question, and individual walkers can adopt a variety of different strategies to suit their interests and circumstances. The whole trail can comfortably be walked within a fortnight, and so this book is structured around 12 stages that are sometimes long but never particularly arduous. The waymarking is good, the going underfoot is rarely a problem, the days are full of interest and the miles fall away easily. So much so, indeed, that strong walkers might be tempted to complete the walk in 10 days at most.

On the other hand, why rush? Why compress an immensely pleasurable journey through the Welsh Marches – an area with an emphasis on the joys of slow living – into just 12 days? Exhilarating though the journey itself is, taking it too quickly can have the effect of relegating the exploration of the border landscape and its complex social and natural history into an undeserved second place. It is very easy indeed to take three weeks or so to complete the whole journey, allowing time to explore the sights along the route and to venture off-trail to experience some of the eclectic towns and villages of the borders.

ALTERNATIVE ITINERARIES

The classic trail itinerary described in this book involves 12 days of walking, with an easy middle section (Stages 7 and 8) bookmarked by more strenuous days at either end. But there's plenty of scope to tailor the trek to individual abilities and circumstances: by way of example, 8-day and 16-day alternatives are described in the Route profile and alternative schedules at the front of the book.

Savouring the Path in sections

This more relaxed approach may appeal particularly to those who want to tackle the trail in a series of separate expeditions – a strategy that is very easy to adopt, given the excellent transport links that survive (so far!) in the Welsh borders.

So, for example, trail walkers can take three or even four days to walk from Sedbury to Hay-on-Wye, savouring impressive and hugely varied landscapes including the Wye gorge, pastoral Monmouthshire and the Hatterrall ridge in the Black Mountains, and taking time to explore the White Castle and Llanthony Abbey. In the middle March the sharply undulating and surprisingly challenging hills of Clun Forest can be tempered with side trips to Clun, Bishop's Castle and Montgomery, while further north an exploration of Chirk Castle, the tourist honeypot of Llangollen and the castle towns of Ruthin and Denbigh can accompany the magnificent traverse of the Clwydian hills.

The Route Summary Table at the front of this guide summarises the key statistics for each of the 12 main stages along the trail, and provides suggestions for how a more relaxed timetable can be constructed based on the time available and personal preferences for the balance of walking and sightseeing.

It should be borne in mind, however, that there are some unavoidably long sections that (unless a driver, or perhaps a taxi, can be persuaded to pick up trail walkers in remote spots) will have to be tackled in a single day. These include the Black Mountains from Pandy to Hay-on-Wye (unless an intermediate stop in Llanthony is planned) and the Clwydian hills from Llandegla to Bodfari.

Accommodation along the route is scarce on other stages, too, and unless this is booked in advance trail walkers will need to prepare for some quite tough challenges, such as the switchback journey across the hills and valleys north of Knighton.

Day walks along the Path

At the other end of the spectrum there are real opportunities for linear day walks along the trail in a number of places, where bus services

The River Dee and the steam railway station at Llangollen (Stage 10)

connect start and finish – for example, between Chepstow and Monmouth, and Kington and Knighton, in both cases facilitating a superb full-day walk along dramatic sections of the trail. Just as good is the walk from Castle Mill near Chirk past the castle, over the world-famous Pontcysyllte Aqueduct and along the Panorama Walk to Castell Dinas Bran and the bus terminus in Llangollen.

South to north, or north to south?

Finally, it's worth bearing in mind that while the most popular direction of travel may be from south to north, it's entirely feasible to make the journey in the opposite direction, possibly into the prevailing wind and the sun but with the compensation of a final day walking above the high limestone cliffs of the lower Wye gorge to Chepstow Castle and the Severn estuary at Sedbury cliffs.

WHEN TO GO

Excellent walking is available in every season, with bluebells and anemones carpeting the woodland floors in spring, wildflowers and butterflies in summer, heather moorlands in late summer and the golden hues of the autumn bracken, and the crisp delights of sunny winter days. Bear in mind, however, that the high hills can sometimes be unforgiving in winter conditions, and that daylight hours in winter may be too short to allow the completion of some of the longer stages.

TRAVEL TO THE PATH

Both Chepstow and Prestatyn are well connected to the national road and rail networks, with Chepstow accessible from the M48 spur of the M4 motorway and Prestatyn easily reached from the M56 and M6 via the A55 North Wales expressway. Chepstow has good train services from Birmingham, Gloucester and Cardiff, while Prestatyn has a particularly good rail service, with direct trains from London, Manchester, Birmingham and Cardiff.

One of the attractive and unusual stone stiles at Tyddyn-y-cyll, with Moel Hiraddug beyond (Stage 12)

TRANSPORT ALONG THE PATH

Rail access is much less convenient at intermediate points along the trail, although Wrexham, Ruabon and Chirk are quite close to the trail in the north; the Heart of Wales line serves Knighton; and Hereford is a key hub in the south, with buses from the rail station to Hay-on-Wye and Kington.

Local bus services are subject to frequent change but are still surprisingly good in the Welsh borders and it is perfectly feasible to reach the start and end points of each stage by bus. Services are, naturally, sparse in the most thinly populated areas – for example, west Shropshire and rural Monmouthshire – but they are often

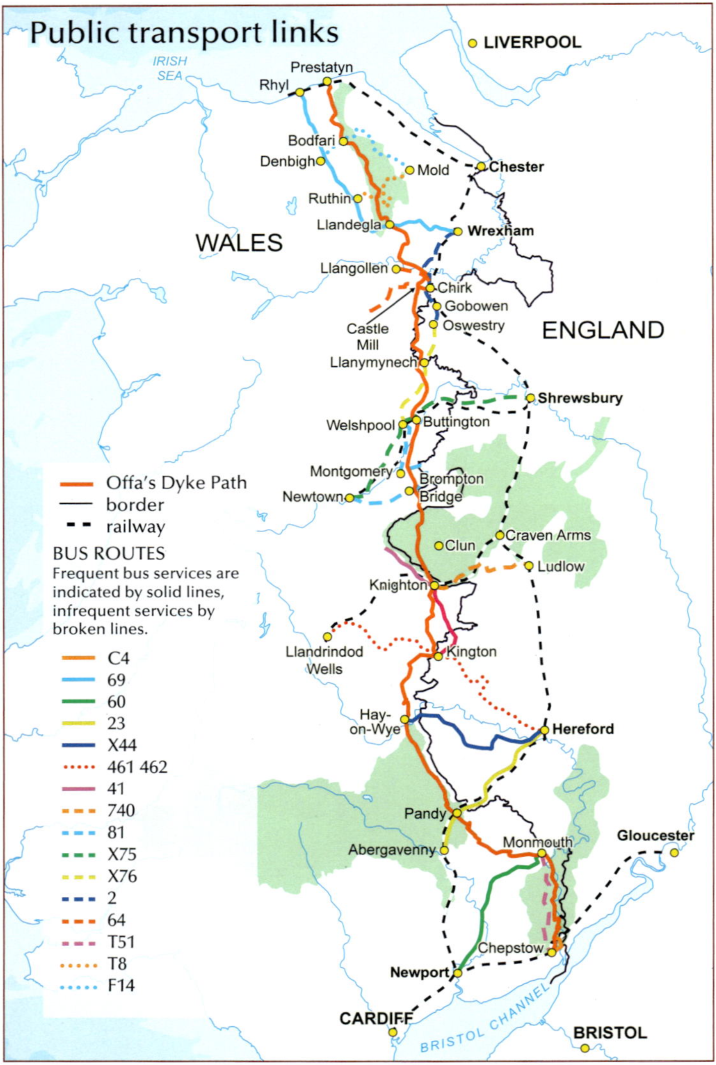
Public transport links
IRISH SEA
Prestatyn
Rhyl
Bodfari
Denbigh
Mold
Chester
LIVERPOOL
Ruthin
Llandegla
Wrexham
WALES
Llangollen
Chirk
Gobowen
Castle Mill
Oswestry
ENGLAND
Llanymynech
Shrewsbury
Welshpool
Buttington
Montgomery
Brompton Bridge
Newtown
Clun
Craven Arms
Ludlow
Knighton
Llandrindod Wells
Kington
Hay-on-Wye
Hereford
Pandy
Abergavenny
Monmouth
Gloucester
Chepstow
Newport
CARDIFF
BRISTOL CHANNEL
BRISTOL
Offa's Dyke Path
border
railway
BUS ROUTES
Frequent bus services are indicated by solid lines, infrequent services by broken lines.
C4
69
60
23
X44
461 462
41
740
81
X75
X76
2
64
T51
T8
F14

excellent elsewhere, and allow the scarcity of accommodation at places like Llandegla and Castle Mill, near Chirk, to be overcome by using early evening and morning bus services to and from nearby towns.

A summary of public transport options is given in the route information box for each stage, and full contact details of the relevant public transport operators are provided in Appendix A, together with details for each of the local councils in the borders, whose websites generally provide very good, up-to-date information on public transport in the relevant area.

FIRST AND LAST NIGHTS

Sedbury and Chepstow

Sedbury is distinctly short of both facilities and attractions to detain trail walkers (there is one pub but otherwise little except the excellent first half-mile of the Dyke, together with the saltmarsh below Sedbury Cliffs, with the 'old' Severn Bridge unexpectedly close at hand). Chepstow is an altogether different prospect, however – amply supplied with eateries and accommodation and well worth a leisurely exploration before getting down to the business of walking the national trail.

The great glory of the town, situated at the lowest crossing point of the River Wye, is its castle – the oldest stone-built castle in the whole of the UK. Its spectacular ruins tower above the limestone cliffs flanking the Wye, while the Great Tower dominates the view from the town and the 12th-century oak doors are the oldest surviving castle doors in Europe.

In late medieval times Chepstow became a market centre and river port, and developed a significant shipbuilding industry, although the growth of Newport and Cardiff during the industrial revolution resulted in a substantial decline in trade. By then, however, early tourism had come to the town's rescue, with the Wye Tour catering for early tourists attracted by the picturesque 'horrors' of the lower Wye gorge. Leisure pursuits are still important now, with Chepstow Racecourse hosting the Welsh Grand National each December.

Prestatyn

Short on historical attractions and dogged by its recent history as a cheap and cheerful holiday resort dominated by holiday camps and outsized caravan parks, Prestatyn may not seem the obvious place to spend extra time at the end (or beginning!) of Offa's Dyke Path, yet it has ample facilities and some hidden cultural gems that repay closer examination. Chief among these, and hidden incongruously in the middle of a housing estate, is a Roman bathhouse – part of a fort situated on the road from Caer (Chester) to Segontium (Caernarfon) – discovered as recently as 1984.

The ancient Hunters Moon Inn on the edge of the churchyard at Llangattock Lingoed (Stage 2)

Attractions in the town, however, are thin on the ground – although the seafront Nova Centre has reopened and offers a variety of swimming and adventure play facilities – but the nearby coastline has excellent beaches together with wildlife sites at Gronant Dunes and Talacre Warren, and each summer the Prestatyn Carnival has a classic carnival parade and a host of other events.

ACCOMMODATION

The opportunity to take a flexible approach to walking Offa's Dyke Path depends to a large extent, of course, on the availability of accommodation and other facilities at key points along the way.

The Stage Facilities Planner gives a summary of the availability of accommodation and other services at each of the key locations along the path, while fuller details are provided for each stage of the walk, with some specific recommendations of places that welcome walkers – especially in more remote locations where alternatives are thin on the ground. See Appendix B for a selection of the accommodation available along the Path.

Facilities

In some places – as shown on the Stage Facilities Planner – facilities are pretty scarce, and a bit of ingenuity may be needed to construct a personal itinerary. Having said that, creative use of bus services can solve many of the problems: for example, the excellent bus service to Ruthin can be used to overcome the dearth of facilities in Llandegla, with the additional benefit of an evening in a delightful Welsh market town.

Information about shops, pubs and cafés on or near the route is provided in the box at the beginning of each stage's description, especially in more remote locations where alternatives are thin on the ground. See Appendix A for websites and contact details of all the tourist information centres and other useful sources of information.

It's important to be aware – as the Stage Facilities Planner makes clear – that there are long stretches of the trail in countryside that may be highly picturesque and full of historic and natural interest but are also remote from towns and services. Facilities are at a premium on several stretches of the walk: between Monmouth and Hay-on-Wye (a minimum of two days' walking) there are no shops or banking facilities and advance planning is essential. Similarly, the direct route between Trevor near Llangollen and the end of the trail at Prestatyn has only one shop and a handful of pubs in a journey of 63km (39 miles).

Baggage transfer

One significant improvement in services for walkers is the increase in the number of providers offering luggage transfer and accommodation booking services, which can take some of the physical (and mental) strain off the shoulders of walkers contemplating the challenge ahead. Full details of these providers are given in Appendix A, while it is also worth checking with accommodation providers, some of whom are happy to transfer luggage to the next overnight stop by prior arrangement.

What to take

A good pair of lightweight walking boots should be able to cope with the whole of the trail, including the moorland and mountain expeditions, while a decent set of waterproofs and spare warm clothing is essential to deal with the unpredictability of the weather in the area. The relevant maps should always be carried, and a compass. A GPS unit is a useful addition (especially in woodland areas and on the moorland in the Black Mountains and on Llandegla moor, which have few landmarks).

Adequate supplies of food and water, a camera to capture the best of the scenery and binoculars for wildlife-watching also need room in the rucksack.

PLANNING DAY BY DAY

The straight track north of Llantilio Crossenny, heading for the snow-capped Skirrid Fawr (Stage 2)

USING THIS GUIDE

The guide is organised into 12 stages based on the availability of transport to and from the starting and finishing points, but also includes information relevant to trail walkers who plan to follow alternative itineraries. The distance walked in a day varies from a sedate 17.3km (10.8 miles) through the Severn valley to a more strenuous 29.5km (18.3 miles) above the lower Wye gorge.

Reasonably fit walkers should have no real difficulty in completing any of the stages, with even the two mountain expeditions consisting largely of moorland walking on good paths. None of this high-level walking is rocky or exposed, but in the Black Mountains in particular it is across its high plateaus with few landmarks where competence in map reading and navigation is required, together with knowledge of the escape routes available if, for example, the weather deteriorates during the day.

For each stage a route information box summarises the practical details associated with the walk, including distance, total ascent, and an estimate of the time required to complete the walk – which will of course vary considerably with the experience, fitness and perhaps the age of the participants. Details of public transport and accommodation options and other services along the trail are also given, together with notes on breaking the journey on the longer, more exposed stages.

A brief introduction to the day's journey then gives a summary of the type of walking involved in that stage and the historical and scenic highlights encountered en route. The walk is then described in detail, with cross-references (in bold) to the accompanying 1:100K stage map provided, an enhanced description of the route at those points where the way forward is a little tricky to follow on the ground, and notes on features of natural or historical interest on or close to the route. In addition, the map booklet included at the back of this guide shows the full route on 1:25,000 Ordnance Survey® mapping.

The topographical glossary provided as Appendix C will help you 'de-code' some of the Welsh place names for your own interest.

Cicerone app and GPX files

This book is available in the Cicerone app on your phone. View GPS-enabled maps you can download for offline navigation, check route details and local points of interest, and plan your adventure with confidence. GPX files are also available to download. See cicerone.co.uk/1279.

MAPS

You may wish to consult the printed versions of the relevant 1:25,000 OS maps extracted in the trail map included in this guide before you set off, although it should not be necessary to carry them with you. The trail is covered by seven 1:25,000 maps:

- Outdoor Leisure® 14 (Wye Valley & Forest of Dean)
- Outdoor Leisure 13 (Brecon Beacons National Park – Eastern Area)
- Explorer® 201 (Knighton & Presteigne)
- Explorer 216 (Welshpool & Montgomery)
- Explorer 240 (Oswestry)
- Explorer 256 (Wrexham)
- Explorer 265 (Clwydian Range)

WAYMARKING

Waymarking is generally very good, as would be expected of an official national trail. The national trail 'acorn' symbol is consistently used, often with fingerposts indicating the next destination. In the few cases where there are ambiguities or obstacles, a more detailed description of how to overcome the difficulties is provided in the text. Of course, changes do occur over time, and where improvement is needed – either to waymarking or to footpath furniture such as stiles and gates – the problem can be reported online to the National Trail Officer, whose details are included in Appendix A. A number of stiles have been replaced with gates, and there is an ambition to do more in this area when resources allow.

The waymark post at the halfway point of Offa's Dyke Path above Newcastle (Stage 6)

WEATHER FORECASTS

Welsh mountain weather is likely to be unpredictable more than a few days in advance, but a detailed weather forecast from metoffice.gov.uk (which includes a mountain forecast for Bannau Brycheiniog/the Brecon Beacons, including the Black Mountains) can prove invaluable as you plan from day to day.

PHONES AND WI-FI

While wi-fi internet access is increasingly available in cafés, pubs and hotels in the Welsh Borders, it is by no means universally available. Mobile phone signals are restricted in coverage and somewhat erratic – especially in the central Marches, where there are quite large areas such as Clun Forest that have virtually no coverage.

EMERGENCIES

The police, fire service, ambulance or mountain rescue can be reached in an emergency by dialling 999 or 112. Mountain rescue services are provided in North Wales by North East Wales Search & Rescue – who cover not just the Clwydian Range but also surrounding areas as far south as northern Powys – and in mid-Wales and south-east Wales by the Brecon and Longtown mountain rescue teams, with the latter team based in Abergavenny and primarily responsible for the Black Mountains, which are traversed on Stage 3 of the trail.

ALL ABOUT THE WELSH MARCHES

The Wye at Redbrook and the wooded slopes of Lord's Grove leading to the Kymin (Stage 1)

GEOLOGY AND LANDSCAPE

Probably the most important factor underpinning Offa's Dyke Path's place as one of the finest of Britain's national trails is its location at the sinuous boundary between upland and lowland Britain. This makes the journey from Chepstow to Prestatyn one of immense contrasts in landforms and scenery, with the underlying geology giving rise to a sequence of contrasting and inspiring landscapes, from high mountain to dissected plateau and fertile lowland valleys.

While Dyke and national trail start above the Triassic marlstone and Lower Lias limestone cliffs at Sedbury, the dominant rock of the first stage of the journey is Carboniferous limestone, through which the Wye has cut down to leave stunning white cliffs towering over a narrow, twisting gorge, with abandoned meanders at Newland and St Briavels left stranded above the present level of the river.

Beyond Monmouth the scenery changes abruptly, with a gently rolling plateau dissected by the Trothy valley – although increasingly the landscape is dominated by the unmistakable asymmetrical peak of Skirrid Fawr (the 'holy' mountain) and the scarp slopes of the Black Mountains.

The high tableland of the Black Mountains is composed of horizontal beds of Old Red Sandstone capped with resistant brownstones that form the slightly higher summits. Saved from monotony by a wild beauty, this remote heather moorland falls abruptly to the Olchon valley and Golden Valley to the east, with dramatic landslips such as the Black Daren on the over-steepened slopes. The northern scarp overlooks the middle Wye valley, with the rolling green hills of Mid Wales and western Herefordshire and Shropshire further north still. A series of ridges, separated by glacially over-deepened valleys such as the Teme and Clun, leads westward to the wild and remote country of the Radnor and Clun forests, with upland pasture on the slopes and discordant conifers on many of the tops.

The hills fall away to the west in the middle March, with the broad vale of Montgomery, a former glacial lake, surrounded by low hills. To the east the unmistakable profile of Corndon Hill – a volcanic phacolith or mushroom-shaped intrusion into the surrounding Silurian rocks – rises in front of the equally idiosyncratic serrated profile of the Stiperstones, its rocky tors a result of periglacial frost shattering. To the north is the very different landscape of the Long Mountain, with a broad and strikingly level summit ridge composed of Silurian shales and siltstones.

The River Severn emerges from the uplands here, taking on some of the characteristics of a mature river as it curves extravagantly across a broad flood plain, the meanders reaching their climax at The Roundabout near Pool Quay, where the river has failed to breach a narrow neck of land and instead twists and turns dramatically across the valley. To the east

Creigiau Eglwyseg from above Rock Farm (Stage 10)

are the Breidden hills, steep-sided and instantly recognisable, plugs of Ordovician volcanic dolerite rising above the flat lands of the Severn but increasingly eaten away to the north-west, where the Criggion quarry is extracting hundreds of thousands of tons of roadstone every year.

The hills reassert themselves once the Severn and Vrynwy are left behind, with a flat-topped Carboniferous limestone ridge extending from Llanymynech to Selattyn Hill, its steep scarp facing west into Wales. The limestone has been quarried ruthlessly and the scars remain, while small-scale coalmining has left its mark on the eastern side of the ridge.

The hills are breached again by the deep, fast-flowing Ceiriog and then the impressive Dee, the river winding across the floor of a deep, well-defined rift valley between the steep wooded slopes rising above Llangollen to the south and the stark limestone cliffs of Trevor Rocks and Eglwyseg mountain to the north.

The jagged rocks of Eglwyseg are the precursor to the long ridge of the Clwydian Range, the hills broken only occasionally by high valleys. To the east the slopes dip gently on Silurian shales, while to the west the slopes are much steeper, dropping dramatically to the wide, flat and picturesque Vale of Clwyd.

Finally, the hills give way to the lowlands bordering the North Wales coastal plain, where drift deposits of boulder clay generally mask the solid geology – although the Prestatyn area has a final surprise with the reappearance of the coal measures in the Carboniferous limestone, still marked by ruined pithead equipment in places.

PLANTS AND WILDLIFE

An eventful geological history and significant diversity of landforms underpins a wide variety of habitats in the Welsh borders, from the spectacular woodlands of the lower Wye gorge to the mixed arable and pasture of the lowlands and the heather moorlands of Ruabon Mountain and the Clwydian hills. More intimate, smaller-scale landscapes include the orchards of Monmouthshire and the species-rich unimproved grasslands hidden among the Mid Wales hills. This diversity naturally translates into a countryside with abundant and sometimes surprising wildlife.

The Wye woodlands are internationally recognised for their rare species, many of them regarded as indicators of the predominance of ancient woodlands in the area, including wild service trees, small- and large-leaved limes, and whitebeams. Beneath the trees are equally special plants, including Tintern spurge – which is only found in this area – and the attractive martigan lily, with two colonies in the lower Wye, one of them right next to Offa's Dyke Path.

Other woodland habitats include the densely wooded valley floor of the Dee, the scattered woodland and richly diverse hedgerows of the Oswestry uplands, the oakwoods and coniferous plantations of Clun Forest, and the orchards of north-east Monmouthshire – some of them quite intensively cultivated under contract to major producers, others small and often neglected. But the most spectacular woods are those of the Leighton estate near Welshpool, and especially the Charles Ackers Grove, where the 30 coastal redwoods planted in 1858 are the tallest redwoods in Europe.

While fragments of lowland heath survive above the cliffs of the lower Wye, upland heath survives much more widely in the Black Mountains, although the semi-natural habitats there are fragile. The characteristic vegetation includes purple moorgrass, heather and bilberry, with sedges and sphagnum in areas of wet heath and blanket bog. Much further

north, the ridge of the Clwydian hills has a similar plant assemblage, with heather dominating the open moorland but with large areas of bilberry, gorse and bracken providing an intensely colourful scene that changes with the seasons.

The Clwydian hills have not, however, always been dominated by heather moorland. The slopes of Moel Llys-y-Coed have provided compelling evidence of vegetation change since the Mesolithic era, when the area was heavily wooded, with hazel, birch, pine and oak predominant, through a period when grassland interspersed with alder carr was the characteristic feature of the landscape to the present open moorland, which itself needs management to prevent encroachment by scrub and small trees.

Entirely different and sometimes quite rare plants can be found in much more specialised and localised habitats, including the limestone cliffs of the lower Wye gorge, where the tiny plateau above the Seven Sisters rocks offers a refuge to bloody crane's-bill and lesser calamint, and the Breidden hills, where a distinctive flora of both acid- and lime-loving species thrives alongside a variety of whitebeams on the crags.

Each of these habitats has attractions for particular birds, from the heather moorlands, where raptors such as buzzards, red kites and (less frequently) merlin fly overhead and red grouse skulk in the heather, to the woodlands of the Wye Valley, with

redstarts, willow warblers and chiffchaffs abundant, and the upper Clun valley, which is particularly important for pied flycatchers and tree pipits. The uplands form important breeding grounds for curlew and snipe, while peregrine falcons breed on the quarry faces at Llanymynech.

Perhaps the most iconic bird of the Welsh Marches is the black grouse. One of Britain's most endangered birds, it has suffered a steep decline in numbers and a remarkable contraction in its range, but a partnership between RSPB and local landowners has reversed the trend on the moors of North Wales. The number of breeding pairs there trebled to more than 300 in just 15 years, and the male's elaborate courtship display (known as lekking) can be viewed at dawn in spring at Llandegla Moor, close to Offa's Dyke Path (booking essential with RSPB rspb.org.uk).

A wide range of butterflies can be found in the area, with woodland butterflies such as the orange tip and speckled wood often seen in the lower Wye valley, and King's Wood near Monmouth being a stronghold of the declining pearl-bordered fritillary. The abandoned quarries at Llanymynech have been transformed into a haven for butterflies, again including the pearl-bordered fritillary but also the grizzled skipper, green hairstreak and small copper, while around Clun specialities include the scarce high brown fritillary and small pearl-bordered fritillary, together with the scarlet longhorn beetle.

The Montgomery Canal, pleasingly remote and long disused, is noted as one of the richest canals in Britain for wildlife, with 14 species of dragonfly recorded along its Welsh length (the stretch on either side of the Vyrnwy aqueduct is particularly rich, with sightings of azure damselfly, banded demoiselle, common darter and others guaranteed in season), while on the River Dee the club-tailed dragonfly is a local speciality.

The relatively quiet borderlands also provide a number of refuges for bats, with the lower Wye specially protected for its bat sites, which harbour large numbers of the declining lesser horseshoe bats, while the old quarries at Llanymynech, already noted for birds and butterflies, also provide roosting sites for greater horseshoe bats.

A number of the border rivers are important for the resurgent otter – none more so than the Dee – while the lower Wye is internationally important for its collection of aquatic species, including salmon (for which it is the best river in England), twaite and allis shad, and white-clawed crayfish. But it is the River Clun that holds perhaps the most surprising secret, with one of the last and perhaps the largest populations in England and Wales of freshwater pearl mussels, together with plenty of young salmon and brown trout.

BORDER PREHISTORY

Accounts of human activity in the Welsh borders before the arrival of the Romans concentrate on a few highly visible sites such as Arthur's Stone above the Golden Valley and the spectacular array of Iron Age hillforts in the region, but they conclude that, with a few notable exceptions, it was almost non-existent. Just how inaccurate that conclusion is has been demonstrated by the painstaking long-term archaeological research carried out by the Clwyd Powys Archaeological Trust in the Walton basin, a tiny area northwest of Kington that is hemmed in by low hills on all sides.

Offa's Dyke cuts an impressive swathe across the eastern flanks of the Walton basin, but it is a relatively late addition to the collection of ancient monuments here. The research has revealed an amazing array of Neolithic sites – most notably the 3-mile-long Hindwell Cursus but also a causewayed enclosure, two palisaded enclosures (one enclosing an area of 34ha and constructed of oak posts set about 6m apart), ring ditches and round barrows. The Romans superimposed their own activities on this landscape, with a complex of marching camps and roads dating from the conquest of Wales in the later first century AD.

Substantial reappraisal is therefore needed, but for the moment the Iron Age hillforts are the most distinctive and unforgettable landscape features left by prehistoric man in the borders, with an extraordinary chain of six hillforts guarding the western approaches to the Clwydian hills, and some exceptionally fine hillforts further south, including Old Oswestry with its concentric defences, the massive fort on Llanymynech Hill, and two superb examples near Clun, Caer Caradoc and Bury Ditches.

The forts were clearly sited and designed to exert military control, but at the same time many of them operated as prototype villages too: domestic dwellings have been discovered inside the huge Clwydian hillfort at Penycloddiau and there are more than 40 hut platforms inside the ramparts of Foel Fenlli a few miles to the south.

The Roman imprint on the higher ground of the western Marches is decidedly faint, but a greater measure of control was exerted further east, with a network of roads including Watling Street (West) between the major Roman forts of Chester, Wroxeter (south-east of Shrewsbury) and Caerleon, together with civil settlements such as Kenchester, on the outskirts of Hereford.

The fort at Forden Gaer south of Welshpool, close to Offa's Dyke Path, was significantly smaller than most but was strategically sited to regulate movement in the middle Severn valley. Where the hills offered important resources the Romans moved in here too, with Roman copper mining proved at Llanymynech Hill and lead mining in Flintshire and probably at Shelve to the west of the Long Mynd.

The collapse of Roman rule left fifth-century Britain fending for itself as the country degenerated into a series of fractious kingdoms in which

Beacon Hill from the south, with the great rampart of the hillfort prominently in view (Stage 7)

Dyke and national trail south of the Kerry Hill ridgeway (Stage 6)

the Roman economic system based around towns and villas fell into decay. 'Welsh' kingdoms such as Gwynedd, Powys, Erging and Gwent were established during this period, while Mercia and Northumbria increasingly controlled the area of the west Midlands.

By the early seventh century Saxon rule had been more firmly established and the Mercian kingdom had become dominant – although its command of the approaches to the uplands in Wales was always fragile. This, then, was the chronically insecure western boundary that Offa inherited when he became king of Mercia in 757.

OFFA AND THE DYKE

The extraordinary earthwork of Offa's Dyke, by some distance Britain's longest ancient monument, is an astonishing feat of construction and even now, more than a millennium after its creation, forms a dramatic landscape feature etched across the rolling hills of the Welsh Marches.

Despite erosion and infilling, the top of the earthen bank still stands 8m above the bottom of the ditch in places, and it would have presented a formidable barrier in early medieval times, when the bank was perhaps revetted with turf or stone to create a near-vertical western face and the underlying rock was exposed by

Offa's Dyke and the national trail on Rushock Hill (Stage 5)

quarrying in places to give the appearance of a substantial stone wall.

Offa's Dyke walkers have an unparalleled opportunity to appreciate the scale of the construction work involved in creating the Dyke, and in particular the way in which it was planned and engineered, as they follow its course for more than a third of the 285km (177 miles) between Sedbury and Prestatyn. The Dyke's planners ensured that it was almost always placed in a dominant position in the landscape, the bank facing westwards into Wales, with a broad western ditch as well, to emphasise the political control exerted by the kingdom to the east.

Yet despite its scale and undoubted impact on the political geography of the borderlands, no contemporary account survives of its construction, so there is still no consensus over the date at which it was erected, with some even doubting that King Offa ordered it to be built. Worse still, the actual extent of the Dyke is disputed – although recent research has very much strengthened the case for the earthwork extending from the Severn estuary all the way to the North Wales coast – and a variety of theories have been put forward to explain its purpose.

The first documentary evidence relating to the Dyke dates back to the late ninth century, almost a hundred years after Offa died, when Bishop Asser referred in his *Life of Alfred* to Offa causing a great dyke to be built 'between Wales and Mercia from sea to sea'. A date of around 780, when Offa was at the height of his powers, still seems most likely, although radiocarbon dating of a recently damaged section near Chirk did little more than confirm that it is definitely post-Roman (the most eccentric of recent hypotheses suggested that it was the lost Roman wall of Severus, although the absence of forts, milecastles or a military road argues convincingly against that theory).

Offa's Dyke appears similar to other linear earthworks regarded as of Saxon origin, such as the Devil's Dyke in Cambridgeshire and Wat's Dyke, which parallels Offa's Dyke near Wrexham, and it also appears to be later than the various short dykes in the Welsh borders; but all these other earthworks are also hard to date with any certainty. The long-held view that Wat's Dyke was built by Offa's predecessor Aethelbald in the middle of the eighth century has now been questioned, with a later date of around 800 suggested for its construction.

No one doubts that the great bank and ditch running between Rushock Hill north of Kington and Treuddyn, near Mold, is the real thing: apart from two short sections where the Severn and the Dee delineate the frontier, the Dyke is virtually continuous and hugely inspiring. Sir Cyril Fox, who published the first significant survey of the Dyke in 1955, agreed with Asser's assertion that it ran 'from sea to sea', but this has been disputed by successive later authors. However, painstaking recent research has established a convincing route followed by the Dyke between Treuddyn and the North Wales coast at Gronant near Prestatyn, with some hitherto unknown stretches of bank and ditch uncovered, for example at Swan Wood near Ysceifiog.

The area south of Kington is much more difficult: again, Fox thought he had found traces of the Dyke at several locations in Herefordshire, together with the much more plausible lengths above the lower Wye gorge and approaching Sedbury cliffs. The route of the Dyke south-east from Kington has been traced as far as the River Wye, which may have acted as the border through Hereford to Ross-on-Wye. Similarly, a plausible line has been traced for the Dyke between Ross and Redbrook in the lower Wye gorge.

The purpose of the Dyke is at the most basic level reasonably easy to discern, since it was clearly intended to demarcate the western frontier of Mercia and by extension to deter incursions from the Welsh kingdoms to the west. As long ago as 1857 Earle perceptively observed that it was too considerable to be a cattle fence but too extensive to be a fully manned fortification.

The extent to which it had a truly military purpose remains uncertain, however; it is just as likely that it was intended primarily as a physical manifestation of Mercian strength and ambition as that it was built to act as a defensive barrier. The debate on this and other aspects of the enigmatic earthwork is likely to continue!

THE WELSH MARCHES AFTER OFFA

Whatever the original purpose and extent of Offa's Dyke, it was clearly not an immutable boundary since control of the frontier zone ebbed and flowed as Welsh attempts to recapture territory succeeded or were repulsed, or as Saxon incursions into the uplands were undertaken. Much more serious, however, was the abrupt decline of the Mercian kingdom in the ninth century, weakened by raids from Vikings and Danes, and faced by a dominant Wessex seizing the initiative and moving towards the establishment of a single English kingdom.

Comparative peace was shattered by William's invasion in 1066, with Norman political and military control quickly established throughout the lowlands. The Normans baulked at the idea of full-scale invasion of the Welsh uplands, instead using the Welsh borders as a buffer zone by creating a vast

The shell keep and motte of Longtown Castle (Stage 3)

The intricate landscape of The Hudnalls seen from Madgett Hill (Stage 1)

number of semi-autonomous lordships that occupied territory on either side of Offa's Dyke and acted as a brake on Welsh ambitions.

In 1067 there were only three castles in the Welsh borders, but by 1215 more than 400 had been built. Many of these were simple earthen mounds (mottes), in use only briefly to subdue border raiders, but others such as White Castle were substantial stone fortresses and lasted longer. By 1105 a boundary between the March of Wales and 'pure' Wales had been established, delineating the frontier between the lordships and the Welsh kingdoms, and although it varied slightly over time it remained more or less intact until the English kings were provoked into more aggressive action in the 13th century.

Even after Edward I's conquest of Wales in 1282–3 the March persisted as a loose confederation of semi-autonomous lordships, until the Acts of Union in the 16th century brought Wales under English control and saw the lordships converted into new Welsh shires or incorporated into the English border counties.

The landscape impact of the Normans can hardly be overstated, from the early motte-and-bailey castles that, as noted above, pepper the countryside of the borderland (at a greater density than anywhere else in Britain) to the later stone-built strongholds such as Chepstow, Ludlow and Chester, many of them with newly planted towns sited alongside.

Towns such as Denbigh and Ruthin established important functions as market and trading centres, but not all of these planted settlements were successful. The failed borough of Huntington with its massive, haunting ramparts is well worth a detour from the trail near Kington, while the boroughs of Painscastle near Hay-on-Wye and Caus on the flanks of the Long Mountain were too remote to make economic sense and failed as well.

The visual impact of later developments was less dramatic, although it included the construction of fortified manor houses such as Stokesay Castle and Tretower Court as the need for outright defence waned, the creation of country houses and of medieval deer parks (a particularly fine example at Lymore east of Montgomery has an unusual duck decoy in one of its lakes and lies next to the trail), and the dissolution of the monasteries in the 16th century, leaving a legacy of ruined abbeys including Llanthony in the Black Mountains and Valle Crucis near Llangollen.

The scars of industry – particularly mining – pockmark the Welsh borders, with the lower Wye valley between Chepstow and Monmouth a centre of iron smelting, tanning, tinplate working, millstone making and wireworks, and the uplands west of Oswestry home to numerous large quarries together with smaller-scale coal mines. Transport developments have intruded, too, with Telford's A5 Holyhead road a feature of the Vale of Llangollen, and the nearby Llangollen Canal crossing the Dee valley on the Pontcysyllte Aqueduct, now a World Heritage Site.

More recently, many of these sites have acquired a benign after-use, becoming themes for the development of the new growth industry of tourism, initially focused on the picturesque (with the Wye Tour, focused on Tintern Abbey and Symonds Yat, at the forefront) and later encompassing the growth of resort towns such as Rhyl and Prestatyn along the North Wales coast.

Latterly the tourism offer has diversified still further – for example into books at Hay-on-Wye, the *eisteddfodau* at Llangollen, food at Abergavenny and Ludlow, and walking and green tourism at Kington – making the prospect of walking the trail yet more enticing.

If you wish to delve a little more deeply into the history and culture of the Welsh Borders, a selection of books is recommended in Appendix D: Further reading.

THE FUTURE OF OFFA'S DYKE

The Dyke has survived over 1200 years but increasingly has suffered from erosion, neglect and occasional acts of vandalism and deliberate damage, so that the fragile earthwork faces an uncertain future. A survey in 2017 found that less than a 10th of the ancient monument was in good condition, and so the Offa's Dyke Association (ODA), with support from Cadw, English Heritage and the National Trail Officer, has established the Offa's Dyke Conservation Project with the intention of supporting management agreements, maintenance work and repairs, particularly to lengths of the monument at severe risk.

In hindsight it is clear that the original decision to position the long-distance path on the crest of the monument was flawed, with the pressure of walkers' boots adding to the problems caused by grazing animals, especially cattle, and burrowing animals such as badgers. A key long-term objective of the Conservation Project is to see the national trail diverted slightly to run alongside the monument, and there are already some stretches where this objective has been achieved.

Since trail walkers can affect the condition of the Dyke, especially in winter when the ground is wetter and soils are more easily damaged, the ODA's popular passport scheme – which enables walkers to log their progress along the trail – operates only from Easter to October each year, discouraging use of the trail in the winter months.

Bad weather above the deep valley of Cwm Ffrydd near Churchtown (Stage 6)

STAGE 1

Above the Lower Wye Gorge

Start	Sedbury Cliffs (ST 552 928)
Finish	Agincourt Square, Monmouth (SO 507 128)
Distance	29.5km (18.3 miles)
Ascent	1025m (3360ft)
Time	7–9hr
Maps	OS Outdoor Leisure 14
Refreshments	Plenty of choice in Chepstow and Monmouth, together with a community-owned pub in Woodcroft, a shop and café just uphill from the path in Brockweir and pubs and a village shop in Redbrook
Public transport	Chepstow has a good train service on the Cheltenham Spa to Cardiff line. Bus C4 connects Chepstow and Beachley, stopping at Buttington Terrace, 0.5km from the start of the trail. Bus 69 runs from Chepstow to Monmouth, calling at Brockweir Bridge, Bigsweir and Redbrook, while there are also services (bus 60) from Monmouth to Newport.
Accommodation	A wide range of accommodation in both Chepstow and Monmouth, but surprisingly little on the path between the two towns, with a few B&B options in Tintern, St Briavels Common, near Bigsweir Bridge and in Redbrook

The first section of Offa's Dyke Path is also one of the best: indeed, it is widely regarded as one of the classic walks of lowland Britain. The walk requires a good level of fitness since it follows an undulating route on the edge of the Forest of Dean, repeatedly descending towards the Wye and climbing again along ridges high above the gorge, and it may be worth considering tackling the route in two stages. In any case, many will find it easiest to aim to time their arrival in Chepstow so that they can tackle the Sedbury section separately, and start from Chepstow Bridge on the following day.

While the national trail, in company with the great earthwork itself, starts on **Sedbury** Cliffs, it is worth beginning the journey on the saltmarsh below, close to

Sedbury Cliffs from the saltmarsh alongside the River Severn

the ancient ferry crossing now superseded by the two Severn road bridges, and under the Lower Lias limestone outcrops of the cliffs, with ammonites and other fossils in the boulders below. A short and easy ascent then leads to the big block of stone marking the beginning of the trail, with a good view of the Dyke dropping down quite sharply to a footbridge and new boardwalk easing the crossing of Slimeroad Pill.

The trail then follows the crest of the Dyke, on a path which has recently been widened through scrub clearance and management to reduce erosion as it makes for the Beachley road at Buttington Tump.

Across the road the path drops down to a ditch, with suburban Sedbury dominating the view ahead. Cross a gravelly lane and a sturdy footbridge and keep straight on to enter suburbia, finding a grassy path on the left and then swinging right on a road which eventually reveals itself as Mercian Way and then Offa's Close.

Keep straight ahead again on a private road, then climb slightly to the right and take a path between a housing estate and the edge of the river cliff above the sluggish, brown Wye. Zigzag left and right across Wyebank Avenue to turn left on the main road, using it to cross the railway line and parallel **A48**.

Another left turn 200m further north leads down an entrance drive; turn sharply left just before the Woodbridge House entrance gates, on gravel and then grass, to reach the top of the river cliff again, this time with excellent views of Chepstow Castle and the elegant old cast-iron bridge over the river.

The views are disappointingly brief, however, as the path is hemmed in by fences as it rises steeply, then runs between high stone walls, descending gently at first but then increasingly steeply until it meets the old main road from Chepstow to Tutshill, now a tarmac path. Turn left here to visit Chepstow, or turn steeply uphill to the right to continue along the trail.

CHEPSTOW

An attractive small town close to the confluence of the Severn and Wye, Chepstow is dominated by the magnificent remains of its castle, begun in 1067. This is the oldest stone castle in Britain and its magnificent Great Tower still stands to its full height, while the 12th-century oak doors are the oldest castle doors in Europe. Later Chepstow became an important river port, importing wine and exporting timber and bark, and was an important shipbuilding centre – although it was eclipsed by Newport and Cardiff during the coal boom. The river was the focus of early tourism, based on the Wye Tour, a picturesque journey along the gorge.

Chepstow has a full range of shops, pubs, cafés and other facilities, and there are also several hotels and B&B establishments.

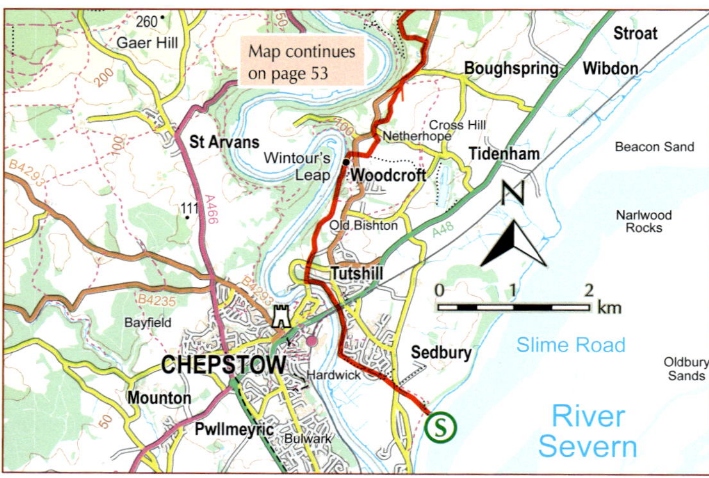

The marker stone at the southern end of Offa's Dyke

The **Wales Coast Path**, a gargantuan long-distance route which was officially opened in May 2012 and runs for over 1400km (870 miles) around the entire Welsh coastline, starts (or ends) on Chepstow Bridge, while the more modest **Wye Valley Walk** follows the western side of the Lower Wye Gorge as far as Monmouth before following the river upstream to Ross-on-Wye, Hereford and eventually the source of the river high on the slopes of Plynlimon in the Cambrian Mountains.

Cross the main road at the top of the hill, keep straight ahead along a lane, and then turn left through a kissing gate to climb across a large field, with the ivy-clad remains of a ruined tower to the right. The tower is actually the remains of a windmill recorded in 1584 but disused by 1769 and converted into a folly; suggestions that it was a watchtower for Chepstow Castle are unfounded. A kissing gate at the far end of the next field leads into a narrow alley; follow this to the right before turning left to cross a field and find a stony path enclosed between a high stone wall and iron railings.

Turn left on the B4228 and left again after 100m under an archway, with 'Moyle Old School Lane' inscribed on the keystone, to follow another narrow path, now with the Wye gorge dramatically down to the left below massive limestone cliffs. The Lancaut nature reserve lies below the path here, with peregrine falcons nesting on the cliffs and superb oak, ash, and yew woodlands, together with rare whitebeams.

The high bank of Offa's Dyke, with the path in the ditch alongside, north of the Devil's Pulpit

The lane climbs gently, with good views of the broad Severn valley away to the right, and passes the massive Woodcroft quarry before intersecting with the B-road again. Immediately to the left is a short lane leading to the sensational viewpoint of **Wintour's Leap**, with a great outlook over the sluggish river as it meanders around the Lancaut peninsula, with the ruined St James's church visible on the riverbank. The sheer cliffs rise 60m above the floodplain here – the supposed site of Sir John Wintour's escape from Parliamentarians during the Civil War.

Turn back to the right along the road for 40m to locate a little path between houses, then cross two fields and turn left to follow the field edge into woodland, then along an access road which leads back yet again to the B-road. Offa's Dyke itself reappears a little to the west here, where the ramparts of the Iron Age promontory fort on Spital Meend were re-used by the eighth-century construction workers.

The trail leaves the road again over a stone stile and runs along the woodland edge and across a maize field, then climbs up to the B4228 for the last time. Keep to the pavement for 500m, alongside the wall of the Dennel Hill estate, but go left when the wall ends, on a long path enclosed between post-and-wire fences until you meet Offa's Dyke again. Follow the Dyke to the right, walking along the rampart itself, with the land falling steeply on the left into the Wye gorge.

Somewhat disappointingly, the thickly wooded slopes mask the spectacular landscape of the lower Wye at first, as the path drops down to an informal parking area and curves left on a wide track. The original line of the path soon left the track to the right, but conservation of the crumbling Dyke is a priority here and a new waymarked path has been created, which gradually approaches the line of the Dyke but keeps below it, both protecting the Saxon monument and providing excellent views of the ditch and rampart.

The trail keeps close to the edge of the great limestone outcrops of Plumweir Cliff and Shorn Cliff, far above the old and long-disused fishery of Plum Weir. In places the trees have been felled to reveal the River Wye and the magnificent sight of Tintern Abbey far below. Another new path with a gravelly surface has been constructed here to preserve the Dyke as it approaches the **Devil's Pulpit**.

> Celebrated as a viewpoint from the early days of picturesque tourism in the Wye valley in the 18th century, the rock pillar of the **Devil's Pulpit**, jutting out from the limestone cliffs above the Wye gorge, is best known for its sensational view of the substantial and picturesque remains of Tintern Abbey. The abbey was built by the Cistercians in the late 13th century, but it was not until much later that the belief that Satan preached at the Devil's Pulpit to try to tempt Tintern's monks from their Christian ways gained credence.

The reconstructed and still gravelly path descends slightly to a junction at the edge of the woods. Ignore the path going through a gate on the right here, but after descending a few steps quickly bear right where the route to Tintern (signposted but not shown as a right of way) peels off to the left.

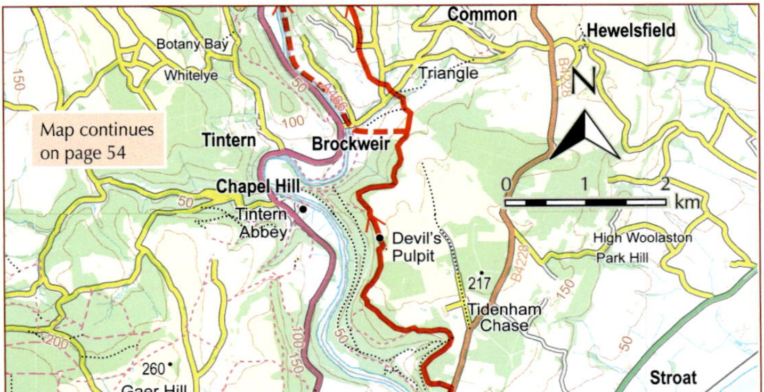

The trail now runs through Passage Grove, alongside and below one of the best preserved sections of Offa's Dyke, with impressive earthen ramparts up to 6m high now threatened by badgers, eventually passing the entrance to Lippets Grove nature reserve – a wildlife trust reserve with ancient trees and a wide variety of wildflowers. The specialities of Lippets Grove include cuckooflower and herb paris, although the most sought-after plant is the martigan lily with its spotted pinkish purple flowers.

The trail continues as a good path parallel to and below the Dyke until it climbs again to run along the crest of the earthwork, with the ground still falling away dramatically to the left. A steep descent of a muddy slope is followed by a right-angled turn to the right as the Dyke follows the contours above the Brockweir valley, then the trail leaves the Dyke, using a newly constructed boardwalk to avoid a steep rocky slope and drop down across rough grassland on the slopes of Madgett Hill.

As the slope eases somewhat a signpost offers two alternatives: the main path across the intricate landscape of the Hudnalls straight ahead, or a left turn to visit Brockweir and follow the riverside path upstream. The two routes are reunited at Bigsweir Bridge some 5km (3 miles) ahead.

Alternative riverside route

Turn left at the signpost and descend steadily on a track that passes to the left of stables and farm buildings. Turn right on a rough track that leads past The Malt House to the main street in **Brockweir** (shop, public transport), passing the pub (closed for several years but now being restored by a community benefit society) to reach the rather utilitarian iron bridge over the Wye, built as recently as 1906 to replace a ferry.

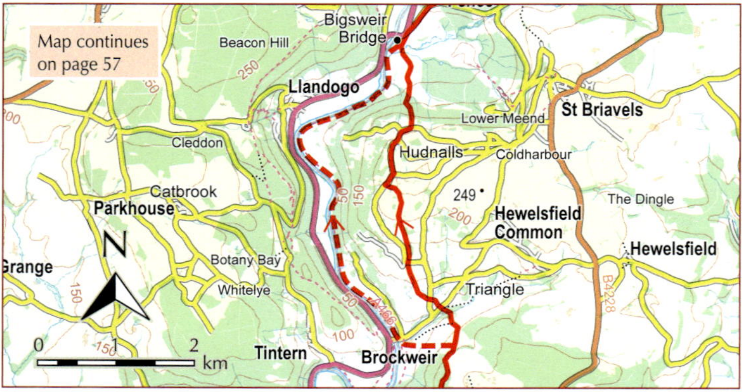

The riverside route north from Brockweir Bridge, with Bargain Wood in the distance

The former river port of **Brockweir** once had a shipbuilding yard and wharf that was used by Severn trows taking goods down the River Wye. Brockweir's gabled Tudor manor house lies amid a cluster of ancient dwellings, while the whitewashed 19th-century Moravian chapel is set alongside a Gothic manse and gabled Victorian Sunday school.

There were once a dozen inns and beerhouses in the village, and in 1832 the newly appointed minister at the Moravian chapel complained that village life was centred on beerhouses, skittle alleys and cockfighting.

A clear track, signposted to Bigsweir, keeps close to the east bank of the Wye, with Coed-Ithel Farm and its old iron furnace and cider house on the opposite bank, and then passes Coed-Ithel weir (where landslips have necessitated a short diversion recently) and hugs the river bank past **Llandogo**.

The path is hemmed in between river and woodland as it heads for Bigsweir House, then it crosses the Mork Brook on a sturdy footbridge and runs through one final field, with salmon fishing on the river and **Bigsweir Bridge** now very prominent ahead. The stylish single-arch cast-iron bridge, with tollhouse on the Welsh bank, was constructed in 1827 to carry the new turnpike road from Chepstow to Monmouth over the river. Leave the river at the bridge and climb up to the main road to rejoin the higher route.

Main route

The main route descends steeply from the signpost to a footbridge, latterly through head-high bracken. Climb the slope opposite, cross a road and take a restricted byway that climbs relentlessly onto St Briavels Common, initially as a green lane but later as a stony track. The route is intricate but generally well signposted as it meanders northwards, twisting and turning along the tiny lanes and tracks, which are characteristic of the ancient landscape of **The Hudnalls**.

> Formerly a large and well-wooded common used for wood pasture, **The Hudnalls** was colonised by squatters in the 18th century and now comprises tiny fields (richly carpeted with wildflowers such as yellow rattle and sheep's sorrel in late spring) and narrow lanes and tracks. There is a real sense of seclusion in this colourful, hidden landscape with its cottages and smallholdings, but there was industry too, with millstones quarried before being rolled down the hillside to be loaded onto barges on the river below.

Go left at a lane, then immediately right before Rock Farm to reach a junction of lanes. Keep straight on here to climb on an excellent narrow track, this time quite stony, to reach the road near Hill Farm. Follow the road round and then leave it to the right, climbing past an old chapel on an ancient walled lane which eventually reaches the plateau as a superb green lane between hedges.

Turn left at a junction of old lanes, cross a field with a colourful corrugated iron hut, then drop down to meet and turn right along a lane that winds through a little hamlet.

Leave the lane by forking left along a hedged path, turn right to join a bridleway and then left along a country lane, following this around to the right – the views northwards along the Wye gorge to the distant Black Mountains are exquisite here – to reach the start of the descent to Bigsweir Bridge. The path is newly re-engineered here, at first simply resurfaced with gravel to withstand visitor pressure but later reconstructed as a steeply descending boardwalk.

Lower down the descent is more natural, on a rocky path and then across two large fields above Bigsweir House to reach the road just to the right of **Bigsweir Bridge**. The riverside alternative comes in from the left here.

The trail uses the St Briavels road for 300m before turning left onto a pleasant path through the woods, cutting through the Dyke and alternating between short climbs and level walking. Cross a somewhat damp meadow and another small wood, aiming to pass to the left of **Coxbury Farm** and climb a stony track. Two paths continue to the north: take the right-hand path to enter the nature reserve at Highbury Wood. The reserve is noted for its cherry, lime and yew trees together with early purple orchids and dormice.

There are occasional glimpses of the Forest of Dean to the right as the path leads along the east side of the ridge, although nearer trees frequently obstruct the views. Turn left through a (somewhat redundant) gate in the deer fence onto a path that clambers over tree roots and eroded building stone as it follows the Dyke, with traces of ditches on either side.

The path follows a gently undulating course through Highbury Wood until the Dyke suddenly turns sharply to the east and the path cuts through it, descending quite steeply past Highbury Farm to cross a track and take a flight of concrete steps leading down past renovated cottages on the right to reach the main road at **Redbrook**.

REDBROOK

A fertile imagination is needed to visualise this quiet village as a busy river port and industrial centre, yet Wyes Green was once a busy wharf exporting the end products of the tinplate and copper smelting works in Lower Redbrook, while there were also corn and paper mills, a malthouse and a brewery, together with tramways and railroads.

The village nowadays has a shop and two pubs (the Boat Inn is actually located in Wales and accessed via a disused railway bridge over the Wye) and B&B accommodation is available.

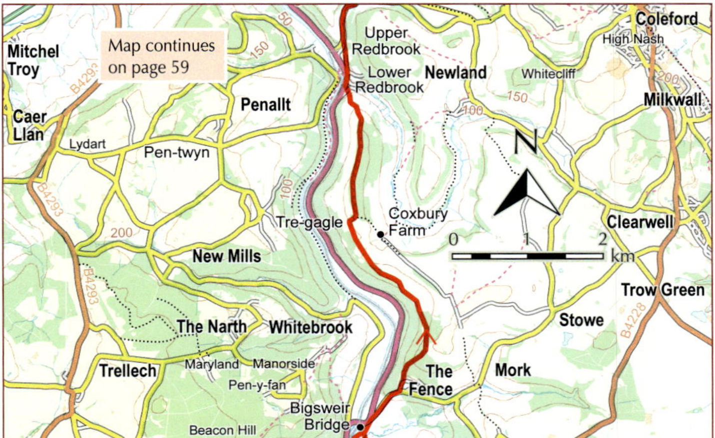

The Round House, built in 1794 on the summit of the Kymin above Monmouth

The way lies north along the road or, more attractively, straight across into riverside gardens at Wyes Green. Take the path along the riverbank, with a good view of the old railway viaduct, to reach the village car park.

Opposite the car park there is a clearly signposted restricted byway which initially gains height alongside the main road, then swings east into the upper Redbrook valley, running to the right of the Incline Bridge, which carried the Monmouth tramway across the valley road at an unlikely angle.

The track converges with the valley road, which leads past a terrace of workers' cottages built on the site of a former tinplate works, heading towards the Mill Pond. Take a track on the left just before the pond, then swing left onto Duffield's Lane to climb past **Upper Beaulieu Farm**, formerly part of a grange farm belonging to the abbey of Grace Dieu.

Take the right fork along the edge of Harper's Grove, with the larches of Bunjups Wood – well known locally for their superb display of autumn colours – prominently in view some distance to the right of the path. The slope eases for the final element of the ascent to the **Kymin**, with an easy but charming walk through woodland leading to a narrow lane and car park.

Walk straight across the lane to reach the twin highlights of the little hill: firstly the Naval Temple, quickly followed by the Round House. The gentlemen of the Monmouth Picnic Club built the Round House (a circular Georgian banqueting

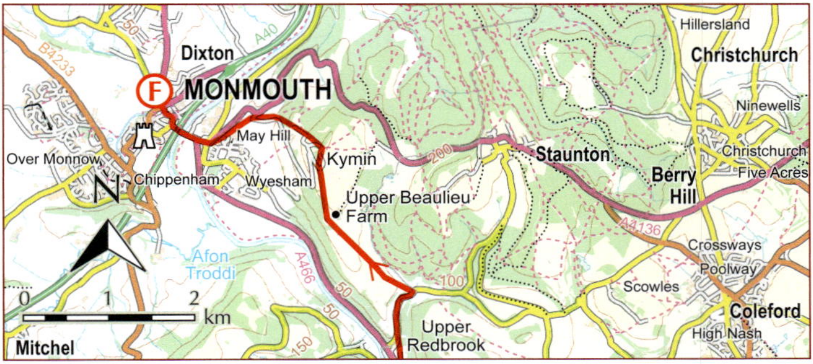

house), while the Naval Temple was built to celebrate the naval victories of the Napoleonic Wars.

A good path leaves the Round House to the north, crossing the plateau to a waymark post. Keep straight on here to descend a few steps by a rocky outcrop and use an ancient holloway that clearly defines the route down the steep hillside. Turn right at another signpost onto a path at the woodland edge to reach a lane, and go through a gate to cross small fields and re-enter the woods.

The descent along the woodland path is gradual and delightful, eventually reaching Good Neighbours Lane, with a sudden panorama northwards and westwards across Monmouth and the Wye valley. Walk along the lane until it bends right, then go straight ahead, going past an orchard, and drop steadily down to join the main road from Gloucester to Monmouth. The road leads across the Wye bridge and through a subway into the attractive market town of **Monmouth**.

MONMOUTH

The old border stronghold of Monmouth has a long history and its Norman castle is best known as the birthplace of Henry V. By far the most impressive monument is the 13th-century fortified bridge over the River Monnow – the only one of its kind in Britain and one of only three left in Europe. Skirmishes in the Civil War revealed a crucial weakness, however, since the river was easily forded upstream and the town's defenders found themselves surrounded. The town was the home of Charles Rolls, co-founder of Rolls Royce and an aviation pioneer who was the first Briton to die in an air crash.

There is a full range of services available, including shops, hotels, cafés and pubs.

STAGE 2

Sheep and cider in remote Monmouthshire

Start	Agincourt Square, Monmouth (SO 507 128)
Finish	Lancaster Arms guest house, Pandy (SO 333 217)
Distance	26.2km (16.3 miles)
Ascent	535m (1755ft)
Time	6–8hr
Maps	OS Outdoor Leisure 13, 14
Refreshments	Nothing en route except the Hunters Moon Inn at Llangattock Lingoed and possibly the Hogs Head at Great Treadam
Public transport	Monmouth has bus connections to Newport, Chepstow and Hereford, while Pandy is served by the 23 bus route from Hereford to Abergavenny, but there is absolutely no public transport at any point along the path between Monmouth and Pandy
Accommodation	Farmhouse B&B along the path at Hendre, Llanfihangel Ystern Llewern and Llanvetherine, together with the Hunters Moon Inn and Old Rectory B&B at Llangattock Lingoed and very limited provision at Pandy

The trail crosses a corrugated landscape of small fields and minor valleys, leaving behind the Wye valley and gradually rising towards the foothills of the Black Mountains. As long ago as the 1870s the predominant land uses were sheep grazing and cider and perry pear orchards, and superficially little has changed. There are few villages and only a scatter of farming hamlets, so there is a surprising feeling of remoteness; the day is a long one, and although the route poses no great challenges, walkers leaving Monmouth will encounter no shops or cafés and only one pub before reaching Pandy.

In **Monmouth**, take Monnow Street down to the river bridge, with its remarkable fortified gatehouse, then turn right along Drybridge Street as the trail endures its last stretch of suburbia until Prestatyn, initially following signs to Rockfield as it goes right at a roundabout, straight on at a second, and then left at a third into Watery Lane. The old route has become the main access road into the Brook housing estate, but after 300m turn left to rediscover the original lane as it aims for

The River Monnow and the fortified medieval bridge, unique in Britain

open countryside, still with houses alongside and with a culverted stream running next to the road.

A sharp right turn heralds the escape from tarmac, with wheat fields all around and Bailey Pitt Farm straight ahead as the trail swings right to follow the right-hand side of a wheat field, with King's Wood looming ahead and the Kymin seen for the last time to the south.

The route crosses two streams on sturdy footbridges, then follows the left-hand edge of a field on a much-improved gravelly path before entering the woodland. Named after Edward III, King's Wood contains wonderful old yews and a number of 500-year-old veteran oaks. Goshawks and owls are often seen, together with hawfinch and tree pipit.

There's quite a climb through King's Wood, on a good path that crosses over two tracks in quick succession and continues steadily upwards as a sunken lane. The slope eases as the route passes an early 19th-century Monmouth parish boundary stone, briefly escapes the trees close to a seat, and re-enters the woodland as a wide gravelly track going straight over a forest road.

A long march along the track ensues, but it is gently and pleasantly downhill until, after passing a barrier, the forest track becomes a stony lane heading for the farming hamlet of **Hendre** (B&Bs, bunkhouse, campsite).

Skirrid Fawr, the 'holy mountain', from the path leading to Caggle Street

Keep to the tarmac road through Hendre, then veer left through a gate and follow a new path that has slightly diverted the long-distance route onto higher ground away from the River Trothy. Pass through two gates, with the site of Grace Dieu Abbey by the river to the left.

Founded in 1226 by John de Monmouth, **Grace Dieu** was destroyed by the Welsh seven years later but limped on until the Dissolution. The substantial 17th-century farm of Parc Grace Dieu, flanked by a two-storey cider house (the first of several encountered along the route) is prominent across the shallow valley of the River Trothy.

The trail crosses a footbridge, with an unexpected picnic table to the right, then snakes across a big field often frequented by white cattle. The old leat, which provided the abbey with water from the river, is represented by pools and green channels to the left as the path approaches and turns left along a country road to cross the Trothy – a quiet river known for its trout, grayling and eels – at Abbey Bridge.

Leave the road to the right after 300m, with the path well waymarked over a series of fields (although it's important to keep straight on across the second field rather than being seduced by a better-defined path going slightly to the right). Drop down across the fourth field to follow the Trothy upstream, eventually reaching a huge meadow which is exceptionally well provisioned with yellow-topped waymark posts, with the substantial stone and slate Court Farm beyond the far bank.

The route passes below Sunnybank Farm and goes through a gate onto the farm's access track to reach the hamlet of **Llanfihangel-Ystern-Llewern**, with the village church just to the left. A tablet in the church records the achievements of Sir Joseph Bradley, who wrote *The History of Monmouthshire*. Turn left along a little tree-lined avenue leading to the church (which has facilities for making hot drinks), but quickly go right to take a path running alongside the raised churchyard, dipping down to cross a stream and then rising to cross a little field with a duck enclosure.

Cross an access lane to a cottage, keep the cottage on the left and keep straight ahead (ignore an inviting route through a gateway to the left: a signpost would clarify matters here). The path through the gateway to the left leads to the B&B offered by Upper Red House Farm but the route lies straight ahead over a footbridge and across three more fields – keep the faith across the second field, where alternatives peel off to the left and right but a stile eventually materialises at the top of the field – to reach a lane by Pen-pwll-y-calch Farm. A short distance to the right, the Quaker chapel within the historic, unaltered hall-house at Pant bears witness to the secret meetings of dissenters in the 17th century.

There's a tedious but unavoidable 500m along the road now, with tantalising glimpses of hills to the west, before the trail takes a path to the right, running through permanent pasture before skirting The Grange. Go straight across the farm's access road, with a sudden panoramic view of the hills above Abergavenny – including the Blorenge, the unmistakeable cone of the Sugar Loaf and the asymmetrical Skirrid Fawr.

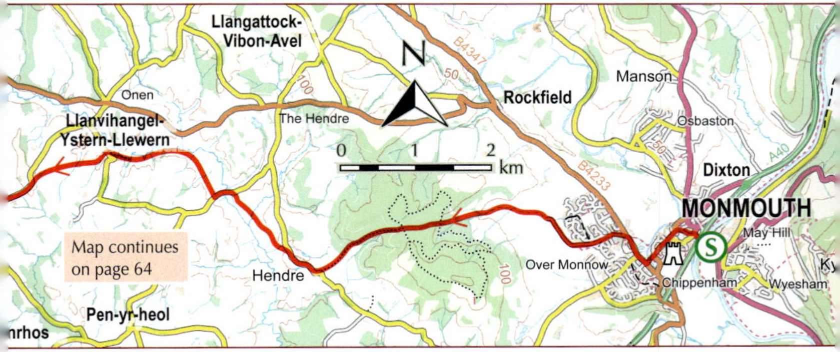

Map continues on page 64

The distinctive jagged profile of **Skirrid Fawr** is almost uninterruptedly in view for the rest of the day. The most easterly of the Black Mountains, it reaches a mere 486m (1595ft) but it is instantly recognisable, with a great gash gouged out of its western side as a result of landslips in the Ice Age. More fancifully, it has been claimed that the mountain was split open during an earthquake which coincided with Christ's crucifixion.

The sparse remains of the medieval chapel of St Michael – once a place of pilgrimage – lie at the north end of the ridge.

Drop down through sheep pastures to find a gate which used to lead into mature cider orchards. Sadly Heineken (the owner of Bulmers) cleared 300 acres of apple trees in 2024, claiming reduced demand for cider but destroying important wildlife habitat (not least for winter thrushes such as fieldfare) in the process. Turn right onto a road that passes **Penrhos** – a renaissance farmhouse with a restored cider house – with the remains of a motte-and-bailey castle lying just to the south. The route eventually crosses the Trothy again close to the disused mill on the edge of the big village of **Llantilio Crossenny** (which, sadly, has no facilities).

The national trail takes a direct route through the village but contrives to miss most of the features of interest here, so instead of slavishly following the official route, which takes a right turn and runs behind back gardens, stay with the lane until it reaches a T-junction, with the former Hostry Inn to the left. The Hostry,

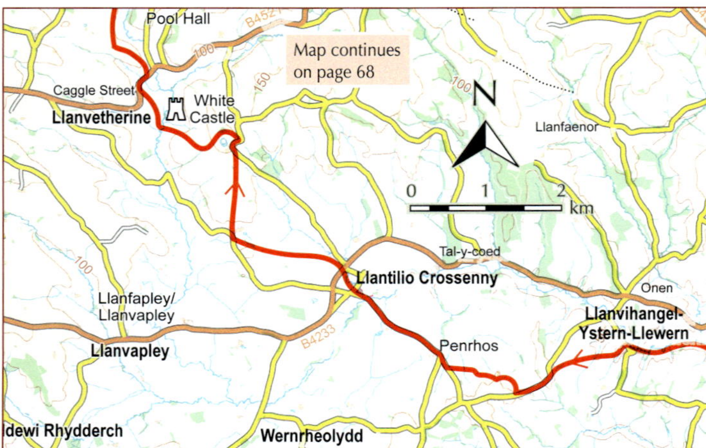

The late medieval former Hostry Inn in Llantilio Crossenny

with its distinctive octagonal chimney, was an inn by 1459 but sadly closed in 2002, contributing to the dearth of pubs in the area.

Turn right at the junction, taking a lane that intersects with the trail, but keep straight on to visit the church of St Teilo, with a notable interior including the medieval parish chest. A path to the left of the churchyard then leads to the B4233, with the site of Hen Gwrt (the Old Court) immediately ahead.

The original building at **Hen Gwrt** was a moated manor house built for the Bishops of Llandaff in the 13th century, although 200 years later the house lay at the south-west corner of an extensive deer park and was used as a hunting lodge. The moat, clogged with bulrushes but still very picturesque, appears to date from the 14th century; it is the only reminder of the former importance of the site, since the house fell into disuse in the 1600s and its site is now open and grassy.

Go back to the B4233 and turn right for 100m to pick up Offa's Dyke Path again as it bisects two large fields on a very clear, wide track. The track fades out and the way lies ahead across two arable fields, the going quite trying at times

The extensive ruins of the White Castle, once part of the lordship of the Three Castles

and the possibility of heading too far to the left all too real. The key is to aim for a copse at the top of the second field, with a gate and waymark to its left.

Descend through a further field and turn left along the Great Treadam Farm access to reach a narrow lane. Turn right along the lane, passing the entrance to the Hogs Head – potentially a useful watering hole, but with restricted opening hours – and turning right along a stony lane past the attractive cluster of late medieval buildings at Old Treadam. The narrow road was clearly more important once, since the metalling survives in places, but it has fallen on hard times now and has reverted to a green lane, climbing quite sharply to reach a plateau.

The lane is a surprisingly long one and runs straight through the site of an Iron Age hillfort – although only the eagle-eyed will spot any signs of this – but ultimately emerges on a road just below the substantial Upper White Castle Farm. Follow the road past the farm and ignore a tempting invitation to visit a (somewhat distant) vineyard's cellar door. The ramparts of **White Castle** are already visible, and the tarmac quickly peters out at the entrance gates.

The 12th-century **White Castle**, its name a reference to the white plaster that once coated its walls, has all-encompassing views of the southern Welsh borderland. The remains are extensive and inspiring, with a square stone keep, powerful round towers and high curtain walls still standing. The inner bailey is defended by a deep and water-filled moat and a gatehouse.

With nearby Grosmont and Skenfrith, White Castle formed part of the lordship of the Three Castles. It was abandoned by the 16th century but gained brief notoriety in the 1940s when Hitler's right-hand man, Rudolf Hess, who was imprisoned nearby, was allowed to feed the swans in the moat.

Offa's Dyke Path makes its way around the eastern and northern ramparts, using a splendid green lane with the solid castle walls to the left and a pretty cottage to the right. Go through a gate to drop down a field, turn right to pass Duke's Barn and very soon left through another gate (the castle now in the distance but still dominating the landscape).

Another left turn has the path heading straight for the Skirrid before the trail bends slightly right to a gate, crosses high above the infant River Trothy on a recently reconstructed and impressive footbridge, and follows a faint path through a big field to reach the B4521 in the hamlet of **Caggle Street**. Only the name survives of the long-closed Vine Tree Inn in Caggle Street, whose name is reputed to mean 'the road strewn with sheep dung'.

The distinctive lime-washed church at Llangattock Lingoed

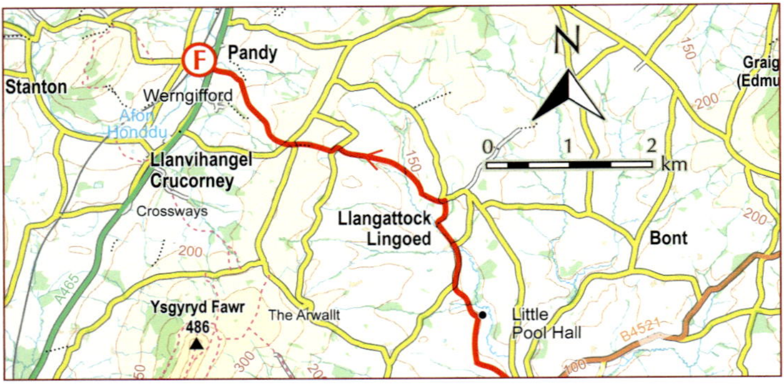

Use the pavement on the right when it materialises, cross the road to take a path through a field often inhabited by horses and then negotiate a second, much larger field where the path winds between thistles. A gate leads into a third field, the path heading for the track at Cockshoot Barn. Turn right here, the track soon becoming a fine green lane through dairying country, with the sadly dilapidated buildings of **Little Pool Hall** Farm in view ahead. Little Pool Hall is an impressive but melancholy sight, with the abandoned farmhouse across a courtyard from an imposing timber-framed corn barn with a flagstone threshing floor.

The trail leaves Little Pool Hall to the left, dips down to cross a stream – the footbridge is usually optional here – and follows a wide strip of green across an arable field, aiming just to the right of a cottage, to reach a narrow lane. Turn right along the lane, passing the entrance to Old Court where the road swings right. A rare survival of a late 15th-century court house, Old Court was the home of the Parliamentarian Sir Thomas Morgan, who later became governor of Jersey. Leave the lane here, going straight ahead along an even narrower (although still roughly surfaced) track to pass cottages and reach Cwm Farm.

The great treasure of Cwm Farm is the virtually unaltered two-storey **cider house** dating from 1754, which contains original fittings including a superb cider mill with circular stone trough and mill wheel, and a cider press with wooden spiral screw and stone trough in which the juice of the pressed apples accumulated. The loft on the upper floor was used for storing apples and perry pears until they were ready for processing.

Opposite the farm a little grassy path drops down to cross a stream and confront an unexpectedly steep climb, going diagonally to the right to find a short tree-shaded lane leading directly into the churchyard at **Llangattock Lingoed** (B&Bs, pub).

Pass the white lime-washed church (comprehensively rebuilt after the near-collapse of the south wall, which revealed fragments of medieval wall paintings) and go through the gates onto the village road, with the Hunters Moon Inn on the right, immediately adjacent to the churchyard. The inn was built in 1217 to house workers building the church next door and still offers B&B accommodation, as does the Old Rectory along the road.

The end of the day's walk is now only 3km away, at first along the road but soon taking a short flight of steps on the right followed by a narrow path between fences, passing the old village schoolhouse.

Beyond a couple of small fields the path descends slightly, with the Skirrid mountain still a dominant feature to the left, to cross the Full Brook and face another climb, with increasingly good views across a deeply incised valley to the left. Pick up a path on a terrace above the stream, crossing fields used to graze horses, to reach a minor road.

Turn briefly left along the road, then right, climbing steadily but with good retrospective views of Great Park and the Full Brook valley. The path continues straight ahead, passing just to the left of Llanerch Farm to pick up its access drive as far as a narrow tarmac lane. Turn right here, then left at a T-junction, now on a rather busier road for 100m or so, with the compensation of an excellent view of the landslip on the north-western face of Skirrid Fawr.

Turn right to cross a field, with the Black Mountains – and especially the distinctive Sugar Loaf and the bulky Hatterrall Ridge – now filling the view ahead. The path is generally well waymarked as it gradually loses height through a number of fields, passing through gates and finally reaching a track aiming for the A465 Abergavenny to Hereford road by the Lancaster Arms guest house in the village of **Pandy**.

PANDY

The straggling village of Pandy includes a scattering of farms, some cottages along the main road and, somewhat incongruously, the modern housing estate of Wern Gifford. The eminent Welsh academic, critic and novelist Raymond Williams was born in a cottage alongside Offa's Dyke Path here, while Owen Sheers set some of his World War 2 masterpiece *Resistance* in the disused Pandy station.

The village has no shop but the 23 bus provides a regular service to Abergavenny and Hereford and there is a limited choice of accommodation on and close to the path.

STAGE 3

Crossing the Black Mountains

Start	Lancaster Arms guest house, Pandy (SO 333 217)
Finish	Butter Market, Hay-on-Wye (SO 228 424)
Distance	26.5km (16.5 miles)
Ascent	715m (2345ft)
Time	7–9hr
Maps	OS Outdoor Leisure 13
Refreshments	There's nowhere to stock up in Pandy, and the only intermediate refreshments involve detours to Longtown and Llanthony (check weekday opening hours), but there is a full range of services in Hay
Public transport	Pandy is served by the 23 bus route from Hereford to Abergavenny, while the X44 service runs between Hereford, Hay-on-Wye and Brecon
Accommodation	There's a good selection of hotels, inns and B&Bs in Hay, together with campsites. The only accommodation en route is at Llanthony (including camping) and Capel-y-ffin, and in Longtown and the Olchon valley, in all cases involving a significant detour from the trail, and additional climbing to rejoin the route.

An exhilarating yet surprisingly easy traverse of the eastern ridge of the Black Mountains, with the Llanthony valley to the west and the Olchon valley in Herefordshire to the east. The 26.5km (16.5 mile) main route requires reserves of stamina, however; and walkers may want to consider breaking the journey in Llanthony or Longtown, and climbing back up to the ridge the following day. In bad weather the low-level route via Llanthony, Capel-y-ffin and the Gospel Pass is a sensible alternative. But in fair weather the ridge walk is a magnificent, sustained high-level adventure.

Start just to the left of the Lancaster Arms in **Pandy**, cross a cow pasture and then use the solid footbridge high above the River Honddu to reach a short path climbing up to a kissing gate by the main Cardiff to Manchester railway line. Take great care here – fast trains hurtle past every few minutes – and hug the left-hand side

The steep-sided motte of the 11th-century castle at Trevedw

of another meadow to reach a country road. Glance back to the left here to see a small but remarkably steep-sided early Norman motte, its summit adorned by ornamental fir trees.

Take the lane straight ahead, passing Trevedw Farm and its massive sandstone barn on the left. Look out for a stile on the right and go diagonally uphill across a field, in the direction of a converted barn and a communications mast. Turn right along the lane and right again at a crossroads (the Beacons Way comes in from the left just before this) to follow a narrow lane contouring above the Honddu valley, and after descending gently for a while take the signposted green lane on the left. The Beacons Way coincides with Offa's Dyke Path for a short part of its 160km journey from Skirrid Fawr through the Black Mountains and Bannau Brycheiniog to the hamlet of Bethlehem near Llandovery.

The lane soon becomes sunken and bouldery as it climbs the hillside to a gate at the moorland edge, with the little estate centred on Trewyn House below to the right. Swing left, now on a green track again, and then curve round to the right, passing drifts of autumn crocuses in season as the track approaches the hillfort above **Pentwyn**. The Iron Age fort defended the Hatterrall ridge from the south, although the northern ramparts are scenically the most impressive.

The path goes right through the fort before using a gap in the northern ramparts to access the lower slopes of Hatterrall Hill. A broad green track through bracken runs to the right of an enclosure described as The Castle – probably the

The southernmost trig point on the Hatterrall ridge and the view north to Hatterrall Hill

site of the manor and chapel of Redcastle, an outlying grange of Llanthony Priory – as it aims for steeper ground ahead.

The way ahead is steep in places but the slope eases as a track joins from the left and leads to the first trig point of the day, at only 464m (1522ft) but with a superb aerial view of the classic border hamlet of Oldcastle down on the right. The path cuts through gorse, bilberry and rough grass on its way down to a minor col, then climbs gently, now running through heather, to reach the summit of Hatterrall Hill (531m/1742ft). Just to the left is the Garreg Las round cairn, with a stone-walled defensive enclosure a little further away and a cross-ridge wall defending the subsidiary ridge to the west.

For 15km (9.5 miles) the national trail follows the crest of the **Hatterrall ridge**, the most easterly ridge of the Black Mountains. The walking is easy yet inspiring, and the views both westwards across the Vale of Ewyas into the dissected upland plateau, and eastwards into the Golden Valley and the ridges and valleys of southern Herefordshire are superb.

The ridge is frequented by sheep, wild ponies and birds of prey, together with hang-gliding enthusiasts and pony trekkers. Pressure from horses' hooves and walkers' feet has required extensive path repairs to avoid further erosion of the fragile peat surface.

Climb up a little, with the first evidence of path repairs in the form of big flagstones set into the peat, and then go round the right-hand side of a little knoll, swinging right at a pile of stones close to a boundary stone. Suddenly the way ahead lies through magnificent heather moorland, with occasional grouse butts hinting at the presence (although in much reduced numbers) of red grouse on the ridge, and with a prospect down to the right of the straggling village of Longtown. The motte and bailey of Longtown Castle is one of the most impressive in the borders, with a solid stone keep protected by a twin-towered gatehouse.

The view ahead is equally extensive, with the main ridge swinging right as it traverses a relatively narrow neck of land and then curving left to climb higher. As the path reaches the narrowest part of the ridge there is a sudden and magnificent view of the Vale of Ewyas on the left, with the extensive ruins of Llanthony Priory clearly seen. The main route keeps to the crest of the ridge here, while the Beacons Way leaves to the left, heading for the priory.

Alternative route via Llanthony Priory and Cwm Siarpal

The way to Llanthony (B&Bs, campsite, pub) descends steadily on a clear track through the moorland before swinging left over a stile close to a stream and cutting through Wiral Wood. Go over a stile out of the wood, with an excellent view of the narrow Honddu valley dominated by the ruins of the priory, and descend

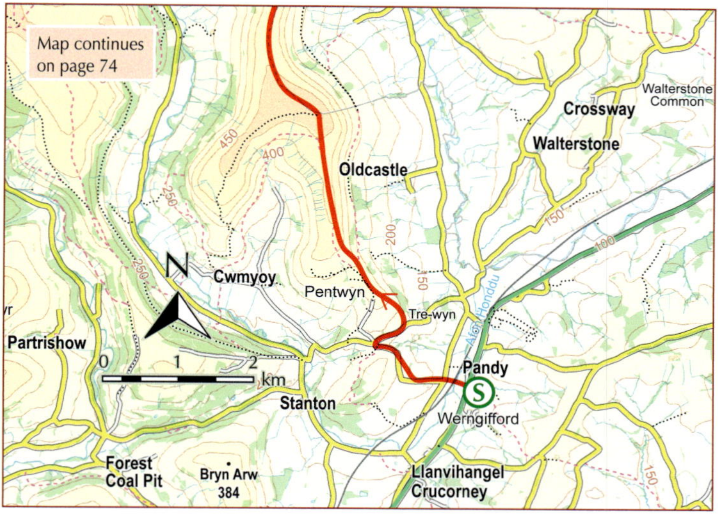

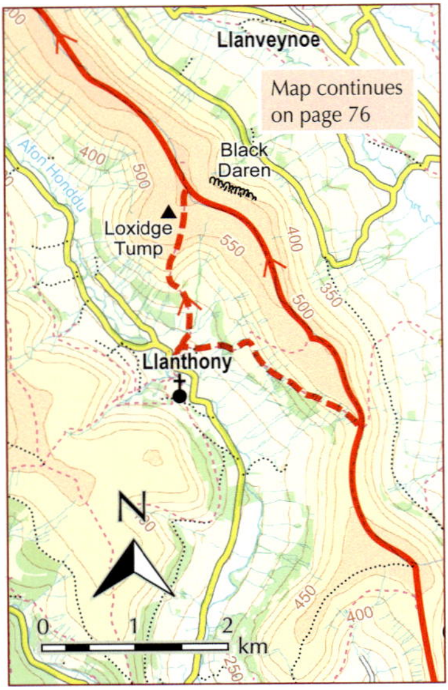

more gently alongside a wall to find a well-used path leading into the priory grounds.

The great glory of **Llanthony Priory** is its sublime situation in a beautiful and peaceful setting deep in the mountains. Possibly founded as a chapel by St David, it became an Augustinian priory in 1108 and now comprises the extensive ruins of the church, chapter house, a medieval gatehouse later used as a barn, fishponds and a dovecote. A tower of the priory church and part of the claustral range became a shooting box and steward's house in the late 18th century, and now form part of a highly unusual pub and hotel.

To regain the ridge go back through the gates and keep left on a waymarked path across fields, with woodland on the left and the unfinished and now ruinous mansion of the poet Walter Savage Landor in Cwm Siarpal over on the right.

The route zigzags up the steep lower slopes above a little quarry, then heads north-east past an irregularly shaped stone-walled enclosure and a prominent Bronze Age burial mound to cross the flat-topped **Loxidge Tump** and rejoin the ridge path.

Main route

The main route follows the ridge northwards, climbing easily past the Rhiw Arw burial cairn, with a solid stone wall enclosing woodland just down on the left. The way lies across heather moorland on a path that is still largely grassy, then there's another gentle climb to a second trig point, at 552m (1811ft) – the heather is still there in patches but now there is also bilberry and rough grassland – with the ridge top now forming a wide expanse of moorland frequented only by birds such as skylarks and wheatears. Another path from Llanthony to the Olchon valley crosses the ridge path at a pile of stones, with yet another burial mound, the Wiral cairn, just beyond.

The trail passes a succession of small muddy pools by the side of the path on the ridge, which is frequented by wild ponies and (especially at weekends) pony trekkers. Below the crest to the right are the cliff faces of **Black Daren** and, somewhat further north, Red Daren. The cliffs form the back walls of 'armchair corries', the result of Ice Age landslips following over-steepening of the sides of the ridge, and support plants such as mossy saxifrage and Welsh poppies. The ridge itself rises almost imperceptibly at this stage, the path sometimes grassy and sometimes gravelly as it crosses heather moorland again.

Occasional cairns – useful in mist – mark the way across the moor, culminating in a big, combined cairn and wall shelter on top of the final Bronze Age burial cairn on the Hatterrall ridge (the Black Daren cairn has been robbed and disturbed, with the cist or stone-lined grave exposed). The heather becomes much more sporadic, with grassland and bilberry dominating, while there is a first glimpse of the Black Hill ridge on the right. The ridge path, repaired with coarse gravel in places, passes another boundary stone and then reaches a big cairn on the left at 605m (1985ft). This marks the point at which the alternative route from Llanthony comes in from the left.

A thin path continues along the ridge, snaking through wide moorland and rising very gently but inexorably (at one point crossing a peaty section on a fairly long stretch of flagstones) to reach the third trig point at 610m (2000ft). The highest

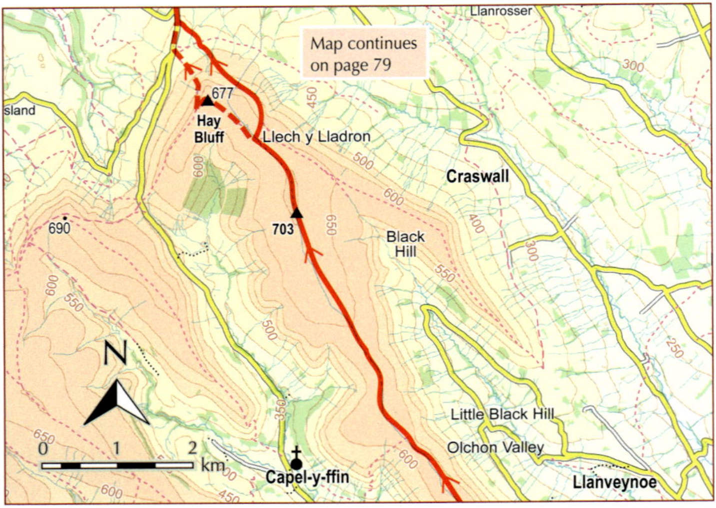

summits of the Black Mountains – the shapely Pen y Gadair Fawr and the higher but less attractive Waun Fach – are now clearly visible across the upper reaches of the Vale of Ewyas, while there is an excellent view to the right across the Olchon Valley to the craggy ridge of the Black Hill, which rises to meet the main ridge as it swings slightly to the right. The remote Olchon valley was the main setting for *Resistance*, a powerful novel by the poet Owen Sheers, which imagined a Britain occupied by Germany in the 1940s.

Beyond the trig pillar the path becomes gravelly and stony again, traversing rough tussocky moorland with one or two pools providing encouragement for bog cotton. Landmarks are at a premium now, although Pen y Gadair Fawr and Waun Fach can still be seen beyond the nearer Chwarel y Fan ridge to the left. Better still is the increasingly intimate view of the sharp, serrated Black Hill ridge across the head of the Olchon valley on the right. Black Hill, also known as the Cat's Back, is a magnificent rocky ridge wholly in Herefordshire but very much a part of the Black Mountains.

Shaggy mountain ponies and their foals often congregate on the slopes here, while red kites and (much more rarely) merlins can be seen overhead. There's a slight rise before a little path comes in from the left, making its way from Capel-y-Ffin and The Vision to Olchon Court.

The **Benedictine monastery** at Capel-y-Ffin was founded in 1870 by Joseph Leycester Lyne, the self-styled Father Ignatius, but abandoned after his death in 1908. Eric Gill, the sculptor and artist, later lived in some of the buildings, while two chapels lie closer to the River Honddu.

In 1880 monks and farm labourers saw visions of the Virgin Mary near the monastery, and The Vision Farm was renamed to mark the event. The name of the farm was appropriated by Bruce Chatwin as the main location for *On the Black Hill*, although he relocated the farm for artistic effect.

The stony path continues along the ridge, with more sections resurfaced with flagstones to take walkers over the worst and wettest of the peat. Unexpectedly, there is suddenly a very bouldery section of path with a plethora of cairns, giving the feel of a mountain climb, although the slope is still very gentle.

Rough gravel takes over again, rather bizarrely piled up as a narrow-cambered path through the moorland, then there are more flagstones, with the slope negligible and the featureless moorland extending in all directions. The Black Hill ridge, now below and to the right, is gradually getting closer from the right, with the green slopes of Dorstone Hill further away.

Another long stretch on flagstones follows, the route winding over moorland with peat on either side and some residual heather, and now with the north-eastern denouement of the dramatic northern escarpment of the Black Mountains prominent ahead and to the left. The highest point of the Hatterrall ridge – and of the whole of Offa's Dyke Path – at 703m (2306ft) is, frankly, a disappointing anticlimax, with nothing to mark the culmination of such a long ascent. Just to the south-east of the highest point is the crash site of a plane that became lost in cloud and failed to clear the ridge in March 1940.

The start of the descent is equally imperceptible at first, but happily the way down then involves a steep and scenic clamber over rocks to reach **Llech y Lladron** (the 'thief's stone') – an outcrop of Old Red Sandstone that projects forward to provide a makeshift shelter. The path forks here, the left branch heading for the summit of Hay Bluff, while the national trail somewhat counter-intuitively heads off to the right.

Alternative route via Hay Bluff

Keep left at the junction of paths and follow the obvious route across the moorland for almost 1km to reach the white-painted trig pillar marking the summit of **Hay Bluff** (677m/2221ft). The pillar has a red Welsh dragon stencilled on all four sides, but a bigger attraction is the extraordinary panorama, from the Bannau Brycheiniog in the west to the Malvern Hills in the east.

The descent from Llech y Lladron to the Gospel Pass

Zigzag left and then right to find the easiest way off the mountain, descending steeply and aiming towards the obvious car park on the Gospel Pass road. Close to the car park is a Bronze Age stone circle identified as recently as the 1960s, with only one stone projecting more than a few inches above the turf. Walk down the road for about 500m to rejoin Offa's Dyke Path as it comes in from the right.

Main route

The main route turns right at **Llech y Lladron**, making for the eastern side of the ridge, at first on flagstones but then on gravel as the path contours round above the extensive Craswall Common. The route loses height gradually, going over a few rocky steps as it keeps to the eastern side of the declining ridge, then swings to the right, away from the mountain, dropping down slightly more abruptly for a while.

Cross the common, with the Gospel Pass car park clearly in view ahead and to the left, negotiate a rather boggy area where several small seasonal streams converge, and take a good path through the bracken. The route crosses a slightly deeper valley, with a little stream in a surprisingly rocky channel, before rising to a junction of paths in a sea of bracken. Take the right fork (unsignposted), reaching the Gospel Pass road a good way below the car park. The alternative route rejoins the national trail at this point.

Go north along the road, ignoring a turning to the left but looking for a thin path that leaves the road to the left just after a field boundary. The path cuts across a grassy area of common land, its direction fairly obvious but not confirmed until it dips down, passes a national trail waymark and climbs briefly up a rutted track to the west of Twyn y Beddau. The round barrow at Twyn y Beddau also marks the site of a 14th-century battle, while nearby Cockalofty was once 'the meanest rural house in the district', but has since been restored.

Keep straight ahead, with a fine prospect of the Wye valley and its patchwork of woodlands and small fields down to the left, and a sensational retrospective view of Hay Bluff and the northern scarp of the Black Mountains.

After passing a second waymark avoid the temptation to follow a green path that heads gradually left, and instead aim to converge gradually with Tack Wood to the right, searching out a gate in the far right-hand corner of the common. Climb up immediately to the right onto a pleasant shady path through woodland, cross a stream on a rock step, and carry straight on past the restored 17th-century farmhouse at **Cadwgan**, with its free-ranging chickens and exhortations not to feed the donkeys.

Go straight ahead on the farm's access lane, but as this goes quite steeply downhill leave it to the right just before Hen-Allt Common, heading diagonally left down a field and going through a thin belt of woodland on an eroded rocky path. Hen-Allt Common has tufa-forming springs, an important population of the increasingly rare meadow saffron, and is the only known Welsh site at which flat-sedge is found.

Cross a narrow lane and take a path past a cottage, follow the right-hand edge of a field and cross a stream on a big footbridge, then turn left to reach a country lane. The lane dips down and starts to rise again, but quickly turn right through a gate. The path is shown as legally diverted here, but the diversion hardly does walkers any favours since it requires a circumnavigation of the field, eventually finding a gate, which could have been reached much more directly.

Hay-on-Wye castle, built by the Marcher lord William de Braose in the late 11th century

Keep ahead through a second field, eventually going through a woodland glade, crossing a high footbridge and through two kissing gates. Take the left-hand option through the next field to find yet another kissing gate, then go diagonally across a final field on a very obvious path to reach **Hay-on-Wye**'s main car park on Oxford Road. An alleyway then leads below the castle to the town square and Butter Market.

HAY-ON-WYE

The Normans founded Hay-on-Wye as a new town shortly after the Conquest, with a motte-and-bailey castle built by the 1090s and superseded by a ringwork with square keep and curtain walls in the 13th century. The town became a minor market centre and might have remained so were it not for the inventiveness of second-hand bookseller Richard Booth, who rebranded the castle as one of many bookshops and inspired the Hay literary festival.

The market still takes place every Thursday, centred on the old Butter Market but spilling into the streets below the castle, while there is a good selection of hotels, guest houses, shops, cafés and pubs in the town.

STAGE 4

Gladestry and Hergest Ridge

Start	Butter Market, Hay-on-Wye (SO 228 424)
Finish	Kington Museum (SO 295 566)
Distance	23km (14.5 miles)
Ascent	680m (2230ft)
Time	6–8hr
Maps	OS Outdoor Leisure 13 and Explorer 201
Refreshments	Apart from tea and coffee in the church at Newchurch, the only chance of refreshments en route is at the Royal Oak at Gladestry. There are plenty of traditional shops, together with cafés and pubs, in Kington.
Public transport	Bus X44 provides a regular service between Hereford, Hay-on-Wye and Brecon, while the 461 and 462 services connect Kington with Hereford
Accommodation	B&B at the Rhydspence Inn and at the Royal Oak and a couple of private houses in Gladestry, with a good choice in and around Kington, including hotels, B&Bs and camping

This section of the trail begins with easy riverside walking – a complete contrast to the preceding stage – but it should not be underestimated since it soon rises to cross the rolling border country of western Herefordshire and south Powys. The route lies across Little Mountain and Disgwylfa to the remote hamlet of Newchurch, but a particular highlight is the trek along the outstanding former drovers' road, Red Lane. The stage ends with a wonderful traverse of the stunning Hergest Ridge, with easy ridge walking and extensive views in all directions.

From the 19th-century Butter Market below the ruins of Hay Castle, drop down along narrow streets on the left to reach Broad Street and then cross the wide, shallow River Wye on the B4351. Turn right immediately after the bridge onto a good path on beaten earth through a thin belt of woodland alive with birdsong, with the wide river surprisingly far below. The path is protected with a wooden fence in places but eventually descends to go through a gate and into a riverside meadow. The temporary Roman marching camp at Boatside Farm, Clyro, lies just to the left here, although it is best observed from aerial photographs.

Beyond another gate the trail continues along the riverbank until, on reaching a small green island in the Wye, it curves left, away from the river, in the direction of a distant metal gate with a reassuring Offa's Dyke Path acorn alongside.

The trail follows the left-hand hedge through the next field, with the hamlet of **Bronydd** straight ahead. Turn left and then immediately right at the end of the field, now following a pleasant green lane with the houses of Clyro (where the diarist Francis Kilvert was the curate) seen climbing the low ridge above the Wye flood plain on the left.

Leave the green lane through a gate on the right, opposite a little copse, and keep left across another large field. Go straight ahead across the next field, heading slightly right at the far end to go through gates and round the barns of Bronydd Farm. Bronydd Baptist chapel, dating from the 16th century and originally timber-framed, can be glimpsed on the left.

Take the left-hand side of a first field, then go straight across a second to find a solid concrete footbridge over a minor stream, then cross a muddy area and climb a bank to approach the busy A438, traffic on which has been audible for some time. Turn right along the grassy verge, quickly enjoying superb views along the Wye, both to the east, in the direction of the distant Clifford Castle on its cliff above the river, and to the south-west, where the massive bulk of the Black Mountains dominates the landscape.

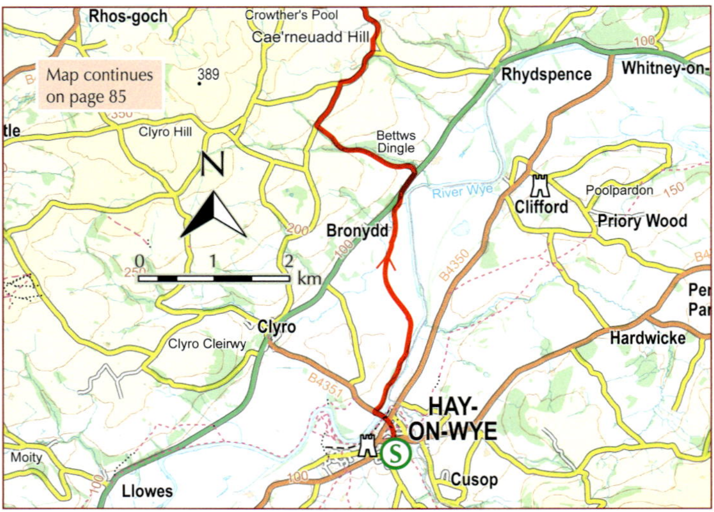

Clifford Castle above the River Wye, viewed from Bronydd

After 300m cross the main road with extreme care and climb a narrow lane, its steepness a shock after the flat valley walking. When the lane bends right carry on ahead on a path that continues to climb before levelling out, with the wooded **Bettws Dingle** (a haunt of drumming great spotted woodpeckers in spring) down to the right, and bracken and then grassland to the left.

The trail runs below Cwm-bwllfa – a medieval cruck-framed hall-house that has recently been restored – and then crests a rise with the partly roofless New Barn to the left. Drop down sharply to cross the Cabalfa brook on a tall, narrow stone bridge, then climb steadily to reach a short section of boardwalk.

Climb a flight of steps here, turn right on a narrow country lane with views down into the Wye valley, and turn right again (signposted to Rhydspence) to reach a junction where a track leaves to the right, passing the chapel of Bettws Clyro on its way to Chapel Farm. Holy Trinity chapel, isolated throughout its history, has ancient origins but was largely rebuilt in the 1870s. Kilvert regularly preached here, walking the three miles from Clyro.

The trail continues straight ahead at the junction described above, the lane cutting through woodland until a gate on the left offers a shortcut across two fields (the path goes sharply right across the second field). Further down the lane is the Rhydspence Inn, a half-timbered 14th-century drovers' inn. There are distant views to the right of Merbach Hill and the hills above the Golden Valley, before a surprisingly elaborate kissing gate leads back to the lane at Cae-Higgin.

Gilfach-yr-heol Farm and the village of Newchurch

Turn left along the lane, dip down to cross a stream and climb slightly to reach Cwm-yr-eithin Cottage.

The trail turns right here, now on Red Lane – part of the old drove road between Newchurch and the Wye valley at Rhydspence. This is for some distance a rutted track but beyond a gate becomes a classic, wide green lane, with a drystone wall that has seen better days to the left and a fence to the right. The surface is muddy where sheep have trampled it, but boardwalks help in the worst places and the going gradually eases until the delightful nature of the lane and the deeply rural scenery can be fully appreciated.

Cross a minor lane, now briefly on tarmac that has also seen better days and soon peters out, then climb gently on grass to reach a junction of green lanes. Turn left, briefly following the course of an unlikely Roman road, then swing right after only 100m by a large pile of stones (the Roman road continues straight ahead in the direction of a mysterious enclosure on the low but colourful hill of Little Mountain).

To the right is the deep and well-wooded valley of the River Arrow, while to the left the hamlet of Newchurch can now be seen beyond the attractive whitewashed farmhouse of Gilfach-yr-heol. Turn very sharply right just before the farm, briefly on a muddy track but then on a quiet, narrow lane that leads directly past Great House and the church of St Mary into the little cluster of houses in **Newchurch**.

NEWCHURCH

While St Mary's is unremarkable, trail walkers will be grateful for the provision of tea, coffee and biscuits in return for a donation. The adjacent Great House is the oldest cruck-framed building in Radnorshire; the timbers for the cruck trusses were felled in the winter of 1449–50. (The date of 1661 above a doorway refers to later alterations.) Around the corner is the Ebenezer Calvinistic Methodist chapel – a much simpler building dating from 1847.

Tea, coffee and biscuits are available in St Mary's church (donation requested) but there are otherwise no facilities in Newchurch.

Turn right just to the north of the chapel to pass a whitewashed house and immediately climb a steep and somewhat stony track to a gate leading onto the common land of Disgwylfa, now grazed only by sheep but once more intensively cultivated, with the remains of leats, field boundaries and cultivation ridges.

The traverse of Disgwylfa Hill is one of the highlights of the day: a wonderful yet not too taxing walk with wide views on all sides. The first section is, however, unrelentingly uphill, until the slope eases somewhat as the clear green track continues through gorse and rough grassland past a long series of waymark posts,

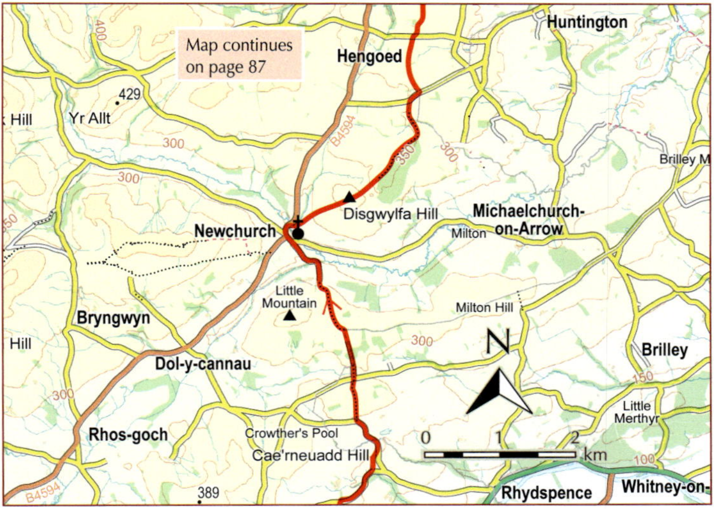

Yewtree Bank, the western edge of Hergest Ridge, from Gladestry churchyard

reaching a very minor summit and then dipping down to a pool and a series of boggy furrows. Baynham Hall, tucked below the eastern slopes here, is a Queen Anne manor house with a hipped roof and tall chimneys.

The trail is very obvious as it climbs steadily through bracken towards the flat summit of **Disgwylfa**, passing a number of frankly unnecessary waymark posts as it runs to the right of the highest point. The landscape is very open, with the Black Mountains still an awesome feature to the south, and a wide outlook eastwards across the Herefordshire plain to the Wormsley hills and the Woolhope Dome.

An easy descent of the northern slopes of Disgwylfa reaches a clear junction where a left turn is well signposted, leading to the edge of the common and a lane running past Hill Farm to a minor road. Turn right here, passing Grove Farm (which has local honey for sale), but after only 200m go left to cross upland pastures, with a splendid view of Radnor Forest ahead and Hergest Ridge to the right.

An easy detour of about a mile from Grove Farm leads along the minor road to **Huntington**, now a quiet hamlet but originally established as a planned borough to succeed Kington, whose castle had been destroyed by raiders early in the 13th century. While Huntington thrived for a while it was soon overtaken by 'new Kington', and all that is left is the evocative but overgrown ruins of the castle.

The Swan Inn (restricted opening hours) is well worth a visit too; a classic unspoilt country inn, it is unchanged since the 1950s and has 17th-century panelling incorporated into the bar counter.

Go slightly to the right across the second pasture to find a gate into another huge field. Cross this and turn right over a stile and briefly along a lane before turning left and taking a narrow path between leylandii and a fence to bypass Fairfields (formerly Stone House barn). Turn left to walk down a pasture, then right through two gates to follow a plain track downhill.

As the solid, Georgian Stone House Farm comes into view, follow the signposted route downhill to the right. Stone House Farm was once owned by the engineer and inventor James Watt, who bought the house in 1798. At first the route lies down a gentle grassy slope but then becomes ridiculously steep for just a few metres before crossing a little stream, going through a gate and joining a narrow lane. Turn left here to follow the lane all the way to the village of **Gladestry**.

GLADESTRY

The village has a number of interesting buildings, including the church of St Mary's and two former chapels, a former drovers' inn with an outbuilding later used as a village shop, the timber-framed 16th-century Corner House and the former Heart in Hand club – a stone 18th-century building with white hand and upturned heart in the eaves. A series of leats and a pond hints at the site of a former corn mill.

Travellers today are catered for by the Royal Oak, which is one of a handful of possibilities for overnight accommodation in the village.

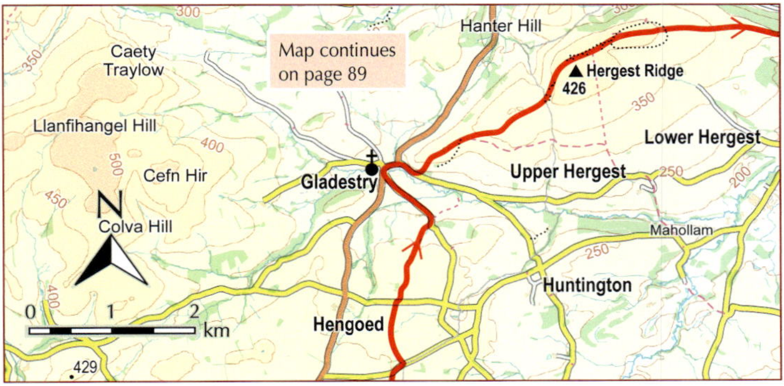

Herrock Hill and Bradnor Hill from the trail on Hergest Ridge

Just beyond the Royal Oak turn right onto a country road, then left after 300m to climb Broken Bank, at first on tarmac and relatively easily. The tarmac peters out at a gate and the climb steepens for a while, following a rough track as the slope eases after a second gate. At one point the track is worn down to the shaly bedrock, but once the trail emerges onto the broad, bracken-covered summit slopes of **Hergest Ridge** the way forward is on springy green turf across the plateau, with gorse on either side frequented by redwing and fieldfare in winter and stonechats in summer.

Welsh mountain ponies and sheep frequent the common, which is criss-crossed with paths and tracks, although the course of the national trail is very clear as it swings towards the northern edge of the ridge, with the outlier of Hanter Hill to the left. Hanter Hill and the adjacent Stanner Rocks are igneous intrusions into the surrounding landscape and are the oldest rocks in Wales, dating back 720 million years.

Hergest Ridge is a wide expanse of springy turf – a great whaleback of a hill with extraordinary views ranging from Radnor Forest in the west through the Clee Hills and Malverns in the east to the blue scarp of the Black Mountains in the south. The birdlife is varied and butterflies abound in summer. Horseracing took place here between 1825 and the 1880s and the track of the near-circular racecourse is still very clear on the ground.

The place has therapeutic qualities too: Mike Oldfield sought solitude in a house looking out towards the ridge after the success of *Tubular Bells*; the tactic worked so well that his second album was called *Hergest Ridge*.

Continue north-east along the ridge, with Hanter Hill now very close on the left and the curious sight of a clump of monkey puzzle trees straight ahead. Slant left before the trees to cross the obvious track of the former racecourse and reach the sizeable detached block known as the Whet Stone. The Whet Stone – a block of gabbro carried by the ice from Hanter Hill – is among the largest of the glacial erratics littering the ridge. There are yet more sensational views here across to Stanner Rocks, with Bradnor Hill and Herrock Hill (crossed on the next stage of the trail) to the right, and the historic landscape of the Walton basin beyond.

The clear green track continues along the broad-topped ridge, intersecting with the racecourse again (there's every chance of seeing waders such as golden plover here) before beginning to descend towards Kington, which can now be seen in the valley ahead.

Offa's Dyke Path on the descent to Kington from Hergest Ridge

Mill Street in Kington, with the market hall and Jubilee tower

The track is rutted in places as it approaches a gate, with Yeld Wood and the Back Brook valley – a meltwater channel in the last Ice Age – to the left and hedgerow birds such as yellowhammer to the right. Go through the gate onto the narrow surfaced Ridgebourne Road, which tumbles down past Hergest Croft. The manor house of Hergest Croft is allegedly haunted by the black dog of Hergest, but is best known for its landscaped gardens with azaleas, rhododendrons and collections of trees.

When the lane meets the old main road into Wales on the outskirts of **Kington**, follow it downhill past the parish church of St Mary and the Georgian buildings on The Square to reach the clock tower and town museum on Mill Street.

KINGTON

The workaday market town of Kington is largely Victorian in character, although the Lady Margaret Hawkins grammar school was built in 1625 for £240. The town lay on busy droving routes out of Wales and is still surprisingly Welsh in character despite its location in Herefordshire, with important sheep and cattle markets and big livestock sales in autumn.

Walkers are very much welcome here, and there is a wide range of facilities, including cafés, pubs (don't miss the Olde Tavern, unchanged for many years) and a variety of options for accommodation, from camping to country town hotels.

STAGE 5

The Radnorshire Hills

Start	Kington Museum (SO 295 566)
Finish	Offa's Dyke Centre, Knighton (SO 285 724)
Distance	22.1km (13.7 miles)
Ascent	735m (2410ft)
Time	6–7hr
Maps	OS Explorer 201
Refreshments	Plenty of options in Knighton, but nothing en route except in Presteigne (3km from the trail)
Public transport	Kington lies on the 461/462 bus route from Hereford, while Knighton has infrequent services on the Heart of Wales railway line between Swansea and Shrewsbury, together with buses to Ludlow. Helpfully, regular buses run between Kington and Knighton, making a day walk based on public transport a feasible proposition.
Accommodation	Knighton has a range of hotels, inns, B&B and camping possibilities, while there is B&B and camping thinly scattered along the route

This is Welsh Marches walking at its finest: not too demanding but full of interest. The scenery is spectacular, with wide-ranging views, and the national trail is reunited with Offa's Dyke after an absence of more than 80km (50 miles), following long stretches of the very well-preserved ancient monument across remote hill country.

The intricate landscape north of Kington, with the path on Bradnor and Herrock Hills above twisting, deep valleys, is especially memorable, while the towns of Presteigne and Knighton are well worth gentle exploration.

Leave **Kington** by taking Church Street and cutting through the surprisingly attractive, dog-legged Common Close, with its Georgian houses and little café, to find the narrow Prospect Road running past whitewashed cottages to cross the Back Brook. Go straight across the bypass and climb gently on a quiet country lane, sunken in places, and turn right through a rusty metal gate to pass to the right of a cottage and enter a pleasant green lane.

When the lane peters out keep straight ahead across a meadow. At the top of the field the way lies straight ahead along a narrow path between hedges, then across a little narrow field to reach the common at **Bradnor Green**.

A very pleasant ascent across the common land, with extensive views westward, is followed by a passage across one of the fairways of Kington golf course – noted for its sunset views and allegedly the highest course in England. The path then crosses a tarmac lane, negotiates practice greens and another fairway, and exits the golf course to the right.

Aim diagonally left across a field, converging with and then walking to the left of a delightful copse, which disguises a long, thin and shallow quarry. Beyond the trees the route lies slightly to the left, on a clear path that dips down to cross the head of a minor valley, with the farm buildings of The Bower just to the right.

Climb out of the valley, with the Herefordshire plain well seen beyond its well-wooded slopes, and with the long ridge of the Black Mountains coming into view as height is gained very gradually across a huge pale upland sheepwalk.

The path approaches the crest of the **Rushock Hill** ridge and a signpost indicating a right-angled turn to the left. Just to the right the Three Shepherds were planted by an 18th-century landowner to honour his daughters. Two of the old yews survive, but the third has recently been replaced. Offa's Dyke comes in from the right here – the first time it has been seen for over 80km (50 miles), although much of its course through Herefordshire has now been identified – and the path

Offa's Dyke above the Holywell valley, with Hergest Ridge and Hanter Hill beyond

now runs along the crest of the low but very conspicuous bank as it aims for a copse on the skyline above Knill Garraway Wood.

Just before it reaches the trees the Dyke turns sharply left, the path now down below it in the ploughed-out western ditch, and begins to lose height, with sensational views ahead into the green Holywell valley in front of the scarp of Stanner Rocks.

Pass through a gate and follow the path down through bracken onto Herrock Common – home to 17 varieties of waxcap fungi – taking a left fork and then veering right by an interpretation panel (the Dyke goes straight on and contours around the western slopes of Herrock Hill) to descend on a superb long green rake with the vast green tree-fringed bowl of the Hindwell Brook valley to the right. The path descends steadily and then becomes a rough track, passing the site of Herrock Cottage (now a hay store) and swinging left to descend towards the valley floor.

The track passes just below a cottage, with the barns of **Lower Harpton** Farm ahead to the right. Look out for a field gate on the right just before the farm and cut across a pasture field to reach and turn right on a path which has recently been created to avoid an unpleasant section of road walking along the busy B4362.

The path follows the left-hand side of two fields, then goes straight across the road and over Ditchyeld Bridge – reconstructed in the 18th century but now bypassed – to the lane leading to the village of Evenjobb. After only 200m, and

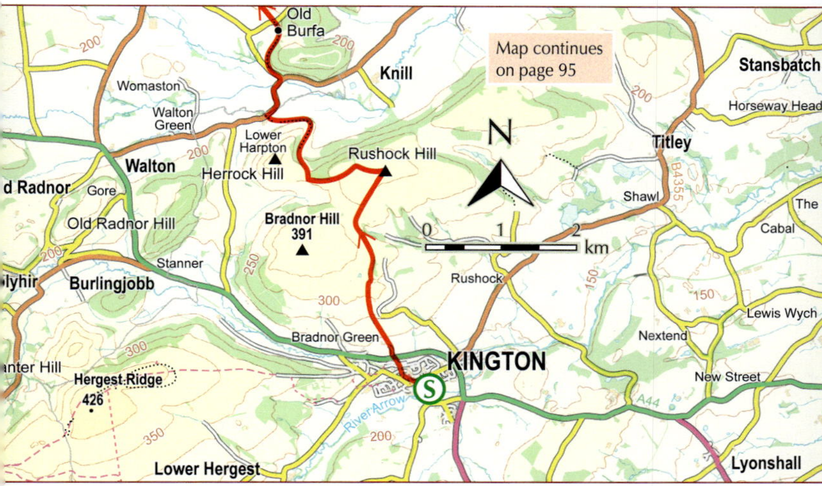

Looking back to the Hergest Ridge from east of Evenjobb

The restored medieval hall-house at Old Burfa

just before the Burfa Bog nature reserve, take a gravelly forest road on the right. Burfa Bog consists of low-lying grassland and alder carr and attracts butterflies such as the dark green fritillary.

The forest road swings round sharply to the right, but the trail lies straight ahead on a wide stony track with a steep forested slope to the right hiding the massive Iron Age hillfort of Burfa Bank, and an improving view of the Walton basin across fields to the left. The track takes a level and unerringly straight course past **Old Burfa** and its extensive barns to reach and turn left for a few paces along a tiny lane. Old Burfa is a cruck-framed hall-house dating from 1487, with exceptional exposed timber-framing inside, painstakingly restored in the 1970s.

Turn right, then go straight ahead on a new footpath to the left of the Dyke, which is on a massive scale here. The scale of the Dyke diminishes as the path continues north-westwards, but it is still an impressive monument. The view to the west, of hills rising above the Walton basin, remains outstanding.

The path goes through a gate and runs along the left side of a field, still with the Dyke for company until the path drops down via a flight of steps to cross the narrow lane that links Evenjobb and Presteigne.

PRESTEIGNE

Although it involves a detour of about 3km (2 miles) from the path, a diversion to Presteigne is worth considering – not least for those needing accommodation. Once the smallest county town in England and Wales, it has a church with a magnificent 16th-century Flemish tapestry, while the curfew is still rung from the church tower every night. The medieval Judges' Lodging is now the town's museum, with courtroom, judge's apartments and gaslit quarters for the servants. The half-timbered Radnorshire Arms, complete with priest's hole, dates from 1616.

There are one or two basic shops together with a few pubs and some B&B accommodation.

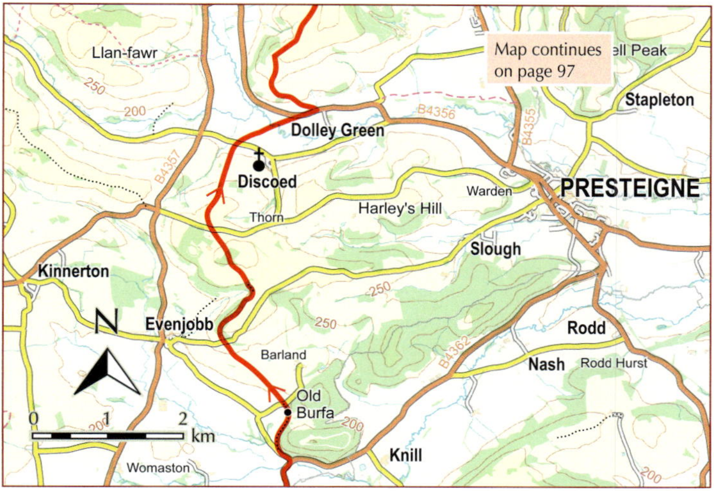

Offa's Dyke Path alongside the Dyke north of Burfa

The trail now enters the Woodland Trust's Granner Wood, climbing steeply at first with the help of a couple of long flights of steps, rebuilt in 2015, to reach a splendid green path that runs parallel to the Dyke, rising gently through relatively open coniferous woodland, with an outlook to the left over green fields to the whitewashed Dunn's Lane Cottage in front of wooded hillslopes.

Beyond a gate signalling the end of Granner Wood the path dips down slightly through bracken to find and turn left along a track worn to the bedrock in places, passing a quarry on the right and then turning very steeply up to the right just before a corrugated iron hut.

The slope eases and the path enters the mixed woodland of Hilltop Plantation, with pheasants skittering between holly, hawthorn and small conifers. Beyond the summit a new vista opens up ahead, with the bracken-covered common land of Llan-fawr and the slopes of Furrow Hill prominent across the wide valley of the River Lugg. Closer at hand, but beyond the farmhouse of Pen Offa, Castlering Wood hides a substantial oval hillfort accessed by a permissive path.

The trail is hemmed in between post-and-wire fences for a while, with the low bank of the Dyke for company, then runs to the left of the earthwork, passing an apparently original gateway in the Dyke (indicated by the arrangement of banks and ditches, meeting at an angle) and then going through a field gate to cross a lane and continue alongside the bank, with excellent views west to the former royal hunting ground of Radnor Forest and south to the Black Mountains.

Keep heading slightly east of north through a series of fields, descending gently with the Dyke (impressive in places) to the left. The bracken invades the path just before it drops down to cross a lane and switch to the western side of the ancient monument, now with an excellent western ditch alongside a high bank.

The ditch is ploughed out where a farm track crosses the Dyke, but the way lies straight ahead to find a hidden gate leading onto a wide country road, with the hamlet of **Discoed** a little way to the right. St Michael's church in Discoed has a 5000-year-old yew tree in its churchyard, while there is very limited B&B available in the vicinity.

Go straight across the road and slant right through a gate onto a good path that follows the hedge line across a couple of fields, and cross the Lugg on the new **Dolley Green** footbridge – a 2014 replacement for a metal and concrete bridge which itself replaced a twin-arched stone bridge washed away in the 1940s. Just before the river bridge a stile on the right provides a way into a delightful riverside meadow, with an informal picnic spot by dramatic, tight meanders. Beyond the bridge the path follows the right-hand edge of a large field to reach and keep ahead along the B4356.

There is no verge alongside the road, but the trail quickly leaves it by turning sharply left onto a rough track that climbs between hedges and becomes gravelly for a while as it swings right and begins to rise more steadily. One final and distinctly steep climb leads to the plateau of Furrow Hill, with the route of the Dyke and accompanying path suddenly very clear for some distance ahead. The little

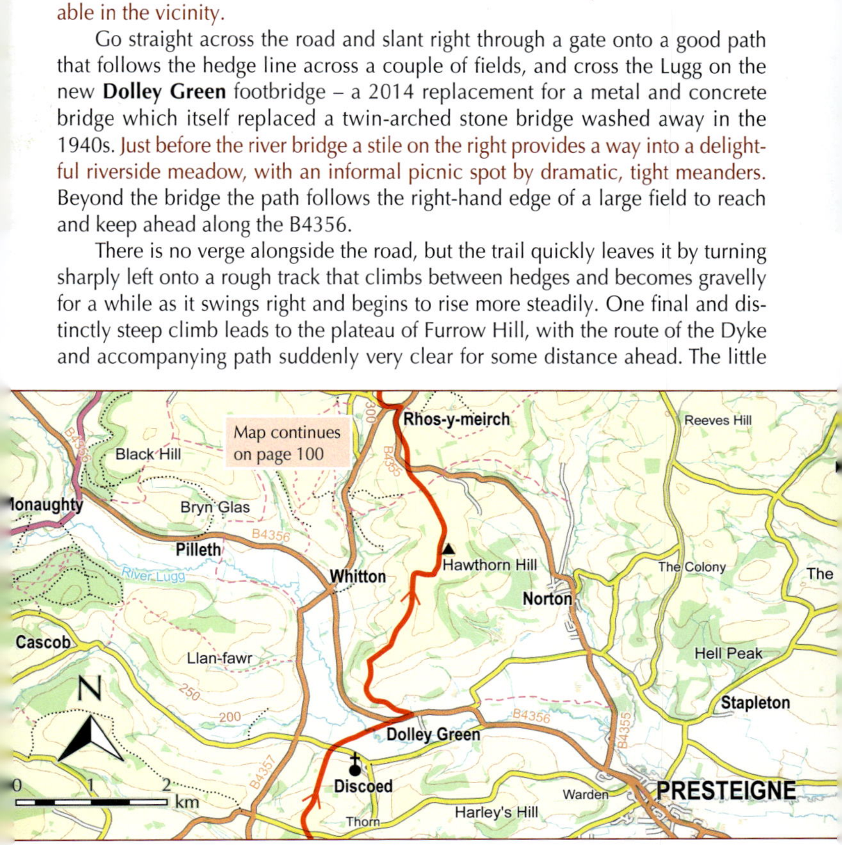

The Price monument on the northern slopes of Hawthorn Hill

Gilfach valley lies down to the left, with the village of Whitton further away to the west.

Keep following the low bank of the Dyke across the common until turning right at an incongruously conspicuous signpost. The views west to Radnor Forest, north to the Kerry Hills and south to Herrock Hill and the Black Mountains are now really impressive, while to the east the Lugg valley and Presteigne can be seen in front of the distant but unmistakable Malvern Hills.

Turn left at the end of the field, go through a gate and climb back up onto the Dyke, which is impressive again here as it skirts an area of coniferous woodland on the rounded summit of **Hawthorn Hill** and runs between upland pastures on the right and arable fields to the left. The view of rounded Welsh hills is still impressively expansive to the west, with the four Wellingtonia redwoods planted to commemorate the battle site at Pilleth clearly in view.

The **Battle of Pilleth** took place on the slopes of Bryn Glas, north-west of Whitton, on 22 June 1402. Henry IV's army, under the command of Sir Edmund Mortimer, Earl of March, was numerically superior to the rebel forces led by Owain Glyndŵr but was outmanoeuvred and all but destroyed, with the English dead left to rot on the battlefield and Glyndŵr's forces pressing on eastwards to attack and burn Leominster. It was one of the greatest victories of the Welsh over the English, and prolonged Glyndŵr's rebellion for several years while destabilising the English monarchy.

Go through a gate to walk just inside another conifer plantation, through another gate to leave it, and then digress slightly to the right to inspect the obelisk that commemorates the achievements of Sir Richard Green Price. The monument acknowledges the role of the MP, JP and Sheriff of Radnorshire in promoting the construction of railways, bringing services to Knighton, Llandrindod Wells and Presteigne.

The commemorative stone with the wrong date!

A further gate leads into a scrubby area dominated by gorse, with stonechats in summer and a final view of the Radnor Forest hills away to the west. A thin path, copiously waymarked, wends its way through the gorse and leads to a crossing of the B4355, with a stone commemorating Offa's efforts (but erroneously dating the construction of the Dyke to AD757) just to the left beyond the road.

Continue northwards on the top of the low, flattened Dyke, negotiating a series of gates while gradually converging with the B-road again. Turn right to go along the road for 500m, then turn left onto the Whitton road for a further 200m. Neither road has a worthwhile verge, and both are quite busy, so the right turn just after a small shelter onto the lane to **Rhos-y-meirch** comes as welcome relief. Even better, the way lies right again after only 50m, through a gate with a tall waymark struggling to be seen above a hedge.

Go straight ahead across a succession of grassy fields. The Dyke has been absent for a while but makes a welcome reappearance north of Jenkin Allis Farm, as a massive bank accompanied by a substantial western ditch, its progress across the landscape marked by a line of ancient trees. Close to the summit of Ffridd Hill the path cuts right through the ditch and Dyke, the earthwork much diminished from this point northwards but with the compensation of an excellent view along the upper Teme valley above Knighton.

The path runs along the flat top of Ffridd for some time, then skirts the western boundary of Knighton golf course as it begins to lose height and descends into a

dry valley with attractive woodland on the left. Eventually a gate on the left leads into Great Frydd Wood, the path now descending steeply on loose earth and leaf litter to cross a little lane and continue as a narrow footpath on the outskirts of Knighton.

Cut through an area of back lanes and garages to reach and go straight across the Llandrindod road and descend Larkey Lane into the centre of **Knighton**, bearing left to reach the Offa's Dyke Centre, managed by the Offa's Dyke Association and home to an excellent exhibition and an information service.

KNIGHTON

Almost at the halfway point of the trail, Knighton is a typical borders town, practical rather than picturesque but nevertheless a very useful service centre. The town has Saxon roots and became a chartered borough with a weekly market and annual fair in 1203, but it endured torrid medieval times, being repeatedly laid waste by the Welsh (with the Welsh princes Llywelyn ap Gruffydd in 1159 and Owain Glyndŵr in 1402 among the culprits). Knighton later became a centre for the farming and woollen industries and lay on drovers' routes to Hereford and London, but has spent much of its existence as a remote and pleasant backwater.

The town has hotels and several good B&Bs, together with cafés and pubs and a variety of local shops.

STAGE 6

Ups and downs in deepest Shropshire

Start	Offa's Dyke Centre, Knighton (SO 285 724)
Finish	Blue Bell Inn, Brompton Bridge (SO 250 932)
Distance	24.3km (15.1 miles)
Ascent	1000m (3280ft)
Time	7–9hr
Maps	OS Explorer 201, 216
Refreshments	None on the line of the route or at Brompton crossroads, but several options in Clun, Bishop's Castle and (3km beyond Brompton) Montgomery – all involving a significant detour
Public transport	Knighton has infrequent services on the Heart of Wales railway line between Swansea and Shrewsbury, together with buses to Kington and Ludlow, but Brompton crossroads has no afternoon or evening buses
Accommodation	Possibilities en route at Newcastle, a wider choice off-route at Clun and Bishop's Castle, and a few B&Bs around Brompton, including at Mellington

This is the toughest section of the trail, with some steep (although reasonably short) climbs and some equally steep descents as the Dyke – superbly preserved in places – heads directly and uncompromisingly across the green hills of south Shropshire, which are unhelpfully aligned from east to west. The scenery is magnificent, from the Teme Valley at the start of the day's walk to the Long Mynd, Stiperstones and Corndon Hill towards the end. The towns of Clun and Bishop's Castle, distinctive and entertaining, are some way from the path but will attract those taking a relaxed approach to completing the trail.

Go to the left of the Offa's Dyke Centre in **Knighton**, dropping down through a little park which has one of the best-preserved lengths of Offa's Dyke anywhere to reach the riverside and turn sharp left, hemmed in for a while between hedges but later following the Teme upstream across fields. Cross the river on a footbridge alongside the Heart of Wales railway line, then turn sharp left across the railway and quickly leave the river to rise past the 17th-century farmhouse at Panpunton and cross a country lane.

Trail walkers approaching the summit of Panpunton Hill

The first of many climbs during the day starts here, at first through oak woodland but then on a clear green path through bracken, gaining height rapidly and unremittingly. Towards the top of the slope there is welcome relief as the path turns left, the gradient much gentler now on a green track and through bracken and gorse as far as a memorial seat and cairn on the western shoulder of **Panpunton Hill**.

The route now lies along the top edge of a series of fields, with wheatears perching on the gateposts in summer and the meanders of the River Teme prominent to the left in front of wooded valley slopes framing the striking Knucklas viaduct – its 13 arches dating from 1865.

A low bank materialises to the right, initially colonised by yew trees but then growing in stature and revealing itself as Offa's Dyke. Beyond a roofless ruin colonised by nesting swallows, the path narrows and works its way around the head of a big side valley, dropping down slightly before clambering up over rocks.

Cross a prominent farm track and take the narrow path which at first contours around the higher slopes of **Cwm-sanaham Hill**, swinging left just before the ruins of an outfarm (outlying barns belonging to a valley farm). The path then heads uphill to reach the trig point at the summit, with the masts on Black Mixen – the highest point of Radnor Forest – now clearly visible beyond the well-wooded Teme valley.

The path and Dyke then drop down, at first gently, with the onward course of the Dyke clearly visible as a line of trees on the far side of a deeply incised valley. The descent steepens, on bare earth and grass that can be slippery after rain, to reach the old stone cottage of **Brynorgan** and use its access track to reach a tarmac lane. Go slightly left here, then up steps into a field with the somewhat austere facade of Selley Hall across the valley.

The trail contours around a knoll, goes through a gate to the left and along the low bank of the Dyke to cross a footbridge, then veers left into the ditch of the ancient earthwork, crosses a second footbridge and climbs a long but easily angled flight of steps to reach a lane. Go straight across, passing **Garbett Hall** and swinging slightly right to rise steadily on a straight stony track. Beyond a gate Offa's Dyke and its ditch reappear on the right on a more impressive scale. From Garbett Hall northwards the Dyke forms a prominent landscape feature for miles, often as a superb bank rising several metres above a scoured western ditch.

The track goes through a gap in the Dyke after the next gate; down to the left is Llandinshop – now only a farm but once a Celtic religious centre. A thin path follows the crest of the Dyke northwards here, but in the interests of conserving the monument the national trail uses a track running a little way to the east.

The way lies slightly to the left at the end of the second field, through a gate onto another track, which appears at first to be little used but which quickly becomes stony, with the Dyke still a little way to the left.

Brynorgan Cottage and the line of the Dyke on Llanfair Hill

Beyond a barn frequented by ravens, the track switches to run on the western side of ditch and Dyke, which presents a striking landscape feature here as an earthwork of massive proportions marching northwards across the slopes of **Llanfair Hill**. Conservation work here has focused on reducing erosion of the ancient monument caused by grazing animals. This is the highest point reached by the Dyke itself during the course of its journey through the Welsh borders.

The track parallels the earthwork for some distance, with views eastwards to the hills beyond Clun and westwards across an intricate network of hedged fields to the upper Teme. The track, now a little further away from the earthwork, loses height gradually and suddenly swings left; go straight on here (a signpost seems to have gone missing) along a delightful green track which all too quickly reaches tarmac.

Keep ahead along the lane, dipping down to cross a stream and climbing back up to reach the lonely crossroads at Spoad Hill. Turn right here, passing Springhill Farm on the right, with a good section of Offa's Dyke in the woodland opposite. The road running east from the farm leads in 5km (3 miles) to the delightful little town of Clun – a rewarding out-and-back detour, not least for those seeking refreshment or accommodation.

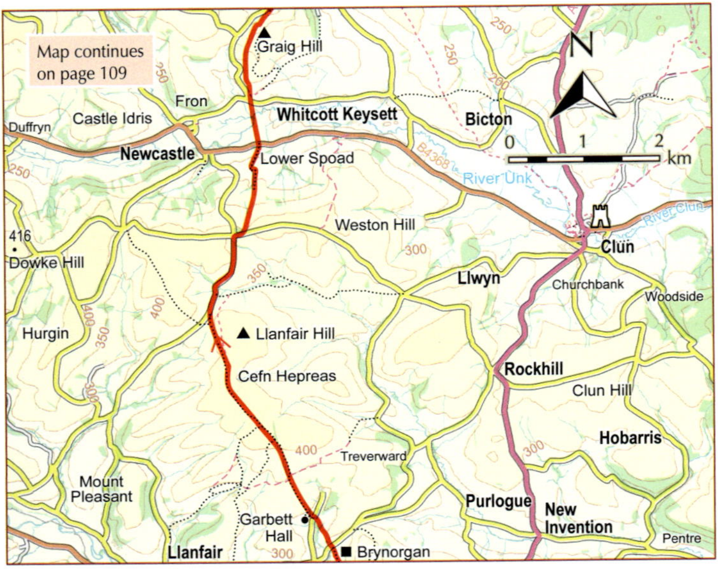

CLUN

One of Housman's 'quietest places under the sun', Clun lay on the line of a prehistoric trackway (later a drove road) heading east to the Clee Hills. The town originally grew around the Saxon church of St George before migrating downhill to the Norman borough established in the shadow of a massive motte-and-bailey castle constructed around 1090. Now picturesque and quiet, with ducks in the river below the narrow medieval bridge, the town is well worth a detour – particularly during the Green Man festival that heralds the arrival of spring with mummers in the town square, Morris dancers and a craft fair.

Clun has a shop and post office together with two pubs offering B&B.

Just beyond Springhill Farm a green lane takes the trail northwards, with the Dyke in bracken on the left and a first view of Corndon Hill – which will become a fixture in the landscape for some time – on the skyline ahead.

Dyke and path descend together, with a fine prospect of the Clun valley and the sprawling village of Newcastle opening out ahead, and the line of the Dyke easily picked out on the far hillslopes. Cross a track and follow a thin path down the left-hand side of a pasture, and drop down a slightly sunken way to join a rough track.

As the track approaches Newcastle there is a fine section of the Dyke to the right, with the village church prominent ahead, before the track unexpectedly turns sharply left (a signpost is welcome confirmation of the route here) to cross a brook and swing right, heading for the farmyard at **Lower Spoad**. Lower Spoad is a medieval cruck-framed longhouse, once a hunting lodge, with a magnificent 16th-century hunting scene carved into the oak beam over the fireplace.

Go across the B4368 at Lower Spoad, now with the Dyke and, unusually, an eastern ditch to the left for only 100m before it abruptly disappears. Drop down to the bottom of the field to find a gate by an old gnarled tree and go around the left side of a big meadow, with the picturesque but somewhat dilapidated wattle-and-daub Bryndrinog Farm ahead.

A big footbridge carries the trail over the River Clun, and a gate on the left leads into another pasture, with the path climbing alongside the Dyke to reach a little lane. Beyond Newcastle church the higher reaches of the Clun valley form an attractively rural picture, with the Iron Age earthworks of Fron Camp out of sight to the right.

A path across the lane is signposted to Hergan and leads past a welcome water point to climb alongside the Dyke to the signpost marking the halfway point in the journey from Chepstow to Prestatyn. Beyond a gate the path runs just above a patch of gorse and then climbs along the crest of the Dyke, which is not particularly impressive here and quite badly eroded on the steeper sections.

Eventually the path meanders to the right of the Dyke, which by now is little more than a break of slope in the middle of a field. The views ahead are quintessentially rural, with the well-wooded rounded hills of Clun Forest – a medieval hunting ground rather than a forest – rising above deep green permanent pasture.

Beyond the remains of a cottage and associated quarries at Bryn-y-Cratch, cross a farm track and follow the Dyke gently downhill, now with a minor road running parallel to the path. To the right is **Graig Hill** – once alive with the mournful sounds of the curlew but now largely deserted.

The path, narrow but well defined across fields above Bridge Farm, crosses another little-used green lane and continues above a pond, negotiating stiles and small fields until it crosses a little stream on a footbridge and climbs briefly to reach a narrow tarmac lane. Turn right here, then quickly left on a slightly more substantial lane for only 100m before taking the access drive to Lower Mount on the right.

Beyond the house, take the green lane to the right of a shed and, just beyond a gate, fork right onto the higher of two footpaths, rising through attractively open woodland. The ascent is quite long but the gradient is relatively easy, with Offa's bank and ditch to the right.

The route climbs to a stile, with the trail continuing forward to reach and turn left at a minor road. Just to the right is Ffynnon y Saint – a holy well in a rock basin whose waters purportedly cured rheumatism. Go to the right through a gate at a junction of lanes and tracks at **Hergan** into a complicated area of banks and ditches, which has been interpreted as a customs post allowing Welsh cattle to cross (on payment of a fee) on their way to markets further east. The way forward is clearly signposted at first, taking a left fork and cutting through the Dyke. It's crucial to turn sharp left immediately here – it's waymarked but the sign is easily missed – to cross a stile, climb up to cross the Dyke and follow it due north.

The path drops down to cross a stream by Eaton's Coppice and then tackles the first of three tough ascents which, coming at this stage of the day's walk, can sap the energy of all but the fittest.

The first hill lasts for only one field but is seriously steep; the route then dips down by the former farm at Middle Knuck before climbing up again to reach a minor road, with the jagged outline of the Stiperstones prominent to the north-east.

Head straight across, dropping down to a gate and then making a steep, muddy descent through the conifers (especially alien here after miles of open hill walking) of Churchtown Wood. A gate at the end of the wood leads to a little meadow followed by a footbridge over the little stream in Cwm Ffrydd, with the tiny, isolated church of St John the Baptist at **Churchtown** immediately to the right.

St John the Baptist, the isolated church at Churchtown

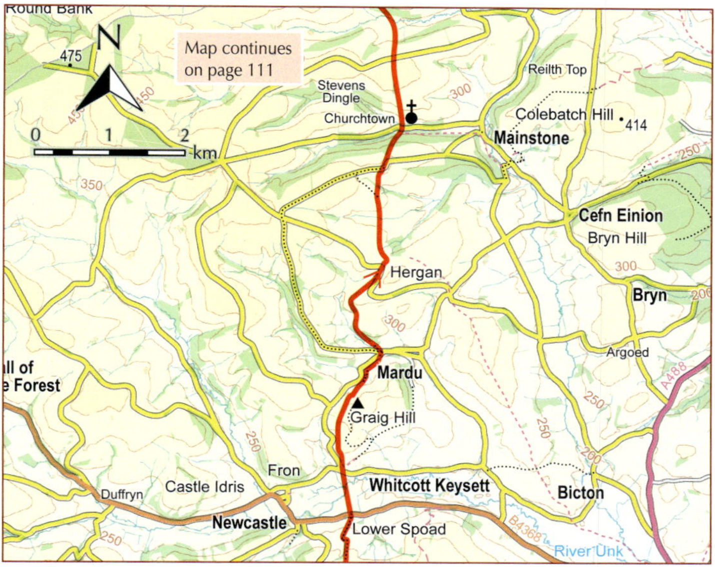

The trail continues straight across the lane at Churchtown, going through a gate leading to the third, longest and toughest of the challenging ascents. The route lies straight up the hillslope, soon reaching a second gate and clambering up past badger setts onto the crest of the Dyke, with improving retrospective views of the deep trench of Cwm Ffrydd in front of Churchtown Wood.

As so often, the slope eases as the top of the hill is approached. Go straight across a gravel track and scramble up onto the crest of the Dyke. This is an exhilarating part of the walk, the earthwork a dramatic landscape feature adorned with wildflowers in summer and the scenery increasingly impressive as the summit of Edenhope Hill is crossed and the unmistakable bulk of Corndon Hill, the rocky crests of the Stiperstones and the great whaleback of the Long Mynd fill the horizon.

Drop down to cross the Edenhope road and continue alongside the Dyke – the bank and western ditch even more impressive here – as it descends increasingly steeply into the glaciated U-shaped valley of the Unk. Cross a substantial bridge over the river, take the track heading to the left but soon look for a path heading over a stile to the right, climbing quite steeply on a narrow path through the commercial forestry of **Nut Wood**, with the sound of warblers and blue tits constant in summer. This is the last climb of the day and is mercifully quite gentle, going through mixed woodland to emerge into a big upland sheepwalk on the southern flanks of the Kerry Hill ridge.

Kerry Hill was a focus of early settlement in the borders and the eponymous **ridgeway**, regarded as 'the oldest road in Wales', was a prehistoric trackway followed by Neolithic axe traders and later adapted as a drove road enabling Welsh sheep, black cattle and other livestock to be transported to markets in the Midlands and London. For 25km (15.5 miles) from the Cider House to Bishop's Castle it follows the crest of the ridge, cutting through early medieval cross dykes and enjoying spectacular scenery.

Follow the left-hand edge of the field to a gate, with the Dyke reappearing as a substantial bank and ditch as the trail continues relentlessly northwards. The woodland falls away on the left, a farm track crosses the Dyke and the path keeps the low bank on its left until swerving through the earthwork and going through a gate onto the Kerry Hill ridgeway.

The fascinating town of Bishop's Castle lies to the right along the ridgeway past Dog and Duck Cottage, and although a visit entails a significant diversion of around 6km (3½ miles) it is well worth making the effort.

Offa's Dyke Path heads down the track to Crowsnest Cottage, with the Dyke on the right (the track follows the line of the ditch) and views opening up ahead of the Vale of Montgomery, and prominent hedgerows indicating the arrow-straight

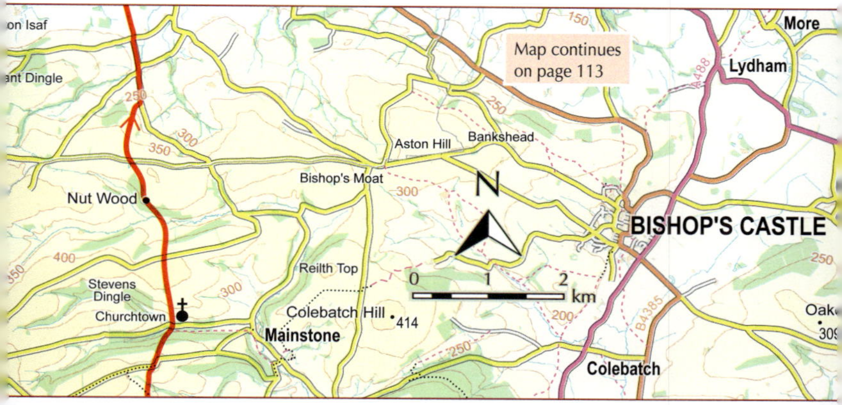

course of Offa's Dyke across the lowland. Closer to hand, the path continues alongside the Dyke, descending quite steeply for a while, with a last chance to take in the dramatic views north-eastwards to the Stiperstones and the Long Mynd.

BISHOP'S CASTLE

A delightfully idiosyncratic little town, it has a curious mixture of black-and-white half-timbered and Georgian brick houses, a cobbled passage spanned by the Tudor House on Crutches, and a working brewhouse (the oldest licensed brewery in the country, dating from 1642) alongside the ancient Three Tuns Inn. The imposing 18th-century town hall has been superbly renovated and there is a superb Elizabethan town house – the Porch House – nearby. Bishop's Castle was a classic rotten borough, with local landowners competing to bribe the town's limited numbers of burgesses in order to secure election as an MP.

Excellent pubs (one brewing its own beer), a classic market town hotel and a number of B&Bs complement an eclectic range of shops in this idiosyncratic borders town.

The trail then accompanies an eroded section of the earthwork where badgers and rabbits have conspired to cause significant damage. The path has now been diverted here to run alongside the Dyke and go through a gate to reach a metalled lane opposite the entrance to Drewin Farm.

The Vale of Montgomery and the Long Mountain from Crowsnest Cottage

Beyond the hamlet of Cwm and its converted chapel – brick-built in 1897 – and timber-framed cottages, the lane reaches a T-junction. Go slightly right here, then quickly climb some steps, go through a gate and cross a farm track. The path runs along the top of the Dyke, which is of pretty modest proportions here, and enters the **Mellington Hall** estate, with a startling contrast between bucolic countryside and distant hills to the left, and the static caravans and chalets of a tourist business to the right. Mellington Hall – now a hotel offering refreshments as well as accommodation – is a Victorian Gothic pile with historic parkland including icehouse, orchard and fishponds.

Sets of steps help avoid some muddy areas as the path runs through woodland that can be spectacular in spring, with snowdrops succeeded by wood anemones and then bluebells. Cross a muddy track and follow the low Dyke until

the trees fall away to the right, then negotiate a couple of fields to emerge on the Mellington Hall drive.

Turn left briefly, then left again to pass through an ornate gatehouse and emerge on the B4385. Keep straight ahead, crossing the picturesque little River Caebitra – which marks the national boundary here – and passing Brompton Mill on the right. Beyond a hedge there is a glimpse of a minor but well-preserved motte and bailey on the right, just before the unspoilt Blue Bell Inn (now closed) and its antique petrol pumps at **Brompton** crossroads.

BROMPTON

Hardly even a hamlet exists at Brompton crossroads now, yet the immediate area contains a Roman fort discovered east of Pentreheyling Farm in the 1960s, and a 12th-century castle sited on the line of Offa's Dyke. There are tourist attractions on tap too, with the working Bachledre flour mill and the Kerry Vale vineyard close at hand.

The Blue Bell's traditional public bar, unchanged since 1949, had a quarry-tiled floor and bench seating – but sadly the pub has been closed since the death of the landlady in 2020, and there are now very few facilities at Brompton.

STAGE 7

The Vale of Montgomery and Long Mountain

Start	Blue Bell Inn, Brompton Bridge (SO 250 932)
Finish	Offa's Dyke Business Park, Buttington (SJ 249 086)
Distance	19km (11.8 miles)
Ascent	425m (1395ft)
Time	5–6hr
Maps	OS Explorer 216
Refreshments	A choice of shops and cafés in Montgomery (involving a short detour), but little else along the route
Public transport	Despite its remote location, the Blue Bell Inn has a useful morning bus service, with two buses from Montgomery (the later one starts from Welshpool) and two from Newtown. The X75 provides a regular service from Shrewsbury to Welshpool, passing through Buttington.
Accommodation	Possibilities en route at Forden, while Buttington has a few options for accommodation, including the Green Dragon (campsite) and Moors Farm, and Welshpool is only 3km away via bus or a canal walk.

The walking on this section of the trail is substantially less challenging than the switchback section through the south Shropshire Hills, with a delightfully gentle passage through the historic landscape of the Vale of Montgomery, with big hedged fields and parkland now occupying the floor of a former glacial lake, followed by the traverse of the Long Mountain. Offa's Dyke Path cuts through a classic high-Victorian estate here, with evidence of some of the innovations that marked out Leighton Park, before climbing to the hillfort of Beacon Ring and descending into the Severn valley at Buttington.

Go north from the **Brompton** crossroads, taking the B4385 towards Montgomery, but after only 150m turn right onto a drive leading to Brompton Hall Farm. Turn left before reaching the farm to pass through a series of fields, some of them pasture and some arable, with an unobtrusive Bronze Age bowl barrow away to the left. Offa's Dyke is a relatively inconspicuous feature at this point, forming a low bank to the right, colonised by brambles, elderberries and sloes.

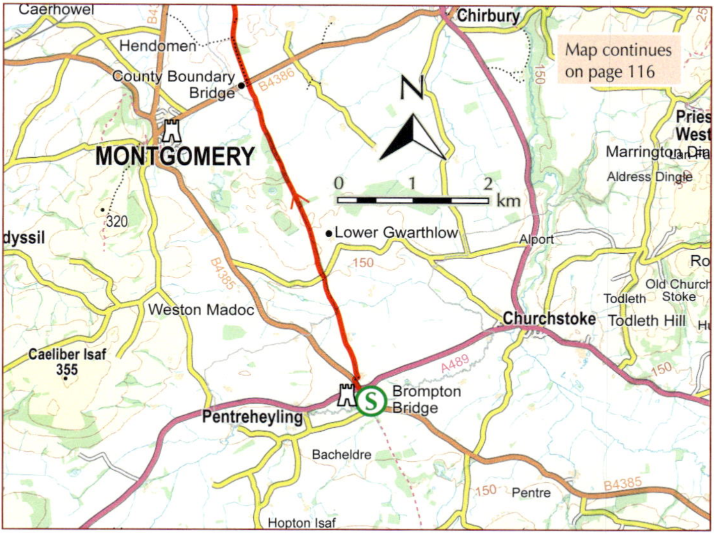

The trail runs through the farmyard at The Ditches, with its impressive 17th-century timber-framed threshing barn, and is then signposted just to the left of the attractive black-and-white farmhouse. At the end of the next field the path climbs up onto the Dyke – which is just a low bank here – and continues arrow-straight to reach a footbridge and farm track, with the brick-built Georgian Pen-y-Bryn Hall in parkland to the left and the silos of Rockley Farm away to the right. Thomas Mason of Rockley was High Sheriff of Montgomeryshire in 1688.

Keep to the right-hand edge of a big cornfield, rising slightly, with the bank of Offa's Dyke now somewhat more substantial and the western ditch separating the bank from the path. Cross a country lane, now walking alongside a thick hedge, but with open views to the left across hedged fields to a range of low hills culminating in Town Hill and the rocky outcrop occupied by Montgomery Castle (prominently in view later in the walk).

The path crosses a track leading to the dairy farm of **Lower Gwarthlow** and its tall grain silos, with bank and ditch still on the right, and the attractive woodland of New Covert and then Boardyhall Wood – a mixed wood with poplar and beech and a central duck-pond – on the left. The trail then crosses a tarmac lane; a left turn leads in 2km to the delightful former county town of Montgomery (a very worthwhile diversion).

MONTGOMERY

One of the finest small towns in the central borderland, Montgomery has a wonderfully old-fashioned feel, with an eclectic mix of half-timbered, Georgian and Victorian town houses, an 18th-century town hall with a little clock tower, and a parish church containing a magnificent rood screen and stunning misericords. A ruined 13th-century castle, towering above the town on a rocky bluff, was the setting for treaty negotiations in 1267, during which Henry III granted Llywelyn ap Gruffydd the title of Prince of Wales. Don't miss Bunners – an incredibly well-stocked, unchanging family-run ironmongers.

The town has a couple of shops, a post office and a few pubs, together with a hotel and one or two guest houses.

The trail, however, goes slightly to the right from the tarmac lane, across a cattle grid, and turns left to follow the eastern side of the Dyke, now with an uninterrupted view of the impressive Corndon Hill. Surrounded on three sides by Shropshire yet situated in Wales, the distinctive landmark of Corndon Hill results from a volcanic intrusion into the surrounding rocks. The way lies along the left-hand margin of a succession of fields, with the Dyke hidden behind a tall hedge and woodland beyond.

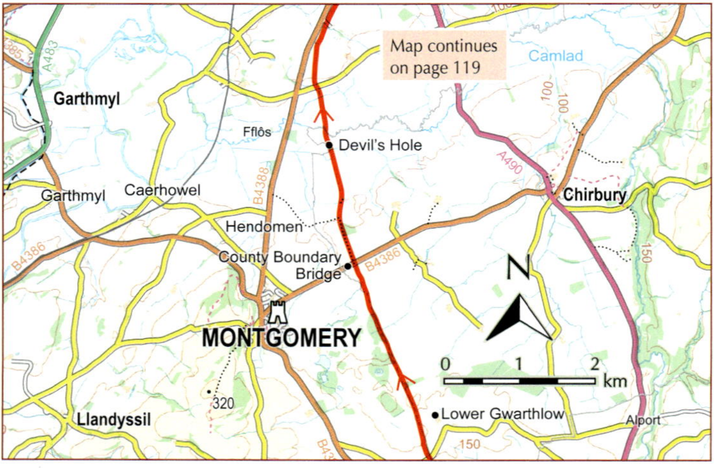

Montgomery Castle

The earthwork is now represented by little more than a hedge line, at a point where a further path on the left gives access across Lymore Park to Montgomery. The big, symmetrical Jacobean black-and-white house at Lymore, used as a hunting lodge, lay in the parkland to the west of the trail but was demolished in the 1930s. The Dyke then reappears on the right by a 'Welcome to Shropshire' sign as the national boundary swings away to the west, while to the left there is a particularly fine view of Montgomery Castle, its ramparts high above the town.

Cross the B4386 just east of **County Boundary Bridge**, keep to the right-hand margin of several big arable fields where the battle of Montgomery raged in 1644, and cut across to the eastern side of the Dyke again, leaving the earthwork to the right but quickly turning left just before Rownal Farm.

Cross a sheep pasture, going towards an old barn, with the Dyke forming the far boundary of the field, and go through a gate onto a path hemmed in between hedges. The route is descending very gently into the Camlad valley, initially as a green lane between tall hedges, eventually passing the **Devil's Hole** – to the east of the farmhouse at Caemwgal – and crossing the river on a fairly new footbridge.

Dyke and path near Cwm Farm south of Forden

Swing left, go through a little gate, briefly with the Camlad (one of only two rivers that flow from England into Wales) to the left, then battle through a field of maize before escaping through a second gate and joining a green lane making for the attractive cottage of Pound House and the end of the flat land, with a fairly short but unexpectedly steep climb past a disused quarry and through a stand of old oaks.

The slope levels off and the route runs through a series of fields, with a first view of the Long Mountain ahead. Cross a little lane to the left of a cottage, going through metal gates in quick succession, and climb another slope, with the Dyke in evidence again to the left as a low grassy bank. Beyond a braided access track the path goes slightly left to reach and turn left along a tarmac lane for 100m.

There is now no alternative to using the B4388 for 600m, although thankfully there is a pavement. Across the first field to the right is the castle mound at Nantcribba, but sadly there is no public access to the site and the view from the road is disappointing. Nantcribba also has the site of a moated mansion, the walled garden of the former Nantcribba Hall and the Victorian barns of a model farm.

The view ahead of the Long Mountain becomes increasingly imposing during the walk along the B4388. (To the left is the site of the auxiliary Roman fort at Forden Gaer, while Forden Union workhouse, infamous for the use of punishments such as the lash and the scold's bridle, lies nearby.) Cross the road onto the opposite footpath, turn right onto the A490, but after only 50m go left through the garden of Fingerpost Cottage.

The path now skirts the village of **Forden** (B&Bs, pub, public transport), running through a number of small fields, the way ahead always obvious on the ground. At one point the path runs along the crest of the flattened Dyke, with the rear gardens of modern houses somewhat incongruously beyond the ditch to the left.

Zigzag left and right across a suburban lane, fork left off a gravelly track onto a path beneath trees and then cross two fields, and go straight ahead on a lane that is not only following the course of Offa's Dyke but is also on the line of the Roman road from Wroxeter (Viriconium) to Forden Gaer, which itself reused an ancient trackway.

The old road ascends the Long Mountain, the ascent not particularly steep but seemingly endless. The Long Mountain – a sprawling mass of high ground reaching 408m (1338ft) at Beacon Ring – was the site in AD630 of a battle between Northumbria and the allied forces of Mercia and Gwynedd. In places the road is sunken into the hillside, with a substantial bank and ditch to the left on the line of the Dyke.

Fork left at a junction towards the top of the hill to enter the Leighton estate, pass a notice indicating that ash dieback disease is a problem here, and immediately turn right onto a rutted track climbing steadily past the late 1850s Tudor-Gothic Greenwood Lodge through woodland, with pheasants in abundance and an excellent retrospective view of the Vale of Montgomery. Another track, more obviously well-used, joins from the right and the route levels off, with mature pine forest down to the left restricting the view of Welsh border hills.

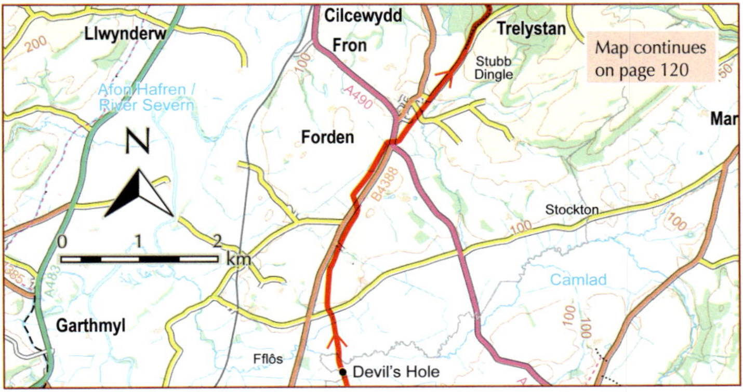

John Naylor's wealthy uncle gave him the **Leighton estate** as a wedding present in 1847. Naylor used the gift brilliantly, developing one of the most extraordinary high-Victorian country estates in Britain, full of far-reaching ideas – including not just a model farm but also an early hydro-electric scheme to power the farm's machinery, and a funicular railway which ran between Leighton Park Farm and an upper station high on the Long Mountain. The estate also included a hall, a church, a series of artificial pools and a plethora of exotic trees.

Keep on the main track above the Poultry House, but just at the point where the track starts to lose height, turn right onto a less well-defined gravelly woodland track. The Poultry House and adjacent Fowl House provided superior accommodation for the estate's poultry-keeper and his charges. Look out for an unexpected signpost to the left, which indicates a path clambering through trees and swinging right onto a path that runs along the ditch of Offa's Dyke. The Dyke is surprisingly impressive here – a tall bank surmounted by ancient trees towering above a substantial ditch deep in the **Leighton Park** woodland.

The path drops down increasingly steeply on venerable wooden steps to reach and turn right on a forest road that is usually awash with pheasants (attracted by the roadside feeders here). Veer left to cross a substantial bridge, with the big brick retaining walls that once contained Offa's Pool – the highest of four reservoirs in John Naylor's former hydro-electric scheme – away to the left.

Keep ahead on a good level track, stony in places, through mature conifers before swinging round to the right. Leave the track to the right at the next bend, using a narrow path that passes a pond clogged with algae and climbing steadily with a wooded slope up to the right and pastures to the left.

The trail through mature conifers north of Offa's Pool

Turn left on a country lane, climb for 100m to reach the crest of the hill, with the town of Welshpool in the valley ahead and wooded hills beyond, then turn right onto a no-through-road by Pant-y-Bwlch Farm. The narrow and poorly maintained tarmac lane rises pretty steeply until the metalling finally runs out at an impromptu parking area where a pleasant, clearly marked green path rises along the left-hand side of a field, with the spruce plantation of Phillip's Gorse to the left.

The path climbs inexorably across the seemingly never-ending field, with the views opening out nicely to south and west as height is gained; at the end turn left to cut through the plantation and rise towards the tree-crowned summit of **Beacon Ring**, with a somewhat less attractive telecommunications mast just to its right. Cross a stile, still climbing steadily, and go through a gate to reach the ramparts of the hillfort.

A big circular hillfort occupied in the late Bronze Age and early Iron Age, **Beacon Ring** has a big defensive rampart and outer ditch. Used as a beacon site from at least the 17th century, the summit of the hill hosted one of the 60 or more beacons that were lit to celebrate the Golden Jubilee of Queen Victoria in 1887, with a bonfire some 5m high. The hilltop was afforested in 1953 to mark the coronation of Elizabeth II.

The western ramparts and ditch at Beacon Hill

The trail goes round to the left, using the outer ditch of the fort – exploration of the interior is possible but somewhat hampered by dense tree cover, at least until the relatively new owners (Clwyd Powys Archaeological Trust) carry out their plans to remove them. Follow the ditch until it becomes marshy, then go left through a gate near another communications station to negotiate an eerily dark plantation, and then wind through young Christmas trees on an easy path through Cwmdingle plantation to reach and go through a metal gate.

Turn sharp left here (ignore a path going straight ahead) to contour around a huge cornfield, keeping above the head of a deep, wooded side valley with yet more pheasants among the gorse, and aim for a five-barred gate in the far corner of the field. There's a large white arrow here to indicate the way forward, but a national trail waymark would be even more reassuring.

Go through another gate, then down the right-hand side of another arable field, now with Welshpool half-left and the Severn valley dominating the view ahead.

The trail steepens through the next two fields, with even more extensive views across and down the Severn valley, then turns right onto an enclosed green lane. When this goes further round to the right, take the path on the left to descend steeply through two more fields and drop down a few steps to cross a minor road.

WELSHPOOL

A church was established here in the 6th century, but the town took some time to develop, with the motte-and-bailey castle near the old railway station dating from the 1190s and the surviving townscape mainly Georgian in character. Attractions include an 18th-century hexagonal cockpit and a restored steam railway, while a delightful short walk from the town leads to Powis Castle. The castle developed into a major fortress in medieval times and retains impressive red sandstone battlements, but also has magnificent 17th-century gardens and extensive parkland.

Welshpool is a sizeable town serving a wide area and so has a good range of shops and pubs, together with hotels and B&B providers.

Keep straight ahead on a path going down the middle of a large field, then diagonally right across a much smaller enclosure to pass a cottage and use its access track to drop down to pass to the left of Stone House Farm.

Once past the farm, leave the track on a footpath dropping down the left-hand side of a field and then cut across, the path very clearly marked on the ground, to the far right-hand corner of the field. Go down the right side of the next field, ignore a flooded gateway and cross a footbridge just beyond it, go diagonally across two more fields and emerge on a green lane leading to the B4388. Turn right to reach the entrance to Offa's Dyke Business Park, with **Buttington** village straight ahead.

BUTTINGTON

The village of Buttington has little more than a church, pub and a few houses, although it was allegedly the site of a battle in 893 when a Welsh and Mercian force defeated a Danish army (another possibility is that the location was at Buttington Tump near Sedbury, at the southern end of Offa's Dyke).

There are one or two B&B possibilities in and around the village, and the Green Dragon pub has a campsite.

STAGE 8

Across the Severn valley

Start	Offa's Dyke Business Park, Buttington (SJ 249 086)
Finish	Llanymynech canal bridge (SJ 265 210)
Distance	17.3km (10.8 miles)
Ascent	55m (180ft)
Time	4–5hr
Maps	OS Explorer 216, 240
Refreshments	Pub at Pool Quay, plus a shop, post office and several pubs in Llanymynech
Public transport	The X75 bus runs between Shrewsbury and Welshpool, passing through Buttington, while Llanymynech has regular services from Oswestry and Welshpool (X76)
Accommodation	The only possibilities en route are at Pool Quay and Four Crosses, but there are a number of inns in Llanymynech

The walking on this stage of the trail is very straightforward, marking the transition between the rolling hills of the middle Marches and the slightly sterner North Wales hills that lie ahead. The respite is welcome but the attractions along the route should not be underestimated, with delightful stretches alongside the River Severn and a towpath walk of exceptional ecological and historical interest on the Montgomery Canal. The industrial archaeology in Llanymynech, centred on a remarkable kiln built to serve an important limeworks, is an added bonus at the end of the walk.

Go briefly north on the B4388 from Offa's Dyke Business Park in **Buttington**, but quickly take a path on the left towards the River Severn, crossing three fields (in the first of them the 1000-year-old Buttington Oak sadly collapsed in 2018) to reach the Shrewsbury to Welshpool railway line. The low bank of Offa's Dyke is away to the left here, but fades away as the river is approached.

Cross the railway and keep straight ahead over another field, with the rusty cast iron girders of the single-span Buttington Bridge now dominant. Climb up to the right of the bridge, left over the bridge itself – take extreme care, since there is no provision for pedestrians here and it's an accident blackspot – and use the verge for 50m until, with some relief, taking a gravelly track past a white-painted house into a riverside meadow.

Plot a straight course across the first field, with the Severn just to the right in front of the profile of the Breidden hills (constant companions for several miles) until it swings further away from the path. To the left the extraordinarily large farm buildings at The Moors lie below wooded slopes.

Go into a second field, with the river now close at hand again, and curve round the outside of a meander – with close views of nesting swans and mallard, and smaller birds such as chiffchaffs – before heading half-left away from the river, converging gradually with the busy **A483**.

Cross the road with great care and head north along the roadside verge for 200m, until the Montgomery Canal comes in from the left and the trail climbs up onto the gravelly towpath. Faint traces of Strata Marcella Abbey, founded by the Cistercians in 1170, can be discerned in a riverside meadow across the A483. At first the canal remains very close to the road, before curving to the left, passing the Abbey lift bridge – a counter-weighted and manually operated accommodation bridge that carries a farm track and footpath over the water.

Buttington Bridge over the River Severn

Offa's Dyke Path uses two sections of the **Montgomery Canal**, which was almost exclusively used to transport lime from the limekilns at Llanymynech to fertilise the fields of the upper Severn valley. It was breached in 1936 and abandoned in 1944, but is being painstakingly restored and two short stretches (at Llanymynech and Welshpool) are navigable again.

Restoration has to take into account the exceptional nature conservation interest of the canal, while there is considerable industrial archaeology to conserve, including locks, canalside cottages, warehouses and a tollhouse together with an outstanding aqueduct over the River Vrynwy.

There is a good view to the east of the Long Mountain, and an increasingly good view of the Breiddens to its left as the canal skirts the hamlet of **Pool Quay** (B&B, pub, public transport) and approaches Top Lock, with its 19th-century lock-keeper's cottage and resident grey wagtails. Pool Quay was once a busy river port, exporting lead ore together with timber for naval shipbuilding. A smelt house, corn mill and flannel factory have all disappeared and only the mill pond remains.

Drop down to the right just before the lock, taking a gravelly lane down to the A483 and using the pavement to go north for 200m. Cross the road to take a path opposite a farm entrance and swing left through a couple of fields, approaching the Severn again with Pool Quay church away to the left.

The Breidden hills from the Tirymynach flood embankment, with Criggion quarry to the left

Climb up onto the flood embankment, with the river and its summer visitors of willow warblers and chiffchaffs to the right and the stark outline of the Breiddens – the left-hand summit topped by Rodney's Pillar – straight ahead.

Cross the raised trackbed of the long-abandoned railway from Oswestry to Newtown, with bridge abutments still visible on either side of the river, and continue along the flood defences between grassland and a maize field, with a few pheasants in evidence at the field edge. Some maps persist in showing the course of Offa's Dyke above the far bank of the river here, but it is much more likely that the river itself took the place of the Dyke for 8km (5 miles) or so from Buttington northwards.

The path continues to follow the broad, low **Tirymynach flood embankment** as it twists and turns across a succession of fields, the placename ('monk's land') indicating that Strata Marcella Abbey was once the landowner. The River Severn is at its gentlest here, with snaking meanders – the most extraordinary of them identified on the 1:25K map as The Roundabout – where the river has failed to break through a very narrow neck of land and instead takes a tortuous, twisting course that has persisted for at least 150 years. The atmosphere here is quintessentially rural and tranquil, with the sluggish Severn framed by the Breiddens to the right, and a patchwork of fields and hedges to the left.

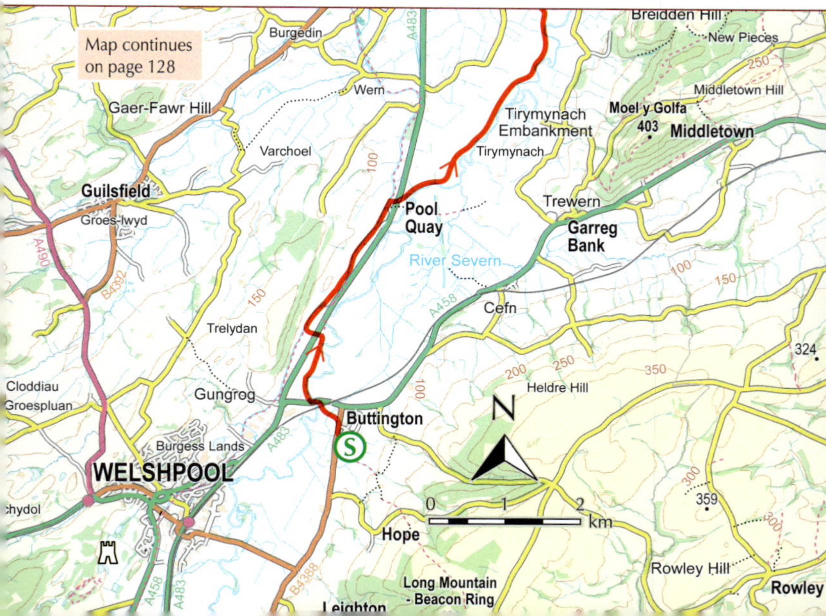

Instantly recognisable from all directions, the volcanic **Breidden hills** rise to 403m (1322ft), with an Iron Age fort on the summit ridge and Rodney's Pillar, erected by Montgomeryshire landowners who supplied timber for Admiral Rodney's fleet, on the northern peak. A golden ball on top of the pillar was destroyed by a lightning strike.

Unusual plants such as rock cinquefoil and shaggy mouse-ear hawkweed thrive on the dolerite soils, while less pleasingly the Criggion quarry disfigures the north-west slopes. Worked by men hanging from ropes until 1967, the quarry now provides up to three quarters of a million tonnes of roadstone every year.

Cross a green farm track and curve markedly left as the flood embankment accommodates a big bend in the river. The path goes through a gate, with a road coming in from the left to run parallel to and below the embankment, which is now pretty substantial as it protects the hamlet of **Rhyd-esgyn** from the river – although the defences failed in December 1960, when terrible floods engulfed Red House Farm, with over 200 animals drowned. A cottage on the embankment at Rhyd-esgyn has a table outside with homemade cakes and jam for sale.

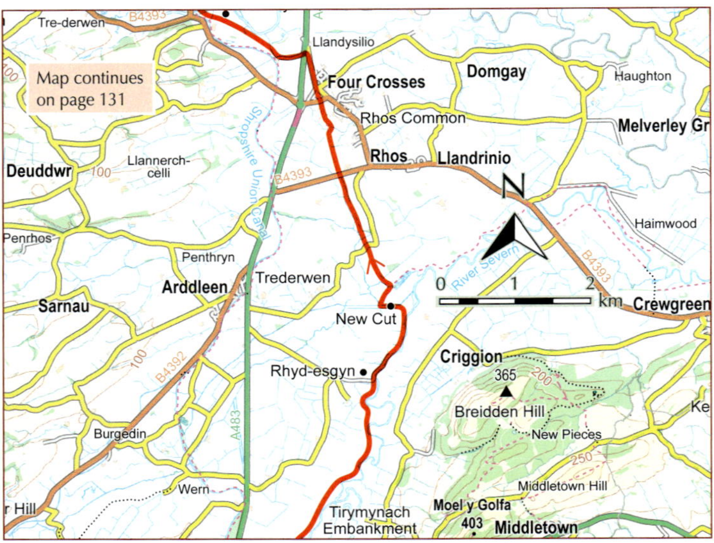

The path on the flood embankment at Rhyd-esgyn

Curve left on the embankment, parting company briefly with the Severn until it once again approaches from the right near a field boundary that has hedgerow trees bursting with birdlife (kestrels hover above the fields here and a grey heron patrols the river). The embankment leads to a curious and almost completely redundant iron contraption carrying walkers above non-existent water and onto the southern levee of the **New Cut**.

Follow the levee upstream and cross the insubstantial stream on Derwas Bridge to find a well-worn path going half-right across a field to a small copse. The flood defences here, locally called argaes, were constructed by the Enclosure Commissioners around 1800. Beyond the copse the trail forks left (the Severn Way leaves here to the right) to find a half-hidden gate and follow the crest of a bank which somewhat surprisingly proves to be Offa's Dyke (the rather inauthentic boulders on its western face probably representing later reinforcements to protect farmland from flooding).

The trail runs between tall hedges on the narrow crest of the bank, with blackberries, sloes and red hawthorn berries providing colour, then drops down with the remnant earthwork to the right and passes The Nea to reach a lane. The Dyke here has been badly eroded by burrowing animals and flood damage, and significant works are planned to secure the future of the monument and the national trail. Go briefly right here, then left to cross fields on a long, flattened-out bank with a sinuous stream on either side.

The attractive top lock on the Montgomery Canal at Carreghofa

Cross the B4393 and continue northwards, the Dyke briefly imposing before reverting to a broad, low bank. At the end of the first field the Dyke keeps straight on but the path diverts to the right to avoid Gornel farmhouse, eventually using its access drive to reach a little lane. Go left for a few steps here, then even further left to cross a field and a disused railway line and rather unexpectedly arrive in the yard of a milk processing plant in the former railway sidings. A diversion to avoid the milk processing yard is planned.

Cross the yard to follow the left-hand margin up to the B4393, now with apartments occupying a former creamery on the left, and keep straight ahead through a sheep pasture to join the street through **Four Crosses** (B&B, public transport). Ty Llew, a B&B located in the former Golden Lion pub, is followed by the village primary school, which was built on the line of the Dyke: the village street occupies the former ditch.

As the street begins to converge with the newly constructed A483 bypass, walkers are directed down to the left to use an underpass under the new road. Turn left on the far side, then right along a narrow metalled lane (the signposting is pretty understated here). The tarmac runs out in the farmyard at Pont y Person and the national trail uses a very short green lane to rejoin the towpath of the Montgomery Canal close to Parson's Bridge with its 'fish-bellied' cast-iron girders.

The canal is spectacularly unspoilt here, with a green path and a waterway that is greatly narrowed in places by bulrushes, reeds and other vegetation.

Dragonflies such as the migrant hawker are particularly abundant here and, together with butterflies such as the comma and red admiral, add colour to the journey along the towpath. The steep northern face of Bryn Mawr, with its hillfort hidden in summit trees, appears ahead until the canal curves to the right, with a sudden view of the limestone cliffs and quarry faces of Llanymynech Rocks beyond **Pentreheylin Hall**.

> **Pentreheylin** was a substantial rural estate, centred on a Jacobean house that was surrounded by substantial barns, a horse engine house, pigsties, a cow-house and a linhay (a hay store and cattle shelter). Farming was not the only occupation here, since the estate embraced the coming of the canal and built a wharf alongside, with industrial buildings including the only surviving salt warehouse in Wales – a particularly attractive late Georgian building with a loading crane still in place.

The towpath leads past Pentreheylin Wharf, complete with salt warehouse, but beyond the wharf the canal narrows and becomes choked with vegetation again as it crosses the Vrynwy aqueduct, the towpath high above the river. The intricate iron aqueduct has repeatedly needed strengthening and occasionally leaks into the river below, but is a fine example of a stone-built, clay-lined aqueduct.

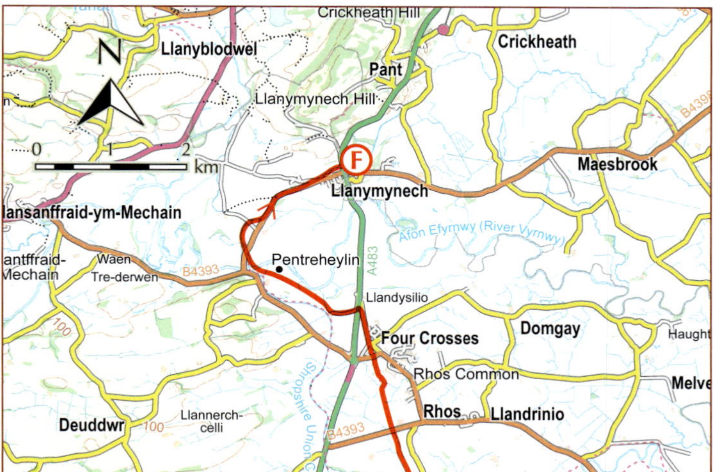

Milepost on the Montgomery Canal

The canal suddenly comes to an apparent dead end where a road crosses its course, but resumes as if uninterrupted on the far side of the road, using a second aqueduct to pass above a much smaller stream before rounding a bend and arriving at the superb restored twin locks at Carreghofa, which marked the end-on junction of the Ellesmere and Montgomeryshire canals. A splendid set of canalside buildings here includes the wharfinger's house, the lock-keeper's cottage and a tollhouse.

Beyond the top lock and its resident swans there is an outstanding view of Llanymynech Rocks, although the canal itself is disappointingly obstructed by vegetation. The towpath is gravelly now as the canal reaches the outskirts of the village of **Llanymynech**, although there is still an attractive outlook to the left of farmland and hills. Straight ahead is the distinctive chimney of the Hoffman kiln, although this disappears behind trees as the towpath reaches an underpass beneath the A483, with the visitor centre at Llanymynech Wharf (open at weekends only) across the canal to the left, and steps on the right leading up to the road and the village centre.

LLANYMYNECH

Straddling the border between England and Wales, Llanymynech is a former industrial village of no great pretensions, although its facilities will be welcome at the end of a day's walking. Unspent energy can be spent on a short excursion to the heritage area, which explores the quarrying and lime-burning history of the village. The centrepiece is the Hoffman kiln, with a tall redbrick chimney and a huge brick beehive kiln with two tunnel vaults entered through 14 round-headed arches. Close by are the remains of two large draw kilns, which were superseded by the state-of-the-art Hoffman kiln around 1900.

Accommodation, food and a shop make the village a useful stop-off for trail walkers.

STAGE 9

Exploring the unknown Marches

Start	Llanymynech canal bridge (SJ 265 210)
Finish	Castle Mill, Chirk (SJ 262 377)
Distance	22.5km (14 miles)
Ascent	725m (2380ft)
Time	6–7hr
Maps	OS Explorer 240
Refreshments	There is a useful post office and shop in Trefonen, together with the Barley Mow (closed weekday lunchtimes), but there are no other facilities on the route
Public transport	Llanymynech has regular services from Oswestry and Welshpool (bus X76). Castle Mill has limited early evening buses on service 64 between Glyn Ceiriog and Chirk.
Accommodation	There is currently very limited accommodation at Castle Mill, but buses can be used to access Glyn Ceiriog, Pontfadog and Chirk, and there are also possibilities scattered throughout the day's walking at Trefonen, Candy and Bronygarth

This is a fascinating day's walking, although it is occasionally difficult to navigate as the route twists and turns through the Oswestry uplands. The waymarking is good, however, and the walking is never difficult, while the variety of landscapes is exceptional. The bare limestone cliffs of Llanymynech Rocks contrast with the gentle slopes and wide panoramas of Moelydd and Selattyn Hill, while Racecourse Common provides a poignant reminder of past pleasures and the Marcher stronghold of Chirk Castle dominates the view north across the Ceiriog valley towards the end of the day.

Walk north along the busy A483 from the **Llanymynech** canal bridge, but quickly turn left up Pen-y-foel lane, passing the shaly rock cutting where Charles Darwin undertook his first geological fieldwork in 1831, using a clinometer (inaccurately!) to measure the angle of slope of the rocks. Continue along the lane, then turn right, more steeply, and when the tarmac peters out take a path on the left going through two metal gates.

The 'Welsh' drum house at the top of an inclined plane leading from Llanymynech quarries

Turn left to climb on the old inclined plane on which wagons of limestone from the quarries were lowered to the canal some 80m below, with the 'Welsh' drum house visible on the skyline ahead. Immediately behind the drum house is one of the extensive quarries that now give Llanymynech Rocks their craggy profile, although to the west the cliff face of Asterley Rocks is more natural. Turn left at the top of the incline, following a level path below the cliffs where peregrine falcons and swifts nest (a very short detour to the left leads to the Border Viewpoint, overlooking the Vyrnwy valley and the Breidden hills).

The nature reserve at **Llanymynech Rocks** straddles the England/Wales border and is home to a spectacular array of flowers, including rockrose, cowslips, wild carrot, several varieties of orchid, and herbs such as marjoram, while the superb late Bronze Age or early Iron Age hillfort on the plateau above is one of the largest in Britain. The ramparts enclose an area of 57ha and excavations have uncovered an Iron Age roundhouse together with traces of Roman lead and copper mining inside the ramparts.

Go through a gate and below a scree slope, contouring below Asterley Rocks before curving left around the edge of the 13th green and 14th tee of a hilltop golf course. The path continues pleasantly but occasionally muddily along the woodland fringe, with the fairway to the right and steep wooded slopes concealing the fine views of the Tanat valley and the earthworks of Offa's Dyke to the left.

The undulating path eventually drops down to a crossroads of paths where the Shropshire Way goes straight ahead to Llynclys Common, but the national trail turns left, descending steeply at first down the Carboniferous limestone escarpment but later more gently past the dairy farm at Blodwel Hall. The hall was once a much larger manor house, the home in the 15th century of the philanthropist 'Gwerful the bountiful'. Only a gateway and a summerhouse survive from the medieval mansion. Turn right onto the farm's access road, pass the old entrance gates to the hall and leave the access road to the left, following the field edge through a gateway and then diverging slightly right across a second field in the direction of an obvious stile.

Cross a long-disused railway – surprisingly the track is still in place – and go slightly right to cross a footbridge over a little stream. The path now curves around the left-hand side of a big field to meet and turn right along a lane, which quickly approaches the A495 at **Porth-y-waen** – home to a well-known silver band.

Cross with care, aiming slightly left, to turn along a track but immediately turn left again on a grassy path across a field and then climb between houses to reach a minor road. Turn left, take the left fork and cross the busy Treflach road, quickly passing the access road to the Tanat Valley Light Railway visitor centre, where the only surviving part of the old Potteries, Shrewsbury & North Wales Railway line is being restored.

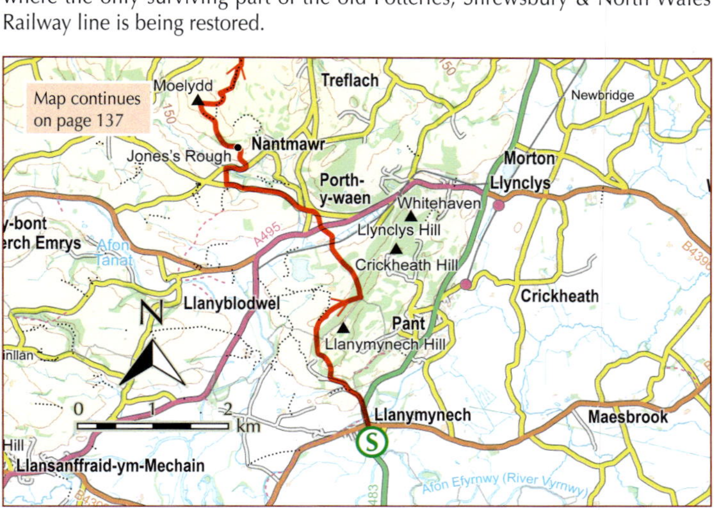

Keep straight ahead, over a level crossing where the ossified track signals the scale of the restoration work ahead. The walk along Cefn Lane is long but saved from tedium by the fine rural views, and eventually ends with a right turn down a field edge and a short descent to a road on the outskirts of the old quarrying village of **Nantmawr**.

Take the road through the village, but turn left immediately before a phone box (the waymark post is unhelpfully hidden in the hedge) to take a stepped path rising past a cottage and through two fields. A right turn leads to a steeper climb to reach a narrow lane.

The trail lies left along the lane, right up an even narrower lane and straight ahead on a track when the metalling ends. Turn right, uphill, just before the metalling ends, to enter **Jones's Rough**. Violets provide food for pearl-bordered fritillaries here, while wild cherries and yews thrive on the steep slopes, with tormentil and waxcap fungi below. Climb steeply through the nature reserve on a stepped path, quickly reaching a gate giving access onto the upper reaches of Moelydd, with extraordinary views west to the Welsh hills.

The trail crosses two fields and passes a ruined farmhouse, then turns left on a track past a house with drinks and ice cream available and forks right off the main track – the route is well waymarked with yellow arrows – to reach the summit of **Moelydd**, where a toposcope details the extent of the panorama.

A wayside cottage at the entrance to the nature reserve of Jones's Rough

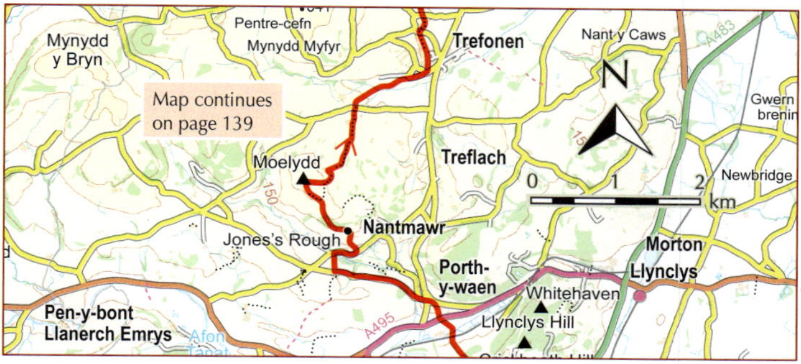

Turn sharply right on Moelydd's summit, with the Wrekin prominent on the horizon and waymarks showing the way. The village of Trefonen, the next objective, is clearly in view to the left. Turn left on a stony track that curves left and right, leaving the track on the second bend to go down two sides of a field and continue straight ahead into woodland.

The trail now lies along a gated tarmac lane past Ty Canol, with its high chimneys, and straight on at a junction to meet a slightly busier road. Turn left here, then immediately right through a wooden kissing gate to follow a path alongside a line of oak trees.

The path is clear across two fields, with a holloway – the original route – a little to the right, then crosses a little stream on a clapper bridge and runs along the left-hand edge of a long field. Small fields on the left, bordering Little London Lane, are named Hyde Park and Piccadilly, because drovers rested their animals overnight here on the long journey to markets in London. Bellan Lane, initially grassy but soon surfaced, lies through a gate and leads directly into **Trefonen**. Offa's Dyke Path turns left into Malthouse Lane, but the village centre lies straight ahead.

TREFONEN

This big, sprawling village was once well-known for coalmining and brick-making. Sculptures near the school mark the site of the Old and New Trefonen collieries, both of which were closed down as a result of flooding. The miners were paid their wages in the former Efel Inn. The nearby Band Box was originally the storeroom for the instruments of the Trefonen band, set up by the rector in 1877 to promote temperance.

The village has a shop and post office, a pub and a couple of B&B providers.

The stone seat built by miners or quarrymen in Candy Woods

When Malthouse Lane curls left, go straight ahead onto a green path behind houses, quickly confined between tall hedges but later becoming a rough track that meets a country lane. To the right is Pottery Row – now a group of cottages but once the drying sheds for the pottery that operated at Trefarclawdd brick-works. Keep straight ahead across two stiles and a field, then bear left along the far hedge to cross a minor lane and continue along the right-hand edge of two fields, with Offa's Dyke now very impressively alongside again as the trail passes Pentre-shannel.

Go steeply down a lane and turn right on the Morda valley road and quickly left in front of a pretty little cottage to pass Glan-yr-afon and climb steeply up through **Candy** Woods on a good path, then even more steeply on a path to the right, picking a way between big boulders. Turn right, then left after only a few steps, still rising but much more gently. The next mile is an absolute joy, on an easy path through delightful deciduous woodland, passing a rudimentary stone seat built by miners or quarrymen. A big cat – allegedly a black panther – was sighted nearby in 2013.

A broad, flat and occasionally damp track, shared with the Shropshire Way, leads to a junction of ways. Turn right here, going through a big gap in the Dyke, and then left on a winding path to enter coniferous woodland through a gap in a stone wall (a wooden seat here is welcome). The wide track through the plantation leads to a stile at the edge of **Racecourse Common**. Oswestry Racecourse was established in Georgian times and the two-mile figure-of-eight course, disused since 1848, is still clearly recognisable as a grassy ride in ridgetop heathland.

Go past the statue of a two-headed horse and then past the scanty remains of the 19th-century grandstand, keeping straight ahead along the old racecourse across three rough tracks and then meeting the **B4580** Oswestry to Llansilan road. Leave the Shropshire Way and the racecourse here, taking Ffordd Carreg-y-big northwards, with the course of the Dyke very clear on the ridge to the left.

OSWESTRY

Despite lying some way east of the path, Oswestry is a possible choice for an overnight stay. It is an attractive old market town with narrow lanes such as English and Welsh Walls but the main attraction is the extraordinarily complex Old Oswestry hillfort, with concentric ramparts (four around most of the enclosure, but up to seven on the western side) enclosing a drumlin, a smooth egg-shaped hill formed by a glacier moving over rock debris during the last Ice Age.

Oswestry has supermarkets and a good variety of local shops, together with lots of market town pubs and a range of accommodation.

After 1km of road walking the buildings of Carreg-y-big (and Oswestry Equestrian Centre) come into view. Skirt around the buildings and when the Selattyn road curves right, climb over a stile on the left to rejoin the Dyke. The trail follows the imposing Dyke through two fields, with an optional diversion in the second to visit the largest standing stone in Shropshire – an irregularly shaped 2m-high limestone block.

Go over a stile to walk along the western edge of a little wood, now on the Dyke itself, although the ditch has been modified and is unusually deep, narrow and water-filled. The Dyke – colonised by bluebells and coconut-scented gorse – is particularly impressive as the trail approaches the isolated farm of Orseddwen. Turn right here, away from the earthwork, then left to take a green track that climbs steadily to reach the summit plateau of Selattyn Hill. A detour to the right here leads to Selattyn Tower, which was erected inside a Bronze Age ring cairn in Victorian times but collapsed in the early 20th century and has recently been restored.

Offa's Dyke Path now turns half-left, however (more explicit signposting would be welcome here), to cross a field and find a signpost at the top of a quite superb green lane that descends gently between tumbledown drystone walls.

There are fine views north across the Craignant valley as the lane descends past Woodside Cottage and through a kissing gate, becoming a gravelly track making a long and slightly sinuous descent. Go right along a minor road for a few steps, then steeply down a narrow lane to reach the valley bottom at **Craignant**.

Cross the stream, continue on the tarmac up to a cottage and then go forward on a stony track to reach a country lane and turn left for 100m, taking a right turn and crossing fields and a tiny lane. Keep ahead alongside the Dyke, its earthen

Chirk Castle from the path above Bronygarth

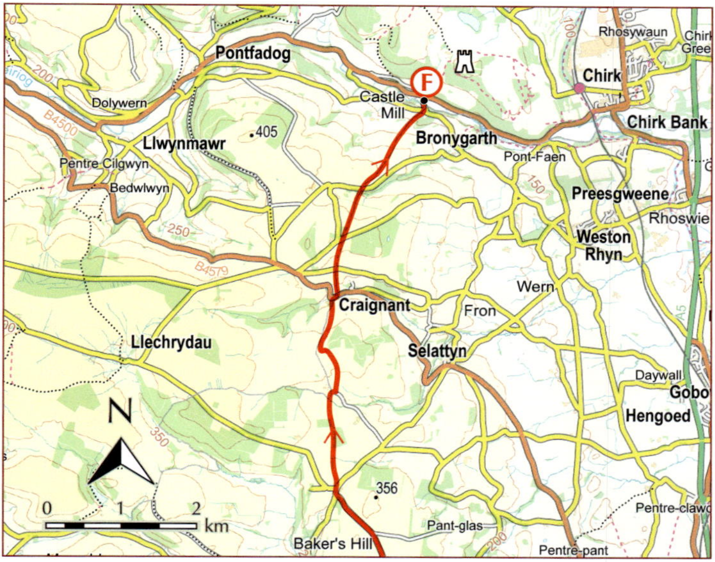

bank and broad ditch once again highly impressive. The sudden surprise of a dramatic view of Chirk Castle on its hilltop beyond the Ceiriog valley adds further variety to the spectacular landscape.

The path abruptly drops down on a long flight of steps to cross the deeply incised Nanteris valley, with a shorter stepped path leading back up to a road crossing. Turn right for a few steps along the road – which is actually a tiny lane overgrown with grass – and go over a stile to the left to rejoin the Dyke, soon going to the right to walk alongside the earthwork.

At the end of the field the path climbs up to the crest of the Dyke and continues on the top of the bank, with good views east to the canal, rail and road aqueducts near Chirk and to the Cheshire plain beyond.

The way continues northwards, across a dusty farm lane used by the Ceiriog Trail, and descends quite steeply with increasingly impressive views of Chirk Castle ahead. The Dyke and ditch are on a massive scale as the descent begins, the earthwork zigzagging slightly down the slope. A left turn down a flight of concrete steps leads to the minor road through **Bronygarth**, with two notably tall limekilns just to the right. Bronygarth has no village hall so two Mongolian yurts were constructed locally in 2004 for community gatherings.

Go straight down the minor road, which crosses the River Ceiriog on an unaltered 19th-century bridge with a high stone arch. A final short climb along the road leads to the B4500 at **Castle Mill**, with the Great Oak at the Gates of the Dead – battered but thought to date from the ninth century – only a few steps to the right.

CASTLE MILL

Castle Mill was the site of the battle of Crogen, fought in 1165, when Owain Gwynedd's forces ambushed the larger army of Henry II, which suffered heavy casualties and was forced to retreat, leading the King to abandon his ambitious plans for the conquest of Wales.

The hamlet has no shop or pubs. The former mill that had become an inn by the time George Borrow ordered ale and bread-and-butter there in 1854 no longer offers accommodation. Early evening buses do, however, provide links to alternative accommodation in the Ceiriog valley to the west and Chirk to the east.

The battered but venerable Great Oak at the Gates of the Dead, Castle Mill

STAGE 10

The Vale of Llangollen and Eglwyseg Rocks

Start	Castle Mill, Chirk (SJ 262 377)
Finish	Llandegla church (SJ 195 524)
Distance	25.9km (16.1 miles)
Ascent	775m (2540ft)
Time	6–8hr
Maps	OS Explorer 240, 256
Refreshments	There are general stores in Trevor and Llandegla, and cafés at Pontcysyllte, together with pubs (some with limited opening times) in Froncysyllte, Trevor and Llandegla
Public transport	Castle Mill has limited early and mid-morning buses on service 64 between Glyn Ceiriog, Pontfadog, Castle Mill and Chirk. The T51 provides regular bus services from Llandegla to Ruthin and Wrexham
Accommodation	There is very little available in and around Llandegla itself, but Ruthin has a good selection of hotels and B&Bs

This is a wonderful and extremely varied day's walking, passing the intact fortress of Chirk Castle and the short-lived, ruined Castell Dinas Bran, crossing Thomas Telford's world-famous Pontcysyllte Aqueduct (an alternative route caters for those without a head for heights!), skirting below the dramatic limestone outcrops of Trevor Rocks and Creigiau Eglwyseg, and crossing heather moors populated by the elusive black grouse on the way to the mountain-biking mecca of Llandegla Forest and the village of Llandegla. In summer, from April to September, there are two possibilities for the first part of the day's walking, using either the main route via Crogen Wladys or an alternative, permissive path through the grounds of Chirk Castle.

Alternative start via Home Farm

The alternative route takes the thin path on the right at **Castle Mill**, passing interpretation boards for the battle of Crogen and climbing the wooded hillside, emerging from the trees to cross a field, then re-entering woodland to reach a track heading for Home Farm. The farm buildings are partly timber-framed and picturesque, but are now used by the National Trust as a visitor centre, with a seasonal tea room. The way, indicated by white-topped posts, then lies past the car park and across upland pastures to reach the buildings and narrow lane at **Tyn-y-groes**, with a fine retrospective view of Chirk Castle across grassland. Newhall lake to the right obscures the line of Offa's Dyke, although the earthwork reappears in times of drought.

Main route

The main route – and the only route from October to March – takes the narrow lane on crumbling tarmac that rises steeply to the west from **Castle Mill**, with the pungent scent of wild garlic very evident and the sound of woodland birds almost deafening. Fork right at Ty Brickly to go steadily uphill to the farm at Crogen Wladys, where the metalling ends.

Climb the rough, stony track until the slope eases, with the Ceiriog valley a dramatic sight to the left, and go through the kissing gate on the right to climb again on a steep grassy path, with bluebells under the trees to the left. The slope eases dramatically at a gate and the trail follows a thin path through three fields, the view ahead improving dramatically, with the distant Peckforton Hills on the skyline beyond the Cheshire plain. To the right Chirk Castle is dominant as the path approaches the house at **Tyn-y-groes**. The alternative path joins the main route here.

Completed in 1310, **Chirk Castle** was Edward I's last statement of raw power over the Welsh following his successful campaigns in North Wales, occupying a strategic and very visible ridge-top site above the Ceiriog valley. It retains its formidable defensive walls and towers but has been much altered internally, with 17th-century Long Gallery, 18th-century saloon and 20th-century library. It was bought for £5000 by Sir Thomas Myddelton in 1595, and his descendants still live in part of the castle, which is surrounded by parkland, with Offa's Dyke running north-east from the castle before its course is interrupted by Newhall Lake.

The trail continues along the lane past The Kennels – an estate cottage with a mock half-timbered barn. After another 300m go through a kissing gate on the left, half-right across a field and slightly left on a well-defined path through a second, larger field. Negotiate a kissing gate and turn right for a few steps, then left, now back on tarmac again. Fork right at a cottage and keep on down an even narrower lane, going straight ahead at a crossroads, accompanied again by the pungent odour of wild garlic in spring.

The road swings left and then right, before a metal kissing gate takes the trail around the right-hand edge of a field and through two more kissing gates in quick succession. Walk diagonally left across the next field to yet another kissing gate.

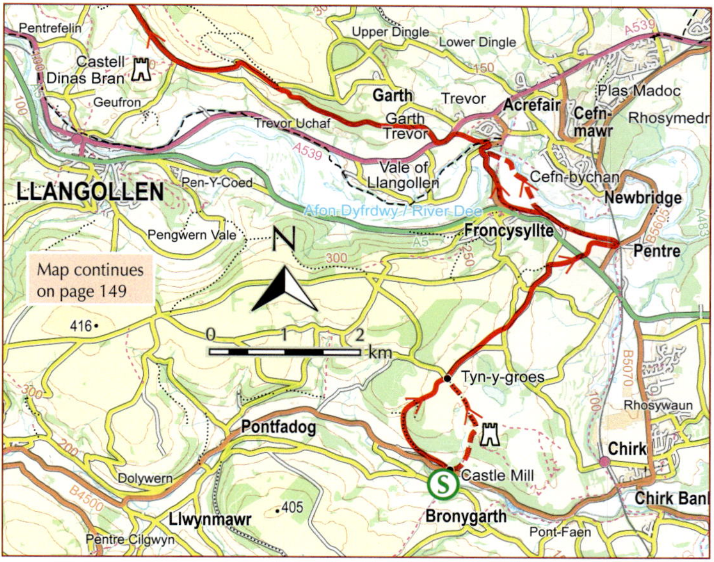

The path lies along the edge of a final field to climb some steps and reach the heavily trafficked A5. The Dyke is to the right here, clearly positioned to overlook routes along the Dee valley. Care is needed here because there is no verge or footway on this side of the road, so cross straight over onto the pavement on the other side, turn right, and after a mercifully brief 20m take the lane on the left, going through a gate to rejoin the Dyke for the final time.

Drop down to find a metal kissing gate at the bottom of the field, cross the Dyke to another gate and keep straight ahead, parallel to but above the Llangollen Canal. The course of Offa's Dyke was cut by the canal, but the earthwork continues northwards through the Wrexham industrial villages on its way to the North Wales coast. The trail reaches the B5605 after crossing two fields; turn left, over the canal, and then left again, downhill, to walk along the canal towpath.

The walking is now very easy as the canal approaches the village of **Froncysyllte**, passing tall, disused limekilns and a miniature canal basin to reach a pedestrian footbridge and vehicular lift bridge in close proximity. Froncysyllte is home to a noted male voice choir. The Aqueduct Inn lies on the A5. Once again there are two choices: the main route crosses the swing bridge and drops down to cross the Dee on a road bridge, while the alternative permissive route (only

The pedestrian bridge and lift bridge at Froncysyllte, where the main and alternative routes diverge

recommended for those with a good head for heights) crosses the river on the renowned Pontcysyllte Aqueduct.

Alternative route via Pontcysyllte Aqueduct

To follow the permissive route, keep to the towpath as it swings right past long-term moorings and approaches the aqueduct, with railings to protect walkers on the narrow towpath but no protection on the far side of the narrow canal. The experience is exhilarating or terrifying according to personal taste.

Once across the aqueduct the canal broadens out into the **Trevor** basin, with canalside warehouses and an attractive bridge over the Llangollen branch of the canal. Trevor has the Telford Inn, together with a general store. A curving path leads back down below the end of the aqueduct and rises to meet a road. Turn right here, cross above the canal and take the far towpath as far as an attractive black-and-white footbridge to rejoin the main route.

Main route

The simpler route crosses the footbridge at Froncysyllte to reach and turn right along the B5434, descending gradually to the stone Cysylltau bridge across the Dee. There is an awe-inspiring view to the right of the Pontcysyllte Aqueduct, followed by a steady climb until the road bends right and the trail goes up a dusty path to the left, later climbing steep steps to reach the canal. Turn left and cross the footbridge. The alternative route comes in along the far bank of the canal here.

Britain's highest navigable aqueduct, carried 40m above the River Dee on 18 piers, the **Pontcysyllte Aqueduct** lies at the heart of a World Heritage Site and is popular with narrowboaters and walkers. Yet the canal system it was built to support was never constructed: the original grandiose plan to connect the Severn, Dee and Mersey was abandoned when money ran out, and it serves only to connect the dead-end Llangollen Canal to the Shropshire Union Canal. Nevertheless it serves as a monument to the creative genius of Thomas Telford, who completed it in 1805.

A roughly defined path crosses the field ahead, aiming for the far left-hand corner, then swings right in a tunnel under a disused railway line, turns right again and follows a tarmac path up to the A539. Cross over and go left along the pavement, turn right into Trevor Hall Road and as the road curves right, take the Trevor Hall drive straight ahead for 100m. Go through a gate to the right and climb steadily through woodland, with a glimpse of Trevor Hall – the family seat of the Trevor family, reduced to ruins by fire in 1963 before being painstakingly restored – below to the left.

The slope eases and the trail follows a long, straight track through coniferous woodland with chiffchaffs and cuckoos audible in spring. Fork left to take the lower path, at first through the conifers but later along the woodland edge and alongside a wall through moorland to a narrow road with the common land of Ruabon Mountain beyond.

Llangollen and the River Dee from the Panorama Walk

Castell Dinas Bran from above the Panorama Walk

Turn left along the road, somewhat unexpectedly known as the Panorama Walk, but named after a path that became popular with tourists in the 19th century. There is heather, gorse and bilberry moorland to the right and a quite staggering prospect opening up ahead, dominated by the detached hill surmounted by Castell Dinas Bran to the left of a rocky escarpment. Once the trees are left behind the view to the left is sensational too, with the town of Llangollen set in the wide rift valley of the Dee, and wooded slopes beyond.

The national trail follows the Panorama Walk beneath the jagged crags of the limestone escarpment, negotiating a couple of sharp bends and then passing below Trevor Rocks. The walking is very easy and there are grassy verges beside the road as it approaches and then passes to the right of **Castell Dinas Bran**, with a minor road on the left giving access to a path leading up to the remains of the fort and castle on the summit. (The road and the summit path can both also be used to reach Llangollen in a little less than 3km.)

The prominent summit of **Dinas Bran** has long proved attractive as a defensive site, with the bulwarks of an Iron Age hillfort especially prominent to the south and west, where they rise up to 8m high in places. A medieval castle was constructed within the hillfort in the 1260s but was burnt by its defenders and then captured by Henry de Lacy, earl of Lincoln, during Edward I's advance into North Wales. The castle was finally abandoned in the 1280s but remains a prominent feature in the landscape of the Vale of Llangollen.

LLANGOLLEN

Some 3km south-west from the Path, this is a classic tourist town with attractions including the river, steam railway and Plas Newydd, the home of the 'Ladies of Llangollen', and is especially crowded during the international eisteddfod in July.

A major tourist destination, Llangollen has plenty of shops, cafés and pubs, together with several hotels and some excellent B&B choices.

Beyond Tan-y-castell the road walking continues, with the magnificent cliffs of Creigiau Eglwyseg increasingly dominating the scene ahead and the green upper reaches of the Dee valley away to the left. After a total of 3.5km the route finally leaves the tarmac, taking a rough track on the right and contouring round underneath the cliffs, which are serrated, layered and hugely impressive here. Cross a rocky stream and take a thin path passing above Bryn Goleu, with peacocks in the yard and a limekiln on the hillslopes above. The well-preserved limekiln dates from around 1800 and was constructed from large blocks of limestone with an arch over the drawing tunnel leading to a brick-built hearth.

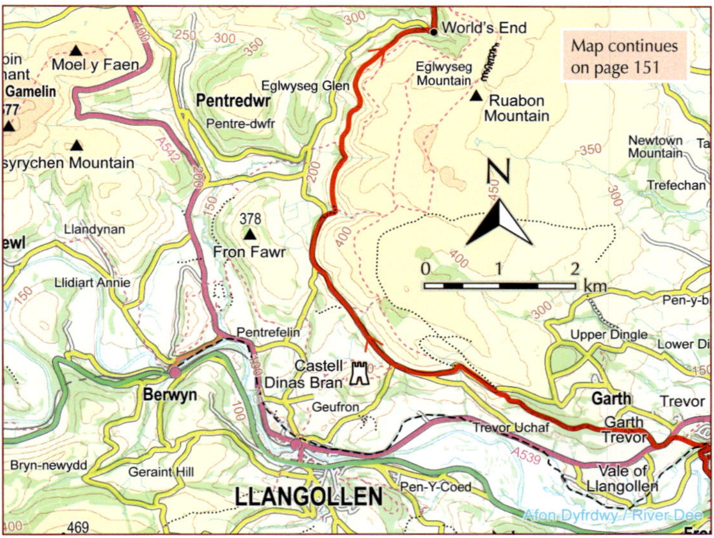

The path crosses the first of a series of scree slopes, although the path itself is perfectly safe, consisting of a gravelly path on a reasonably wide ledge cut into the mountainside. A brief respite on grass at another stream crossing is followed by another journey on a good path through the scree, with the solid Plas yn Eglwyseg farmhouse and attached stables in the valley below and the smooth slopes of Llantysilio Mountain beyond.

Another grassy interlude leads to a further stream crossing, with the dramatic grey, stepped escarpment of Craig Arthur above and the forbidding bulk of Craig yr Adar ahead. Behind and to the left is the Eglwyseg valley, with the deeper trench of the Dee beyond and the tops of the Berwyn Mountains on the southwest horizon, while ahead to the left is the southern edge of the grouse moor which the trail is heading towards.

An obvious junction of paths below Craig Arthur may cause some uncertainty, since the upper path heads promisingly below the cliffs and has the advantage of avoiding a steep section of road walking. However, Offa's Dyke Path takes the lower path, just above a little plantation and then well above Plas Uchaf. Plas Uchaf is an attractive half-timbered manor house dating from 1563, once the home of John Jones, who signed the death warrant of Charles I.

The path now descends to pass through a gate onto the valley road at **World's End** – a picturesque spot at the head of the Eglwyseg valley, although once the site of a lead and silver mine. Cross the ford and continue along the narrow road, which is pleasant enough on weekdays but can be a nightmare on summer Sundays, when it becomes a very popular leisure drive. There is a brutal but

The superb path through the screes near Bryn Goleu

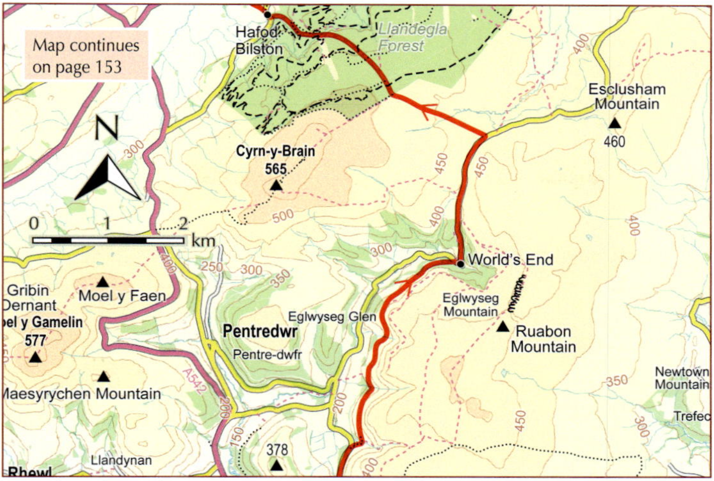

reasonably short ascent, but beyond a cattle grid the slope eases and the route lies across the heather moor.

The road walking ends when the head of the shallow valley to the left is reached: look out for a low stone national trail marker pointing the way left through the heather and bilberry dominating the sprawling plateau of Cyrn-y-Brain. The path is narrow but much improved, with railway sleepers providing a boardwalk across the dampest parts of the route, and a stony path elsewhere. Ahead is **Llandegla Forest**, with a huge area of clearfell and replanting highly visible.

The moorland of Ruabon Mountain was once reserved for grouse shooting and red-legged partridge are still reared as game birds on the eastern slopes, but to the west **black grouse** are specially protected. The species has declined significantly in recent decades, but half of the Welsh population of black grouse can be found here, and the last few years has seen the local population increase significantly. Dawn visits to the lekking sites where the male birds display in spring are provided by the RSPB (rspb.org.uk).

When the moor ends, climb over a ladder stile into the plantation. Keep straight ahead on a wide stony track that crosses two cycle routes in quick succession and then narrows to a well-surfaced path as it enters the forest, using a small gap between lines of conifers. Llandegla Forest, planted in the 1970s

Crossing the boardwalk on the heather moorland of Cyrn-y-Brain

and covering 6km^2, consists largely of Sitka spruce with some larches and is now home to a hugely popular mountain-biking centre.

Cross a forest road, shortly followed by a cycle track, and commence a long, gentle and winding descent on a good path to reach a clearing in the forest. Use a plank bridge to cross a stream, go slightly left to cross two more cycle tracks in quick succession and take the path straight ahead, which is briefly stonier and somewhat steeper.

An easier section follows, on a wide track carpeted with pine needles and cones, with a final stony track leading down to the edge of the forest, next to information boards by a wooden gate. The path beyond the gate is steep and worn to the bedrock in places as it curves left, but once it bends right the gradient eases and the trail meets and turns right along a country lane running through the hamlet of **Hafod Bilston**, centred on a 17th-century gentry house with mullioned windows.

Just beyond the last buildings go left to follow a track running along the right-hand side of the field. At the field boundary don't be tempted by the gate leading

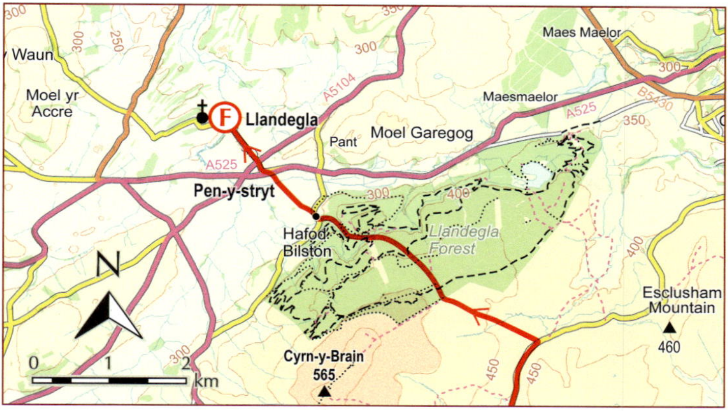

straight ahead; instead go slightly to the right, through a kissing gate, and cross the sheep pasture, aiming for a pylon straight ahead. Just beyond the pylon, use another kissing gate to cross the field to the left, aiming for a footbridge over a little brook and crossing a final field to reach the A525 just to the right of a house.

After an unpleasant 50m along the well-worn verge, cross with care and use a narrow footpath to reach a much quieter road. Turn left along this, then straight across a second major road (the A5104) to reach and walk along the main street of **Llandegla**, with the church about 400m ahead.

LLANDEGLA

Situated on a key droving route through North Wales and once noted for its cattle fairs, Llandegla had a village blacksmiths and several inns but is now a quiet backwater. St Tecla's church lies on a river terrace above the River Alyn, while St Tecla's well is a low-key pilgrimage site 200m away, its waters once favoured as a cure for epilepsy.

There is a post office and village stores, and the church offers simple refreshments. The Crown on the main A525 is some distance from the village and provides food but not rooms, while there is very little B&B accommodation in the vicinity. However, the T51 bus runs every hour to Ruthin, where there is a good selection of accommodation.

STAGE 11

The Clwydian Range

Start	Llandegla church (SJ 195 524)
Finish	Bodfari (SJ 097 701)
Distance	28.2km (17.5 miles)
Ascent	990m (3250ft)
Time	7–9hr
Maps	OS Explorer 256, 265
Refreshments	The only possibilities for refreshments along the route involve significant detours to nearby villages such as Llanarmon-yn-ial, and a considerable climb to regain the ridge. The Dinorben Arms in Bodfari serves meals all day.
Public transport	The T51 provides regular bus services from Ruthin and Wrexham to Llandegla, while Bodfari has a few early evening services (bus F14) to Denbigh and one to Mold
Accommodation	Several B&B providers together with camping in and close to Bodfari, with other possibilities in Denbigh. Intermediate options in Llanarmon-yn-ial, Llanferres and Llangynhafal all involve a significant detour from the route.

The journey along the long, undulating ridge of the Clwydian hills – the narrow range dividing industrial Deeside from rural Denbighshire – is one of the highlights of the entire walk. A near-continuous scarp slope to the west divides the ridge from the Vale of Clwyd, centred on the medieval castles and market towns of Ruthin and Denbigh. The trail uses a succession of green lanes in the Clwydian foothills, rising to the ridge at its central, highest point to visit the iconic Jubilee Tower on Moel Famau, and passing a string of superb hillforts crowning most of the major summits.

Leave **Llandegla** along the lane between the church and the old rectory, keep straight on at a gate and cross an extraordinarily long field, with the River Alyn just to the left. Cross the river on a footbridge, turn right across a field and then left to drop down past a little wood and keep ahead across a second footbridge, with the Alyn reappearing from the right.

The landscape here is curious, with little hills and limestone outcrops interspersed with small woods, as the route goes left through a kissing gate but immediately right along a relict field boundary to reach a little hedged green lane, passing between more limestone outcrops before going straight across a quiet country lane. Caves in some of the limestone outcrops were occupied in the Neolithic era, and later used as burial sites.

The trail follows the access track to Chweleiriog Lwyd around a right-hand bend and then left through a sheep pasture before taking a sensible diversion away from the farmyard, instead rising through two fields – notices rather bizarrely request no picnicking or even stopping here – to turn left at the top of the second. An RAF Washington bomber inexplicably crashed nearby in 1953, with the loss of 10 lives. The tail section of the plane came to rest in woods above Chweleiriog Lwyd.

Keep to the lower edge of a succession of small fields, with an excellent view back to Llandegla Forest and Llantysilio Mountain, and pass Tyddyn-tlodion, with the remains of a cruck-framed 16th-century hall-house down to the left of the path, to reach and turn right along a narrow metalled lane.

Follow the lane, awash with bluebells in spring, for 800m until it swings left, passing the entrances to the Pen-y-Ffrith coarse fishery (the exotic bird park here has now closed) and the Gweryd fishing lakes, then taking a track along the left edge of Nurse Fawr Wood as far as a transmitter station. The surfacing ends here and a green track continues alongside the attractively open upper reaches of Nurse Fawr, with a tumbledown slate wall now supplemented by a fence.

The woodland falls away to the right and the way lies straight ahead through a gate, with the first serious climb of the day heading for the western ridge of **Moel y Plas**. The retrospective view over Llyn Gweryd provides a diversion during any rest breaks.

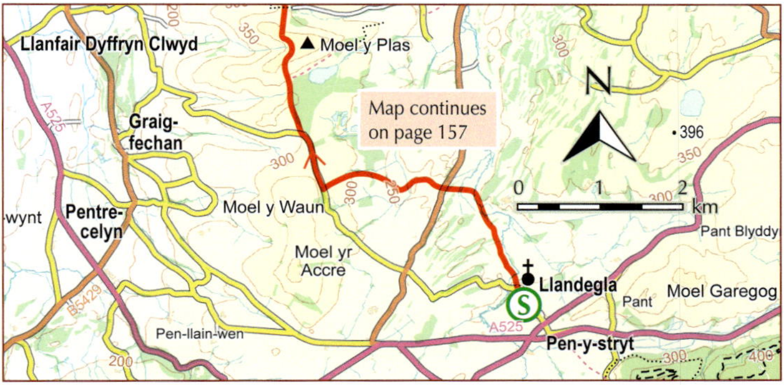

The descent to the Llanarmon road, with Moel Llanfair beyond

Go briefly right at a fence, then cut through heather and bilberry moorland above a deep cleft which leads towards the Vale of Clwyd – a classic rift valley with fertile alluvial soils. Keep straight ahead as the path starts to lose height, with a good view of the village of Llanarmon-yn-ial to the east, and descend more steeply past a lone tree to a rough track in an obvious col, with old piggeries and the farm of Ty'n-y-mynydd to the right and two burial mounds straight ahead.

Once a droving centre and later reliant for employment on its limestone quarries, **Llanarmon-yn-ial** was the ancestral home of Elihu Yale, whose gift of books, a portrait of King George and nine bales of goods helped to establish Yale University. Nearby is Tomen y Faerdre, an imposing motte 6m high on a rock outcrop above the River Alyn.

The classic rural inn here – **the Raven** – was rescued by villagers and is run as a community enterprise, offering local real ales and overnight accommodation.

Take the really excellent green lane contouring around the western slopes of **Moel Llanfair**, with a superb view of the medieval town of Ruthin to the left. The medieval borough of Ruthin, centred on its red sandstone castle, dominates the upper Vale of Clwyd, and was once an important cloth-working centre. Turn sharply right at a stile, with a prolonged and quite steep climb on a roughly surfaced track, now largely reclaimed by grass, and with the delightfully wooded Plas-y-nant side valley down to the left.

Just before the top of the slope take the timber kissing gate on the left to cut across the top of the valley. A wide path from Llanarmon comes in from the right close to the marker stone of Garreg Lwyd and the trail follows this (it becomes another magnificent green lane) around the western shoulder of **Moel Gyw**, with an excellent view northwards to the hillfort on the summit of Foel Fenlli.

The green lane ends at a stile. Turn half-left here, following an indistinct path across the pasture in the direction of a low waymark post, and keep to the same direction through a patch of gorse, with the distant Ruthin church directly ahead. Go slightly right across the next field, meeting and turning right along a lane that becomes metalled, passes cottages and climbs briefly to meet the A494 at **Clwyd Gate**. The name of Clwyd Gate recalls the location of a former tollgate on the Ruthin to Wrexham turnpike road. Sadly the motel and restaurant here closed in 2017.

Turn right along the main road, briefly on a narrow pavement but then on the road edge past Bwlch-uchaf before crossing the road and taking a roughly surfaced farm track leading past a cottage and up through gorse on the eastern slopes of Gyrn. Swing left off the main track, crossing a stile and taking an excellent path through a little coniferous wood thick with bluebells in spring. The path continues straight ahead beyond the wood, passing above the roofless barns of Moel-eithinen Farm to reach a crossroads of footpaths at the far right corner of the field.

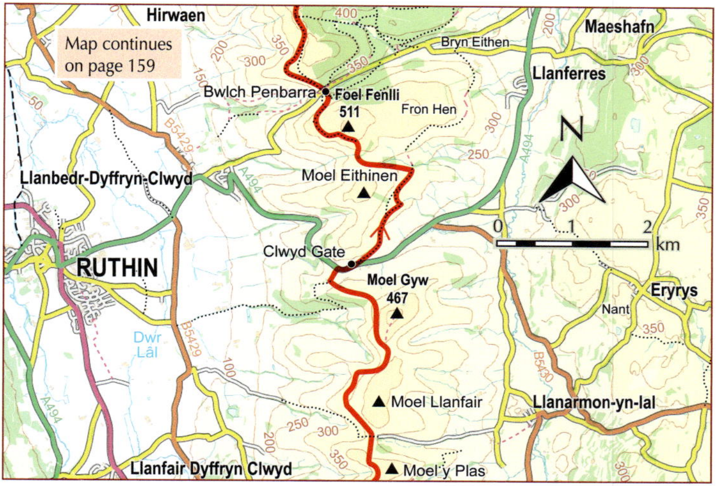

Turn sharply left, rising to walk past Clwyd Nurseries (a plantation rather than a garden centre!) with the hillfort crowning Foel Fenlli now very prominent ahead to the right. Go steeply up the next field, curving to the right to find a stile in the top corner, and drop down with conifers on the right and gorse and bilberry on the left to cross the minor col of Bwlch Crug-glas – once somewhat fancifully called Bwlch Agricola on the dubious grounds that the Roman general crossed here on his way to Anglesey.

The way now lies up the abrupt southern slopes of **Foel Fenlli**. This is proper hill-climbing for a while, steeply up on a mixture of rock, gravelly scree and slippery grass as far as a waymark post. Go straight on here, contouring around the western side of the hill again rather than attempting a direct ascent to the hillfort (a tactic discouraged on conservation grounds, but reinforcing the feeling that the southern Clwydians are being rounded rather than conquered outright). The retrospective view along the ridge is excellent, however, with Llandegla Forest still in view and the bleak moorlands of Hiraethog and the Migneint now clearly in view to the south-west.

The trail gains height very slowly on the western shoulder of the hill, arriving at a waymark post with a stepped path on the right leading up to the hillfort. The hillfort – the most impressive in the Clwydian Range – was defended by two or three ramparts, with an intricate in-turned entrance to the west, around 40 house platforms and evidence of Roman pottery and coin hoards. The trail heads downhill to the left, however, also on steps for a while before taking a grassy path around the hill.

Moel Famau and Foel Fenlli from the western slopes of Moel Llanfair

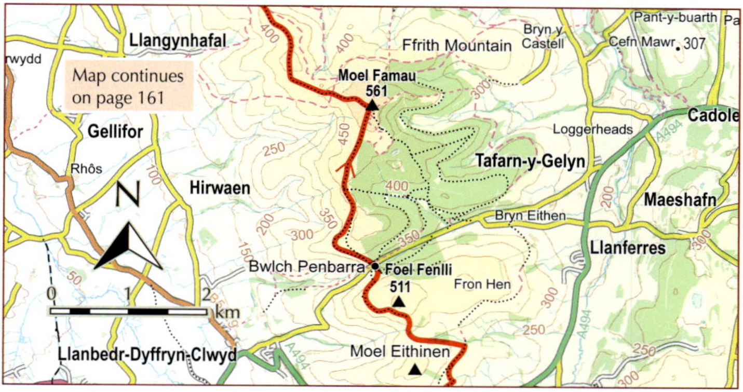

The green trod becomes stony and surprisingly turns left, downhill, but only for 100m before swinging right to resume its northward course, with a sudden surprise view of the highest hill in the Clwydians, Moel Famau, beyond the rather obtrusive car park at Bwlch Penbarra, once the summit of the main road from Mold to Ruthin.

The path zigzags down the grassy slopes towards **Bwlch Penbarra**, passing picnic benches and crossing the road and the car park to take the lower route, again well below the Clwydian ridge. Sadly the shepherd's hut in the car park, which provided light refreshments, closed in early 2021. The track is wide, gravelly and very well populated most of the year, with casual walkers making the short trip from the car park to the Jubilee Tower on the summit of Moel Famau.

Ruthin still dominates the view to the west, but as the track swings right and begins to climb steadily the northern Vale of Clwyd appears. The track levels off across the moorland before a steeper section on loose stones marks the final climb to **Moel Famau**'s summit.

The highest summit in the Clwydian Range, **Moel Famau** is also the centre of a country park and the summit viewpoint attracts some 200,000 visitors annually. The current rather squat remains of the Jubilee Tower, restored in the last few years, are distinctly disappointing compared with the original – a two-tiered Egyptian-style edifice constructed in 1810 to celebrate the Golden Jubilee of George III. The tower was badly damaged during high winds in 1862 and the upper stages collapsed onto the pyramidal base.

Cader Idris, Yr Wyddfa, the Carneddau, the Dee Estuary and Beeston Castle on its sandstone ridge are among the highlights seen from the viewpoint.

The steep descent from Moel Llys-y-coed, with the hillfort on Moel Arthur beyond

The path going north-west from the summit of Moel Famau quickly braids, with a rough, steep descent by a wall to the right and a slightly more circuitous route to the left finally descending on steps, the routes coming together very quickly at a minor col with the little pool of Pwll-y-rhos and the remains of sheepfolds used by drovers just to the right.

A gravelly track, which later becomes grassy, gains height and passes between two enormous cairns – one marking the summit of Moel Dywyll – with an excellent retrospective view of the Jubilee Tower from the more easterly of them.

The path continues easily down the northern slopes of Moel Dywyll through yet more heather and bilberry, the heather gloriously purple in August and harbouring secretive red grouse throughout the year. An old drystone wall, constructed by the Penbedw Estate in the early 19th century, forms a prominent feature to the right. The wide wooded valley of the Nant Gain lies to the right, the foreground dominated by a sizeable reservoir. The Penmachno mine in the upper Nant Gain valley was one of several opened during the short-lived (and unsuccessful) 'Cilcain gold rush'.

Go straight on at a walkers' crossroads, where a path drops down to Llangynhafal on the left and a broad track heads east to Cilcain, then head towards Moel Llys-y-coed, still with a wide panorama back along the ridge and, after a turn to the right, somewhat contrasting views north-east to quarries and an industrial landscape in the far distance. To the left is the distinctive summit of Moel Arthur, topped by another of the Clwydian hillforts.

A very steep descent on an engineered but still somewhat eroded path, with big boulders placed strategically, leads to a minor road (formerly another drove route through the hills) and a little car park. Walk through the car park to find a narrow path, which rises steadily around the eastern shoulder of **Moel Arthur**, arriving at a slate monolith where an easy path leaves to the left to reach the hillfort. The earthworks on Moel Arthur's summit slopes cover a much smaller area than others in these hills but were occupied from the early Bronze Age for several centuries.

The trail continues straight ahead, towards another minor road crossing, now with the massive hillfort of Penycloddiau dominating the scene ahead beyond the woodland of Coed Llangwyfan, with old field boundaries and lynchets hidden among the trees.

Drop down a grassy slope to turn right along the narrow road, then slant left through the Coed Llangwyfan car park and take care to select the highest of three routes, a narrow path rising along the eastern side of the wood. Beyond the trees there is an excellent view towards the distant peaks of Eryri, while after crossing a stile the path climbs easily to pass through the southern defences of the massive hillfort of **Penycloddiau** – one of the largest in Wales. The superb multiple ramparts and ditches of Penycloddiau, especially impressive at the north, enclose an area of 21ha, with the foundations of houses scattered within and alongside the inner ramparts.

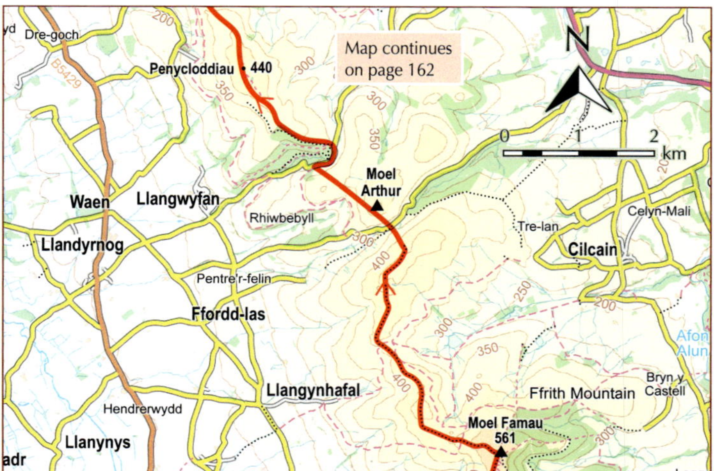

Denbigh Castle and its imposing gatehouse

A wide grassy path runs right through the interior of the hillfort, with a magnificent retrospective panorama of Moel Arthur, Moel Famau and, to the right, the more southerly Clwydian summits. After 800m the trail passes a curious modern ring cairn and then descends through the superb northern defences, descending through a series of ramparts and ditches.

A splendid path, braided in places to avoid muddy areas, now leads gently down the northern slopes, with another excellent view of the Vale of Clwyd and

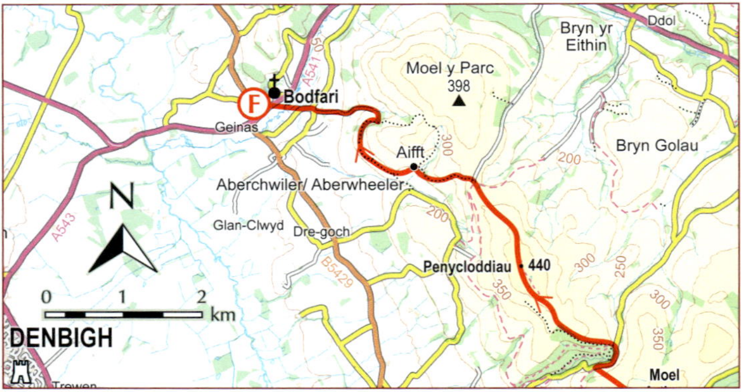

The lane from Aifft around the western slopes of Moel y Parc, with the Vale of Clwyd beyond

the town of Denbigh to the left, going slightly right below a rocky outcrop and then negotiating a complex junction by going right through a gate and then left down a stony lane past the wreck of a farmhouse. The lane drops steeply down, curves to the right and runs through the hidden, tranquil hamlet of **Aifft**. The hamlet has a number of ruined farm buildings and a little disused chapel, suggesting that settlement here was more extensive in the Victorian era.

> The hilltop town of **Denbigh** is well worth a visit, with a spectacular castle, medieval town walls with a wonderful outlook across to the Clwydian hills, the bulky Burgess Gate – built in the 13th century complete with portcullis, bridge and ditch – and the ruins of Leicester's Church, built in the 16th century and intended as a cathedral church to replace St Asaph's. The old market place around Back Row, and the more recent grand houses along Vale Street, show how the town moved away from its original hilltop site to a more convenient location.

Stay on the track as it starts to climb, but quickly leave it to the left to use another of the area's excellent wide green tracks, once again contouring around the western shoulder of high ground – this time the rounded hill of **Moel y Parc**, with a TV mast below its summit. The landscape to the left is of little irregular fields, while to the right there are abandoned field boundaries covered by bracken and gorse in the common land of the higher slopes.

Quite suddenly the village of Bodfari is in view ahead, with its white-painted church on a little rise beyond the village centre. Take the left fork at a junction of paths here, dropping down through gorse to find a stile and turn right across a field. Go straight across the next field to a hidden stile, maintain the same direction across a further field to locate an even more cunningly concealed stile among the gorse bushes in the far corner, and keep straight ahead to a further stile. The gaunt buildings of Grove Hall – a hotel and a residential home in recent years – lie away to the left.

Turn right along a little lane, then immediately left on an equally narrow lane, and zigzag right and left across a staggered crossroads. Immediately beyond Aberwheeler Farm go through a metal kissing gate on the right and take the narrow path alongside a ditch to cross the River Wheeler on a footbridge. Glance right when crossing the footbridge to check for grey herons: large numbers visit here, attracted by the trout farm upstream. The A541 Mold to Denbigh road and the village of **Bodfari** is now straight ahead across a final field and through a kissing gate.

BODFARI

A former industrial village with a haematite mine, Coed-y-llan quarry and several limekilns, Bodfari expanded along the railway and the turnpike road from Mold to Denbigh in the 19th century but is now a quiet commuter settlement, with its whitewashed church the focus of the village. The sad wreck of the Dinorben Arms and its former brewhouse next door has happily been superbly renovated by a local pub group.

There is no shop but there are several B&B and camping options; the Dinorben Arms offers evening meals.

STAGE 12

Northern hills and coast

Start	Bodfari (SJ 097 701)
Finish	Prestatyn seafront (SJ 060 837)
Distance	20km (12.4 miles)
Ascent	620m (2035ft)
Time	5–6hr
Maps	OS Explorer 265
Refreshments	Pubs (some with limited opening hours) just off-route in Rhuallt and Gwaenysgor, with a wide choice of shops, cafés and pubs in Prestatyn
Public transport	Bodfari has useful morning services (bus F14) from Denbigh and Mold. Prestatyn has good rail connections to Manchester, Birmingham, London and Cardiff
Accommodation	There is limited accommodation in and around Rhuallt, while Prestatyn has a number of hotels and guest houses

This final stage of the trail occasionally needs care in route-finding as it twists and turns among the low hills and valleys in the northern part of the Clwydian Range. The walking is easy, however, on lanes and field paths, with an increasingly impressive panorama of Eryri and the North Wales coast from the Great Orme to Deeside, together with the wind turbines and oil and gas rigs offshore.

The last Clwydian hillforts, the industrial landscape around and above Marian Mills, and the descent into the seaside town of Prestatyn make for a very varied final day.

Head east along the main road for 150m from the kissing gate in **Bodfari** and take the seriously steep lane opposite the former Downing Arms, climbing past cottages before following it round to the left and immediately looking for a stile on the right. Cross this to find a path going straight up a field, again very steeply, but swing round to the right above a patch of woodland concealing a small quarry and then follow the path up the right-hand field edge.

A right turn leads to an excellent, shady path on a hillside terrace below the southern ramparts of the Moel y Gaer hillfort – where excavations have revealed a substantial stone-built rampart above a big ditch cut into the rock – and then to a stepped path swinging left and climbing below the eastern defences.

Cross a track and take an obvious path across the field ahead, turn left onto a tarmac lane, immediately left again onto a rough track and just as quickly leave the track on a hairpin bend to go over a stile and straight ahead across a field. Some care in route selection is needed now: the path veers slightly right across the next field, full of buttercups (ignore the temptation to use the path going straight on).

Turn right along a little lane – a signpost exists but is high up and set back in a tall hedge – but after only 30m take the lane on the left opposite Adwy-wynt, climbing steadily to a crossroads where a bench has a great prospect over the Vale of Clwyd, with Denbigh the centrepiece and to the right the 'marble' church at Bodelwyddan with its tall limestone spire. Adwy-wynt dates from at least 1765, when it included a bakehouse, and part of it was later used as a slaughterhouse.

Continue along the lane through the dispersed hamlet of Sodom, still with an excellent view north-west towards the North Wales coast as far west as the Great Orme beyond Llandudno, and with the mountain summits of Eryri somewhat further to the left.

The trail passes the Scots pine plantation of Sodom Covert, with a view eastwards towards the failed town of Caerwys with its grid street pattern, but when the road bends left and then right, look carefully for a path going straight on (the waymark post is easily missed). This is a delightful, shady path on the edge of woodland, although the tree roots are a trip hazard.

Pass a single wind turbine at the top of the wood and go straight across one field, then diagonally right across a second, seeking out an inconspicuous stile on the far side. The rounded, low summit of Cefn Du is on the left here, although there is little sign of the ancient settlement on its upper slopes. The route lies slightly left across a third field, joining a lane and going straight ahead, passing a wildlife pond at Penuchaf. Cross the Tremeirchion road, going left for 50m and then right, climbing steadily to find a splendid bridleway under trees on the left.

Just before the trees end, cross a stile on the right and follow the path through a kissing gate, easing through gorse thickets on the slopes of **Moel Maenefa** with the cathedral city of St Asaph and, less pleasingly, the A55 North Wales expressway straight ahead.

The cathedral in **St Asaph**, which has much more the feel of a village rather than a cathedral city, developed from a monastery founded in 550 by St Kentigern, the first bishop of Glasgow. Twice destroyed by fire, the cathedral is the smallest in England and Wales, with a tower that was rebuilt after its predecessor was destroyed in an early 18th-century storm. Historically regarded as a city because it was the centre of a diocese, St Asaph only formally regained that status in 2012 as part of the Queen's Golden Jubilee celebrations.

The trail crossing the buttercup field below Adwy-wynt

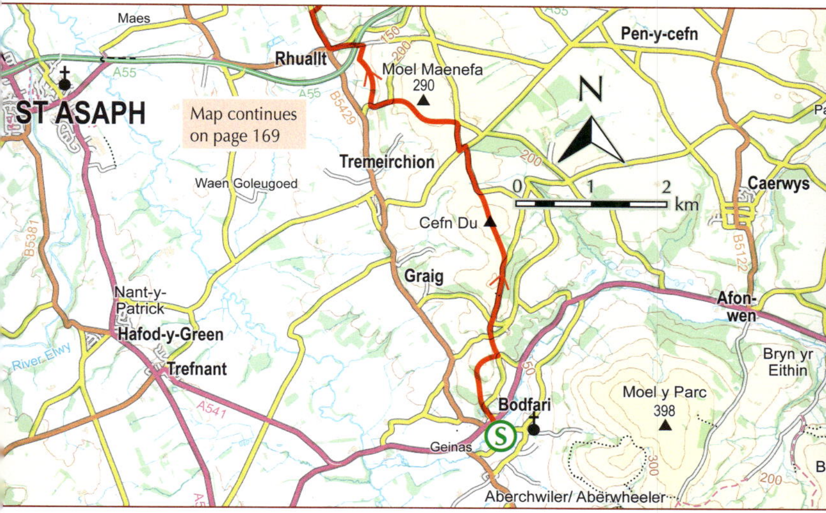

The Vale of Clwyd from Brynllithrig Hall on the edge of Rhuallt

Further kissing gates lead onto a pleasant path through open deciduous woodland, with plenty of bluebells, and then to a country lane. Turn left here, steeply downhill (the signpost is hidden in the hedgerow and is not easy to locate when coming from the north) then just before St Beuno's College climb up a short flight of steps on the right into the first of several sheep pastures, with the path both obvious on the ground and clearly waymarked past the remains of Maen Eva Farm (it's worth keeping well to the right in the third field to avoid marshy areas around springs). The Jesuit poet Gerard Manley Hopkins spent three years training for the priesthood at St Beuno's, while the explorer HM Stanley lived for a while at nearby Ffynnon Beuno Farm.

Cross a little footbridge, walk up a narrow path between fences and swing right to follow the hedge alongside and above the A55, invisible behind the hedge but noisily intrusive. Turn left at the top of the field to cross the dual carriageway on a high footbridge above a massive cutting slicing through the hills, then go straight ahead down steps and along a lane (unremarkable but on the line of the Roman road from Chester to Caernarfon) into the village of **Rhuallt** (B&B, pub).

Turn right at the crossroads, passing the former Smithy Arms, and climb the lane as far as Brynllithrig Hall, with its coach house and terraced gardens. Percy Pratt, the then owner of Brynllithrig Hall, had the distinction of crowning the first Carnival Queen of nearby Rhyl on the promenade in 1891. The path leaves the road here, climbing very steeply through woodland and then up the right-hand

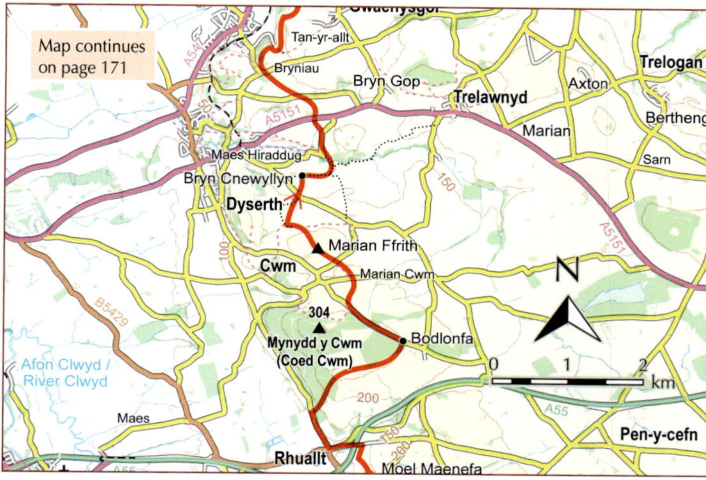

side of a long, narrow field with foxgloves in the wall. At the top of the long field a very short walled lane leads into an area of scrub, with gorse, bracken, brambles and plenty of birdlife including pheasants.

A gate just above Pen-y-mynydd leads to a rough and stony track, with Moel Maenefa very prominent to the right. The track runs just above another cottage, with the conifers of Mynydd y Cwm to the left (the proposed line of Offa's Dyke Path ran through the plantation but was rejected) and reaches a country lane at **Bodlonfa**. Turn left here to follow the lane for around 700m, initially quite pleasantly with wildflowers in the verge and a distant view of the big village of Trelawnyd below the tree-capped Gop Hill, but then more drearily through woodland. The 14m-high cairn on Gop Hill is the largest Neolithic cairn in Wales, and it is now clear that the hill was traversed by Offa's Dyke as it approached the coast.

Soon after the trees finally end on the left, a very distinct path on the right runs along the right-hand boundary of a big field to reach and go straight across a narrow lane. The path through the next field, on closely-cropped grass, is much less distinct, but lies slightly left (aim for the chapel that soon comes into sight) to reach a kissing gate and climb a slope up to the road through the hamlet of **Marian Cwm** opposite a converted chapel. Turn left along the road, then almost immediately right by a telephone box to cross a stile and enter a field with low limestone outcrops, much favoured by the local tawny owls.

The path through the fields to Bryn Cnewyllyn, with the ridge of Prestatyn Hillside beyond

The way ahead is not immediately clear, but after passing through a gap in the post-and-wire fence the first of a series of low waymark posts showing the way across the low rocky hill of **Marian Ffrith** can somewhat belatedly be located. The hill is part of a barrier reef formed some 330 million years ago, and the hard limestone has survived glacial erosion to form a distinctive undulating landscape. To the left is a low burial mound, while to the right there are caves, quarry pits and the remains of lead and copper mining. More recent industry is clearly in view too: ahead are the giant wind turbines of the North Hoyle wind farm, lying around 8km (5 miles) offshore. North Hoyle was the first offshore wind farm in the UK when it opened in 2003 with a maximum capacity of 60 megawatts.

Drop down in the direction of Tyddyn-y-cyll, with the hillfort on the summit of Moel Hiraddug behind, and tackle the first of a series of six stone stiles that provide welcome diversity in the landscape. Moel Hiraddug, the most northerly of the Clwydian hillforts, is famous for the second-century bronze plaque found under the ramparts. Its northern slopes have been badly disfigured by limestone quarrying. Beyond the second stone stile a lane leads past the farmhouse, and after a further 50m the way lies right, down a little valley and then left around a big pasture to reach a rough track leading to a metalled road at Morwyllfa. Go left here but then immediately right, this time over a wooden stile, to cross an arable field on a clear path.

Cross another, narrower field and turn right on a track just east of **Bryn Cnewyllyn**. The track becomes an excellent gated green lane, with views back to Moel Hiraddug and the quarry etched incongruously into its northern slopes. The lane swings round to the left and then left again, with the first of the industrial artefacts of the Marian Mills complex – the hub of the Felin Fawr mill wheel – now visible on the right.

The area of Marian Mills is fascinating for its **industrial archaeology**, although several of the old buildings have been demolished. Much of the flour mill at Felin Fawr has disappeared, but the original wheel shaft is still in place; originally the spokes of the wheel were wooden. The only trace of the adjacent Felin Fach mill, which was demolished in 1947, is the watercourse, and Pandy Mill has gone completely, but there are substantial remains at Grove Mill further down the valley.

Go past a trout hatchery and when two metalled lanes diverge take the higher, right-hand option, with the ruins of Grove Mill down to the left. Grove Mill was

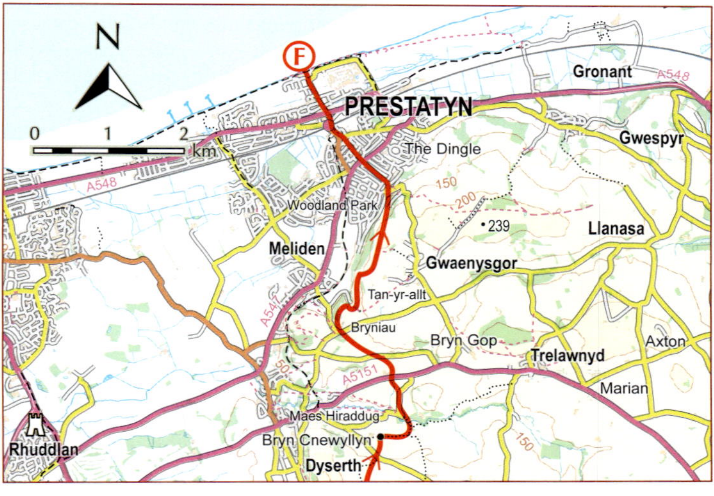

Welsh	English
nant	stream
plas	mansion
pont	bridge
rhiw	hill/slope
rhyd	ford
sarn	ancient road or causeway
ty	house
ynys	island

APPENDIX D

Further reading

Andrew Allott *Marches* (Collins New Naturalist Library, 2011)

Bruce Chatwin *On The Black Hill* (Jonathan Cape, 1982)

Myrddin ap Dafydd *The Welsh Marches from the West* (Gwasg Carreg Gwalch, 2019)

John Davis *Hanes Cymru (A History of Wales)* (Penguin 1990, revised 2007)

Cyril Fox *Offa's Dyke: a Field Survey of the Western Frontier Works of Mercia in the Seventh and Eighth Centuries AD* (Oxford University Press, 1955)

Max Lieberman *The March of Wales* (University of Wales Press, 2008)

George Peterken *Wye Valley* (Collins New Naturalist Library, 2008)

Keith Ray & Ian Bapty *Offa's Dyke: Landscape and Hegemony in Eighth Century Britain* (Windgather Press, 2016)

Trevor Rowley *The Landscape of the Welsh Marches* (Michael Joseph, 1986)

Owen Sheers *Resistance* (Faber & Faber, 2007)

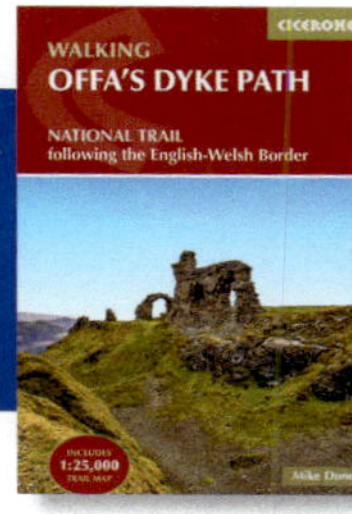

Other British long-distance guides

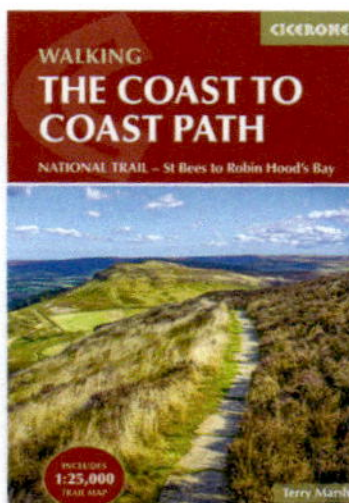

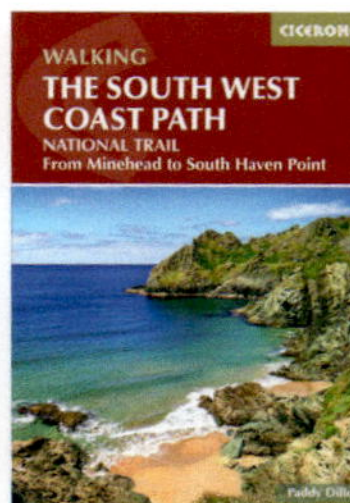

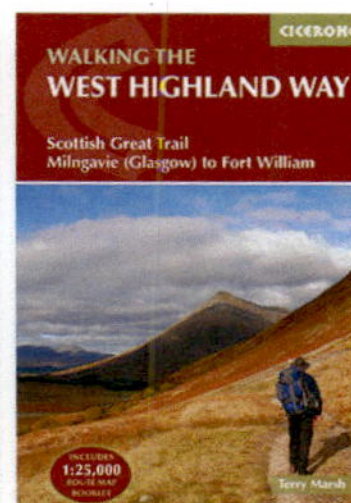

Other guides to this region

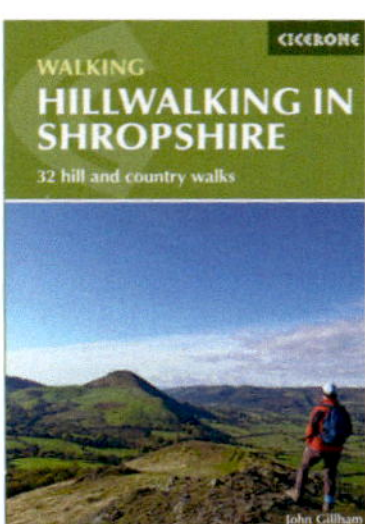

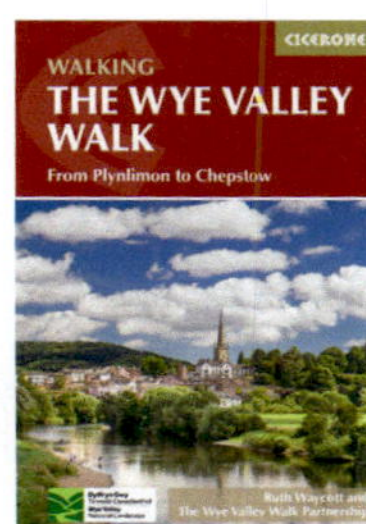

Hello, and thank you for choosing a Cicerone guide!

It takes the combined dedication of many to create the book you now hold. Our authors explore the world to find the best routes; they research, write, record data and take stunning photos on the trail to inspire and guide new adventures. Then, our talented team work together with authors to create the best products for our readers, whether digital or printed. The final part of the picture is you; we deeply value hearing from Cicerone customers with ideas and updates from the trail. Your input helps us to improve and innovate across our guides.

Cicerone is proud to be a family business. Exploring the outdoors has always been central to our lives, and we are passionate about sharing our love of walking, trekking, cycling and climbing. If you have any feedback or just want to say hello, please get in touch – we would love to hear from you.

Happy adventuring,
Joe & Maddy

Contact us at

hello@cicerone.co.uk **cicerone.co.uk/contact**

The Cicerone story

1969 Cicerone is founded by Walt and Dorothy Unsworth and Brian and Aileen Evans, publishing Lakeland guides printed on a garage press.

1977 The *Tour of Mont Blanc* guidebook defines the modern trekking guide and establishes Cicerone internationally.

1999 Jonathan and Lesley Williams take over, bringing a deep love of the outdoors.

2011 Cicerone produces its first eBook.

2022 Joe and Maddy Williams take the helm, keeping Cicerone independent, family run and rooted in real adventure.

2026 The Cicerone App launches, bringing decades of trusted route knowledge, GPS-enabled maps and planning tools directly to your phone.

Discover more at **cicerone.co.uk/about-cicerone**

The Cicerone story

1969 Cicerone is founded by Walt and Dorothy Unsworth and Brian and Aileen Evans, publishing Lakeland guides printed on a garage press.

1977 The *Tour of Mont Blanc* guidebook defines the modern trekking guide and establishes Cicerone internationally.

1999 Jonathan and Lesley Williams take over, bringing a deep love of the outdoors.

2011 Cicerone produces its first eBook.

2022 Joe and Maddy Williams take the helm, keeping Cicerone independent, family run and rooted in real adventure.

2026 The Cicerone App launches, bringing decades of trusted route knowledge, GPS-enabled maps and planning tools directly to your phone.

Discover more at **cicerone.co.uk/about-cicerone**

Radnor Forest from the northern slopes of Hawthorn Hill (Stage 5)

OFFA'S DYKE PATH

This trail map describes Offa's Dyke Path National Trail, a 177-mile (285km) long-distance route along the English–Welsh border between Sedbury (near Chepstow) and Prestatyn on the North Wales coast. One of Britain's classic trails, this ancient route is long but not particularly strenuous, making it an ideal challenge for first-time backpackers.

Contents and using this guide

This booklet of Ordnance Survey® 1:25,000 Explorer® maps has been designed for convenient use on the trail and includes:

- a key to map pages (page 2) showing where to find the maps for each stage
- the full and up-to-date line of the National Trail
- an extract from the OS Explorer map legend (pages 76–78)

In addition, the companion *Offa's Dyke Path* guidebook describes the full route from south to north, alongside all the information you need to plan a successful trip and lots of incidental information about local history, geography and wildlife.

Second edition 2026
First edition 2016
ISBN-13: 978 1 78631 280 8

Printed in China on responsibly sourced paper on behalf of Latitude Press Ltd.
Cicerone's EU representative for GPSR compliance is Easy Access System Europe, Mustamäe tee 50, 10621 Tallinn, Estonia. Email gpsr.requests@easproject.com.

OFFA'S DYKE PATH

Route symbols on OS map extracts

route

alternative route

start point

finish point

start/finish point

For OS legend see pages 76–78.

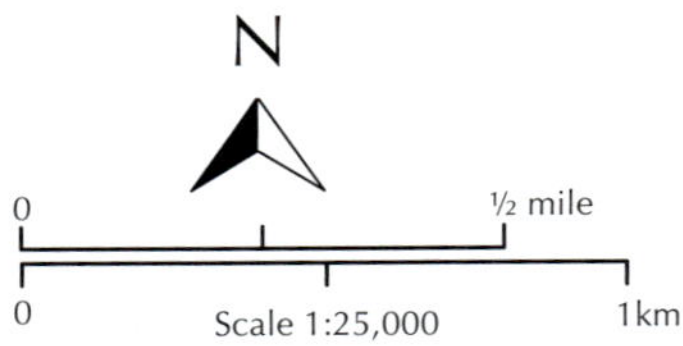

GPX files for all routes
can be downloaded free at
cicerone.co.uk/1279/GPX

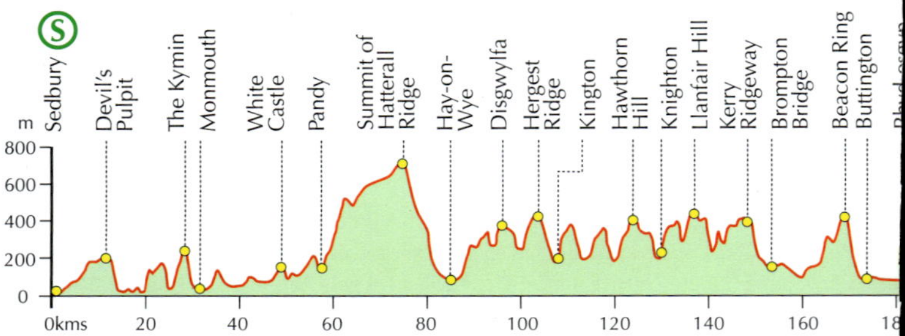

IRISH SEA
68-74
LIVERPOOL
Prestatyn
ANGLESEY
Bangor
Caernarfon
Denbigh
Clwydian Range
Ruthin
61–68
0 20 km
0 10 miles
54–61
Wrexham
Porthmadog
Llangollen
ERYRI
Oswestry
49–54
44–49
WALES
ENGLAND
Shrewsbury
Machynlleth
Welshpool
39–44
Montgomery
34–39
Shropshire Hills
Aberystwyth
Clun
Ludlow
Knighton
29–34
Kington
24–29
Hay-on-Wye
Hereford
Wye Valley
15–24
10–15
Abergavenny
Monmouth
4–9
Chepstow
Newport
CARDIFF
BRISTOL CHANNEL
BRISTOL
Moelydd
Selattyn Hill
Castle Mill
River Dee
Llandegla Forest
Llandegla
Moel Famau
Bodfari
Marian Ffrith
Prestatyn
200
220
240
260
280

4

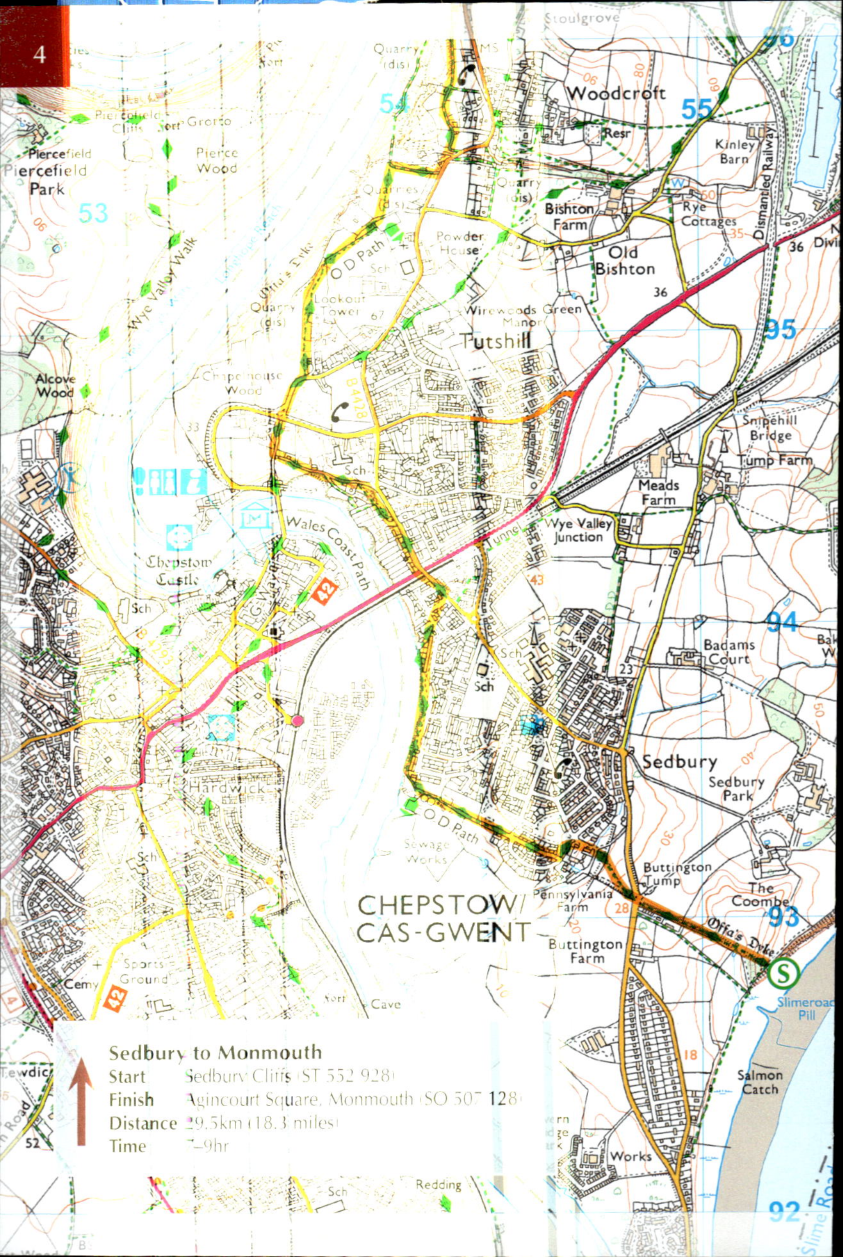

Sedbury to Monmouth

Start Sedbury Cliffs (ST 552 928)
Finish Agincourt Square, Monmouth (SO 507 128)
Distance 29.5km (18.3 miles)
Time 7–9hr

5
Madget
Hotels
Passage Grove
Sheepcot
227
237
Clayton Wood
Miss Graces Lane
Sheepcot Brake
Ash Grove
Devil's Pulpit
Quarry (dis)
Reddings Farm
Spr
Sprs
The Park
Quarries (dis)
217
Shorn Cliff
High Wood
Plumweir Cliff
Offa's Dyke
Cairn
Worgan's Wood
Chase Farm
191
Tidenham Chase
Boatwood Plantation
A466
ack Cliff Wood
Black Cliff
Black Morgan's Wood
River Wye / Afon Gwy
MS
Quarries (dis)
Parson's
James's Thorns
The Slade
Tintern Quarry (disused)
B 4228
183
Quarry (dis)
Hut Circles
East Vaga
98
Dismantled Railway
Liveoaks Grove
Dennelhill Farm
Quarry (disused)
Wyndcliff Wood
ynd Cliff
Livox Cottages
BS
Dennel Hill
Beverston Farm
Liveoaks Brake
Liveoaks Grove
Cockshoot
Boughspring
Wallhope Farm
Ppg Sta (dis)
Offa's Dyke Path
Prior's Reach
Ban-y-gor Rocks
Resr
122
Tunnel
Gloucestershire Way
Ban-y-gor Wood
Wallhope Grove
Spital Meend Fort
Lancaut
Lancaut Nature Reserve
Offa's Dyke
Asheberry House
97
St James's Church (remains of)
Netherhope
Cross Hill
Netherhope Lane
Wintour's Leap
Broadrock
Mean Low Water
Piercefield Cliffs
Stoulgrove
Fort
Quarry (dis)
MS

The Nedge
Tyersall
Knoll Farm
Chapel Farm
Hudnalls
Hudnalls Farm
Hart-hill Farm
Sandy Lane
Windward House
Coed Ithel Weir
Birchhill Cottage
Spring Farm
Hollyside Farm
Hart-hill Grange Farm
Offa's Dyke Path
St Briavels Common
Grove Farm
Pewgreen Farm
Brockweir House
Hill Farm
Brook Farm
The Triangle
Bay
Coed Beddick
Mill Hill
Rock Farm
Cows Hill Wood
Wye Valley Walk
Park Glade
Brockweir
Beech Knoll
Lower Chase
Market Garden
Madgett Hill
Hotel
VINEYARD
Quarry (dis)
Madgetts Farm
Beeches Farm
The Old Station
Caswell Wood
Ash Weir
Tintern Abbey (Cistercian)
Lippets Grove
Hotel
32
A466

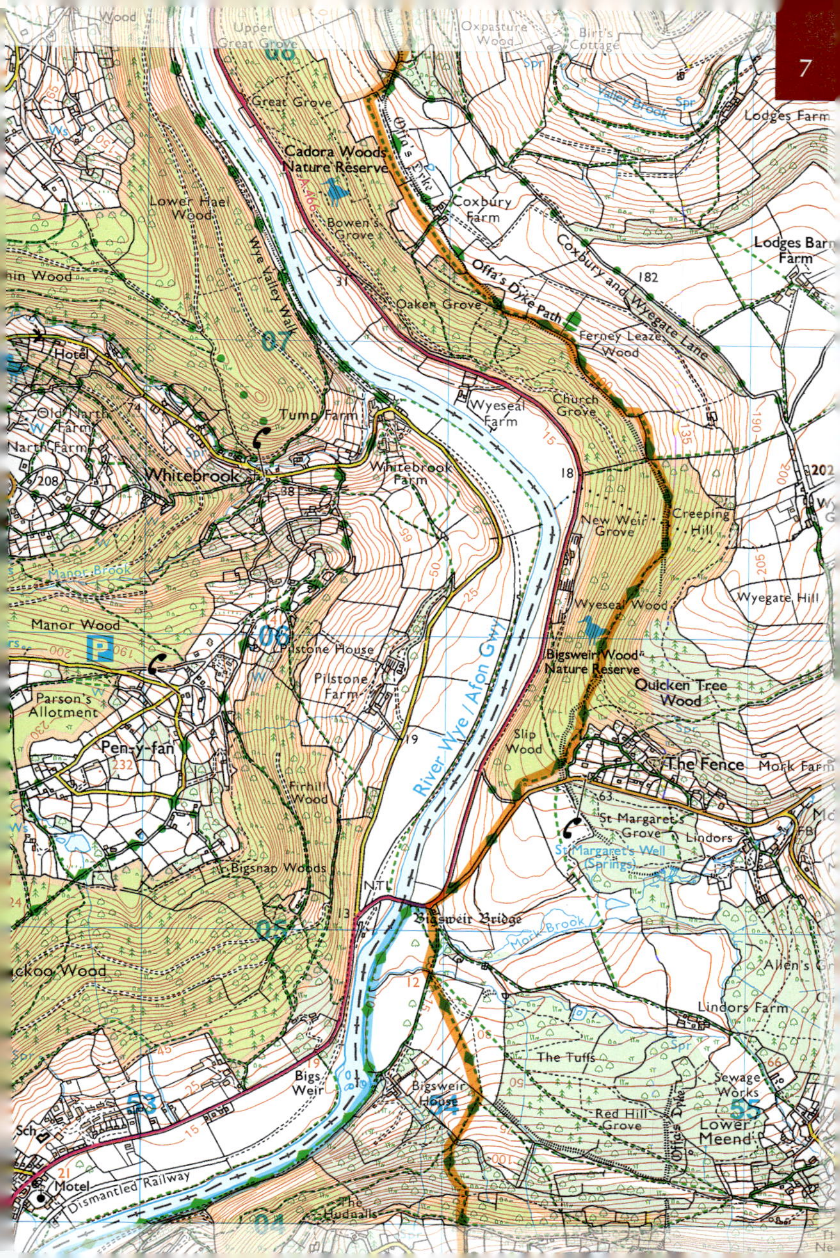

Upper Great Grove
Oxpasture Wood
Birt's Cottage
Great Grove
Valley Brook
Lodges Farm
Cadora Woods Nature Reserve
Offa's Dyke
Lower Hael Wood
Bowen's Grove
Coxbury Farm
Lodges Barn Farm
Coxbury and Wyegate Lane
Offa's Dyke Path
Wye Valley Walk
Oaken Grove
Ferney Leaze Wood
Hotel
Church Grove
Wyeseal Farm
Old North Farm
North Farm
Tump Farm
Whitebrook
Whitebrook Farm
Creeping Hill
New Weir Grove
Manor Brook
Wyegate Hill
Wyeseal Wood
Manor Wood
Pilstone House
Bigsweir Wood Nature Reserve
Quicken Tree Wood
Pilstone Farm
River Wye / Afon Gwy
Parson's Allotment
Pen-y-fan
Slip Wood
The Fence
Mork Farm
Firhill Wood
St Margaret's Grove
Lindors
St Margaret's Well (Springs)
Bigsnap Woods
Bigsweir Bridge
Mork Brook
Allen's Grove
Lindors Farm
The Tuffs
Bigs Weir
Bigsweir House
Sewage Works
Red Hill Grove
Offa's Dyke
Lower Meend
Motel
Dismantled Railway
The Hudnalls

STAUNTON CO
Adventure Centre
Staunton Meend
Harper's Grove
Upper Beaulieu Farm
Cockshoot Ash Barn
Bunjups Wood
Knockalls Lodge
Knockalls Inclosure
Wye Valley Walk
Livox Wood
Lord's Grove
Offa's Dyke Path
Duffield's Lane (Track)
Duffield's Farm
Dismantled Railway
Penallt
Church Farm
Lower Wood
Jordan's Barn
Mill Pond
Furnace Grove
Jackston Farm
Birches Road
Washing's Wood
The Birches
Upper Redbrook
Old Hills Wood
Church Hill Common
Pwl-mawr Wood
Blackbrook Wood
Llananant Farm
Newbarn Wood
Luggas Wood
Hazel
Probyn's Allotment
Glyn Farm
Upper Glyn Farm
Lower Redbrook
Forge
Highbury Terrace
Wyeswood Common Nature Reserve
Young's Grove
Pentwyn Farm
Highbury Farm
Waterfall
Pen-twyn
Lone Lane
Lone Farm
Highbury Wood
Prisk Wood
Glyn Farm
House
Graig Wood
David's Grove
Highbury Wood National Nature Reserve
Highbury Plains
Coxbury Lane
Cadora Grove
Fruid Wood
The Argoed
The Grove
Upper Hael Wood
Upper Great Grove
Oxpasture Wood

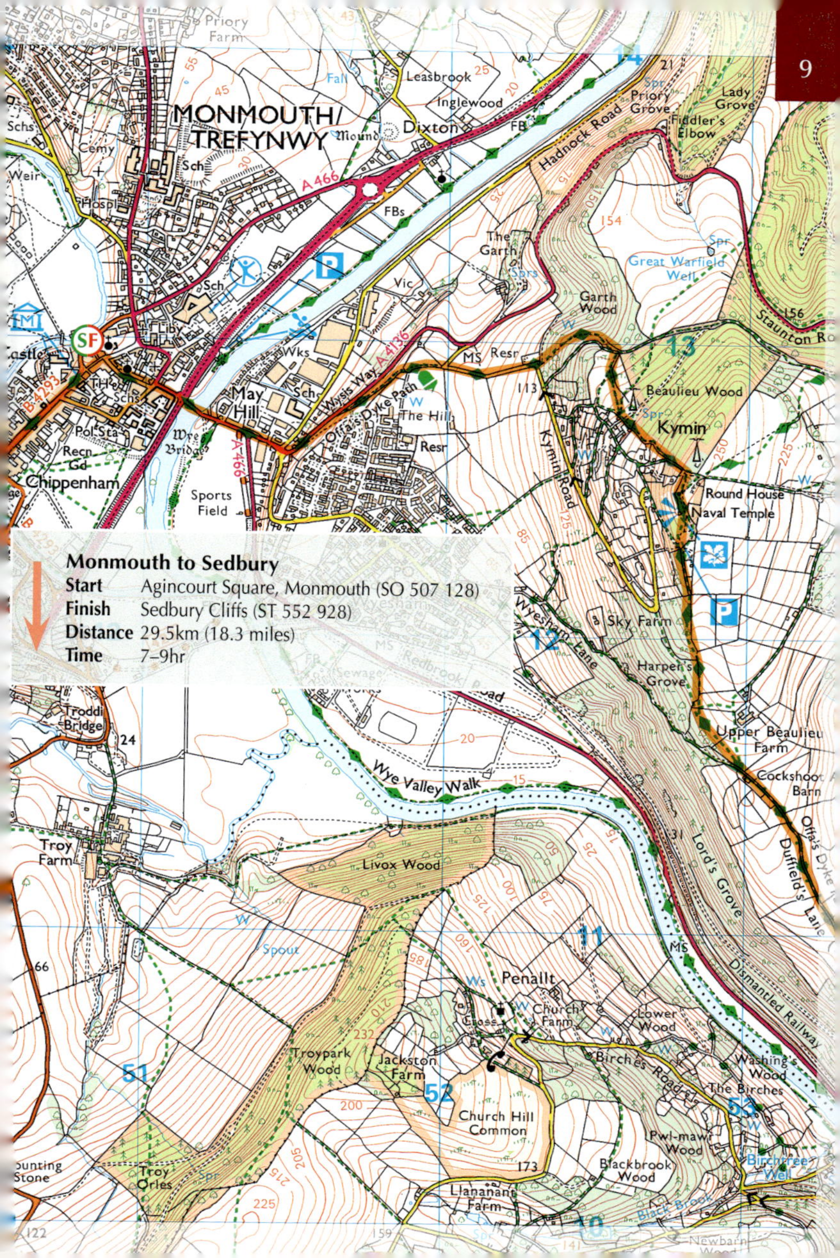

Monmouth to Sedbury

Start	Agincourt Square, Monmouth (SO 507 128)
Finish	Sedbury Cliffs (ST 552 928)
Distance	29.5km (18.3 miles)
Time	7–9hr

Monmouth to Pandy

Start Agincourt Square, Monmouth (SO 507 128)

Finish Lancaster Arms guest house, Pandy (SO 333 217)

Distance 26.2km (16.3 miles)

Time 6–8hr

Parsonage Farm
Court Wood
The Old Rectory
Sunnybank
Cefn Wood
Yewtree Cottage
Llymon Bridge
River Trothy / Afon Troddi
Offa's Dyke Path
Abbey Bridge
Abbey Cott
Parc Grace Dieu
Tregare Mill
Cefn-garw Farm
Ty Newydd Farm
Hillbank Cottage
Pen-y-lan Cottage
Pen-y-lan
Twyn-y-waste
Tumplands
The West
Nant Ffin
Parlour Farm
Grace Dieu Court
Nant Wachan
Ford
Upper Llantrothy
FBs
Hendre Farm
Site of Grace-Dieu Abbey (Cistercian)
Abbey Meadow
Middle Hendre Farm
Raglan Lodge
Tumulus
Bowling Green Wood
Beech Grove
Summer House
Rolls of Monmouth Golf Club
Deer Park
Hillside
Lower Hendre
Hendre Great Wood
Limekiln Wood
Panterris Wood
Panterris
Millburn Wood
Calling Wood
Dingle Wood
Telltale Wood
Allan's Little Wood
Floodbrook House
The Oaks
Peartree Cottage
Gorse Cottage
Worthybrook

Llantilio Crossenny
Llandeilo Gresynni
Dyke Path
Park Farm
Moat
Weir
Mill Covert
Llantilio Mill
Nantyderri Farm
Llandroptby Farm
Perry Orchard Cottage
Holly Lodge
Gwraig
Penrhôs Farm
Farm Brake
Great Bottom
Maendy
Motte & Bailey
Cross Elms
Elms Farm
Commin
White House
Little Grange
The Grange
Pen-twyn Wood
Pont-yr-ychain Farm
Pont-yr-ychain
Pont-yr-ychain Wood
Tal-y-coed
Tal-y-coed Court
Pen-y-parc
Tal-y-coed Park
B 4233
White House Farm
Rosedale
WHITECASTL
Pant Wood
Marl Hill
The Pant
Pen-pwll-y-calch Cottage
Pen-pwll-y-calch Farm
Pen-pwll-y-calch Wood
New House
Red House Wood
Upper Red House
The Oaklands
Llanfihangel Ystum L
Mill House Farm
Pant-llwyd Wood

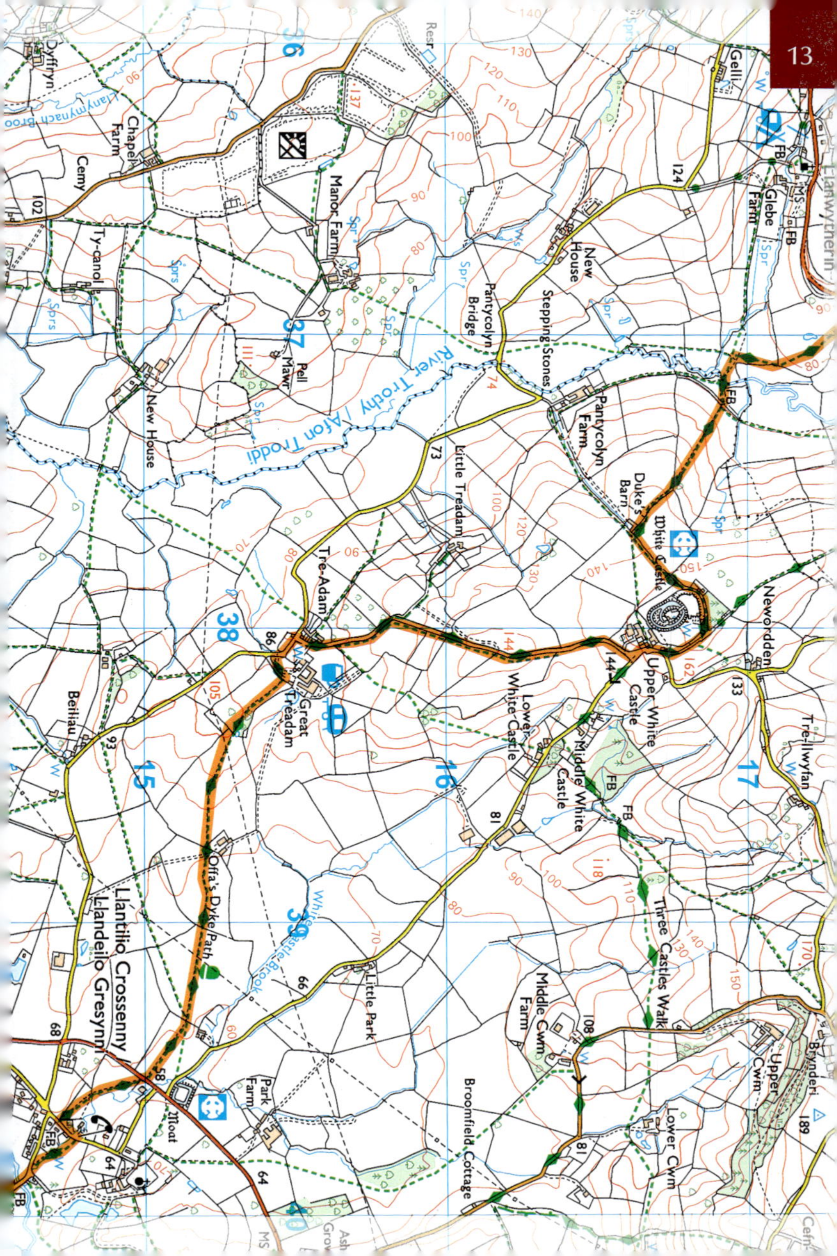
Dyffryn
Llanymynach Brook
Chapel Farm
Cemy
Ty-canol
Manor Farm
Pell Mawr
New House
River Trothy / Afon Troddi
Pantycolyn Bridge
Stepping Stones
New House
Gelli
Glebe Farm
Llanwytherin
Pantycolyn Farm
Duke's Barn
White Castle
Little Treadam
Tre-Adam
Great Treadam
Newordden
Upper White Castle
Lower White Castle
Middle White Castle
Tre-llwyfan
Beiliau
Offa's Dyke Path
Llantilio Crossenny
Llandeilo Gresynni
White Castle Brook
Little Park
Three Castles Walk
Middle Cwm Farm
Upper Cwm
Brynderi
Park Farm
Moat
Broomfield Cottage
Lower Cwm

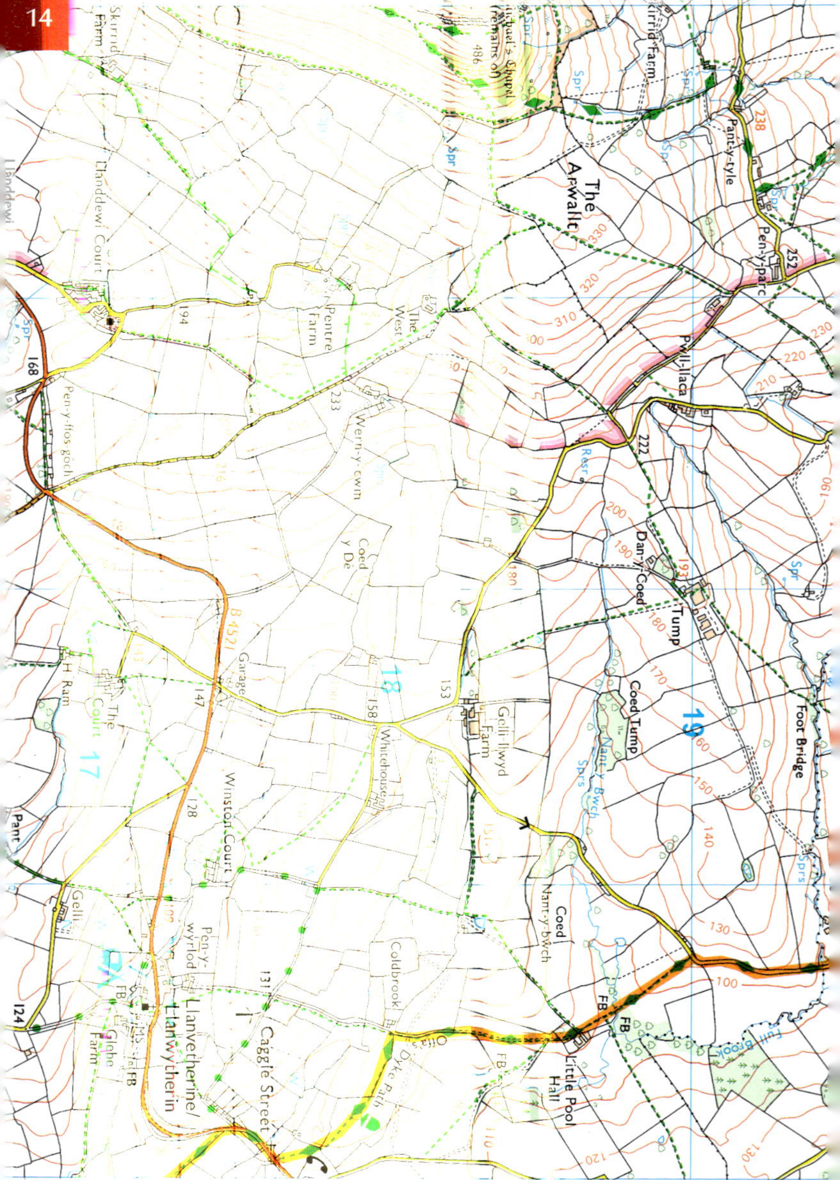
Skirrid Farm
St Michael's Chapel (remains of)
486
The Arwallt
Pant-y-tyle
Pen-y-parc
Llanddewi Court
Pentre Farm
The West
Pwll-llaca
Pen-y-ffos-goch
Wern-y-cwm
Coed y Dê
Dan-y-Coed
Tump
Coed Tump
B4521
Garage
H Ram
The Court
Gelli-llwyd Farm
Whitehouse
Foot Bridge
Nant y Bwch
Winston Court
Coed Nant-y-bwch
Gelli
Pen-y-wyrlod
Coldbrook
Llanvetherine/
Llanwytherin
Caggle Street
Dyke Path
Little Pool Hall
Glebe Farm
Full Brook
Resr
Llanddewi
Pant
17
18
19

Pandy to Hay-on-Wye
Start Lancaster Arms guest house, Pandy (SO 333 217)
Finish Butter Market, Hay-on-Wye (SO 228 424)
Distance 26.5km (16.5 miles)
Time 7–9hr
Pandy to Monmouth
Start Lancaster Arms guest house, Pandy (SO 333 217)
Finish Agincourt Square, Monmouth (SO 507 128)
Distance 26.2km (16.3 miles)
Time 6–8hr
Pandy
Ty-newydd
Pwll-y-wern
Werngifford
Wern-Gifford
Llanteems
Gilboa
Whitehouse
Court Wood
Campstone
Llanerch
Berry Bach
Upper Park
Cherry Orchard
Great Park
Old Park
Offa's Dyke Path
Full Brook
Hendre
Cherry Tree Cottage
Great Campston
Little Campston
Upper Kathlea
Holly Wood
Llangattock Lingoed
Ransley
Pentre
Crossway Cottages
Great House Cottage
Cwm Farm
Pen-rhôs
Common Farm
Pen-y-parc

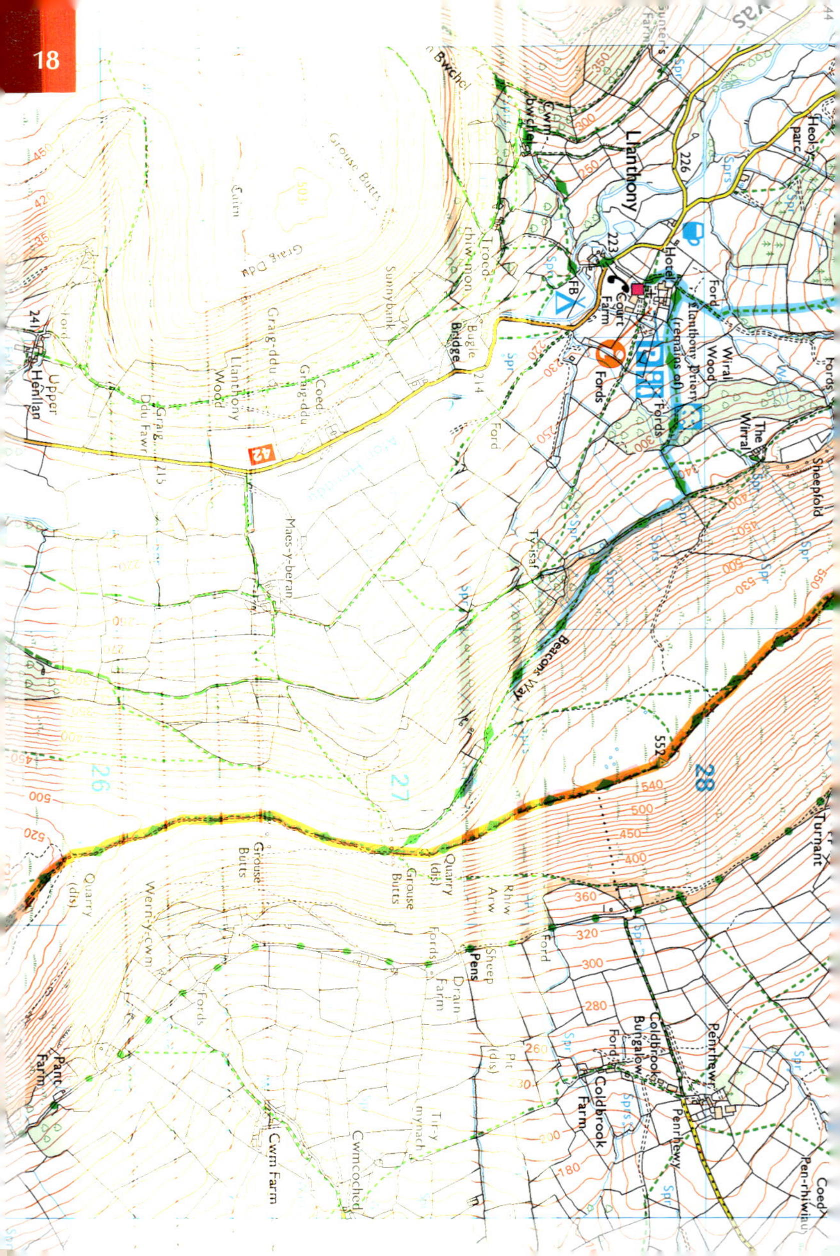
Llanthony
Llanthony Priory (remains of)
Hotel
Court Farm
Fords
Wirral Wood
The Wirral
Sheepfold
Heol-y-parc
Cwm-bwchel
Grouse Butts
Cairn
Graig Ddu
Sunnybank
Troed-rhiw-mon
Bugle Bridge
Coed Graig-ddu
Graig-ddu
Llanthony Wood
Graig Ddu Fawr
Upper Henllan
Maes-y-beran
Ty-isaf
Beacons Way
Turnant
Quarry (dis)
Rhiw Arw
Wern-y-cwm
Sheep Pens
Drain Farm
Pant Farm
Penrhewr
Penrhewy
Coldbrook Bungalow
Coldbrook Farm
Pit (dis)
Tir-y-mynach
Cwmcoched
Cwm Farm
Coed Pen-rhiwiau
42

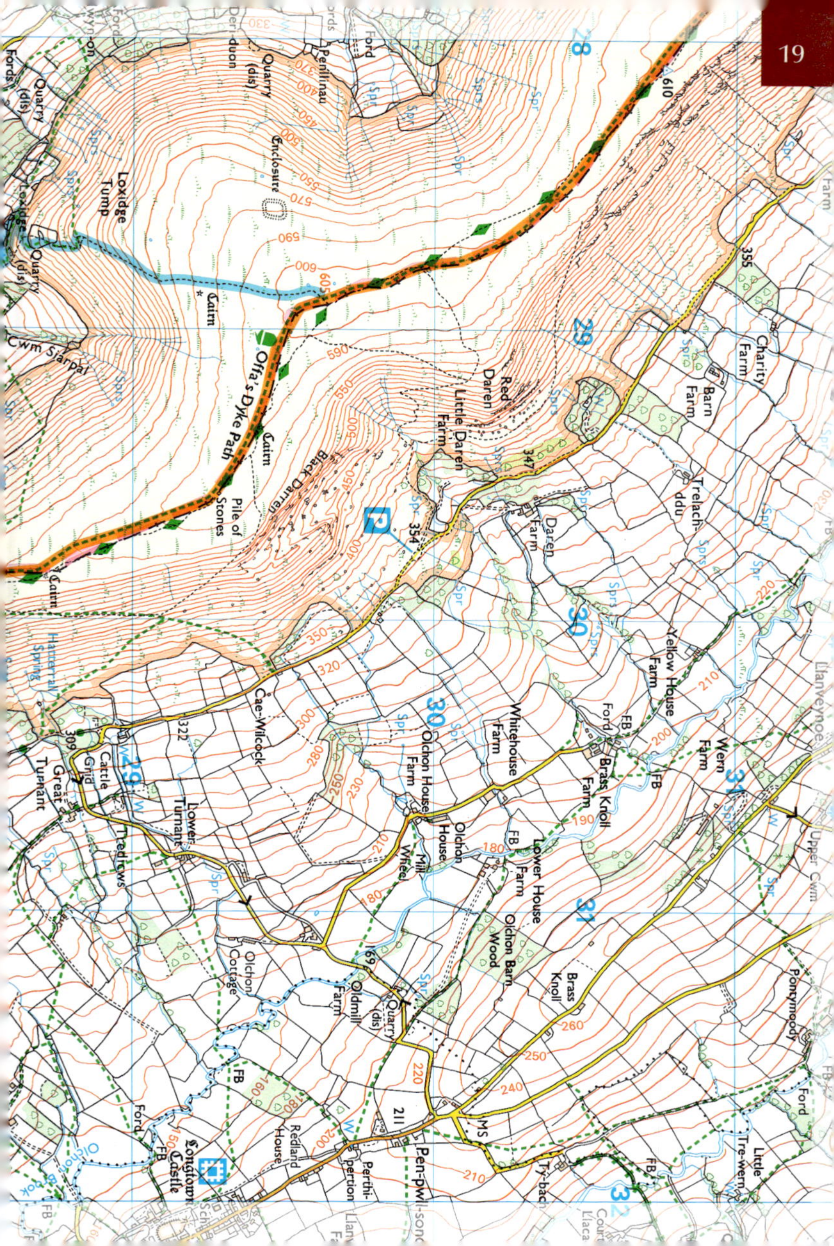

Offa's Dyke Path
Loxidge Tump
Cwm Siarpal
Enclosure
Cairn
Pile of Stones
Black Daren
Red Daren
Little Daren Farm
Daren Farm
Hatterrall Spring
Cae-Wilcock
Great Turnant
Cattle Grid
Lower Turnant
Tredrews
Olchon House Farm
Olchon House
Mill Wheel
Whitehouse Farm
Brass Knoll Farm
Lower House Farm
Olchon Barn Wood
Brass Knoll
Yellow House Farm
Wern Farm
Trelach-ddu
Barn Farm
Charity Farm
Llanveynoe
Upper Cwm
Pontymoody
Little Tre-wern
Ty-bach
Olchon Cottage
Oldmill Farm
Quarry (dis)
Redland House
Perthi-pertion
Longtown Castle
Olchon Brook

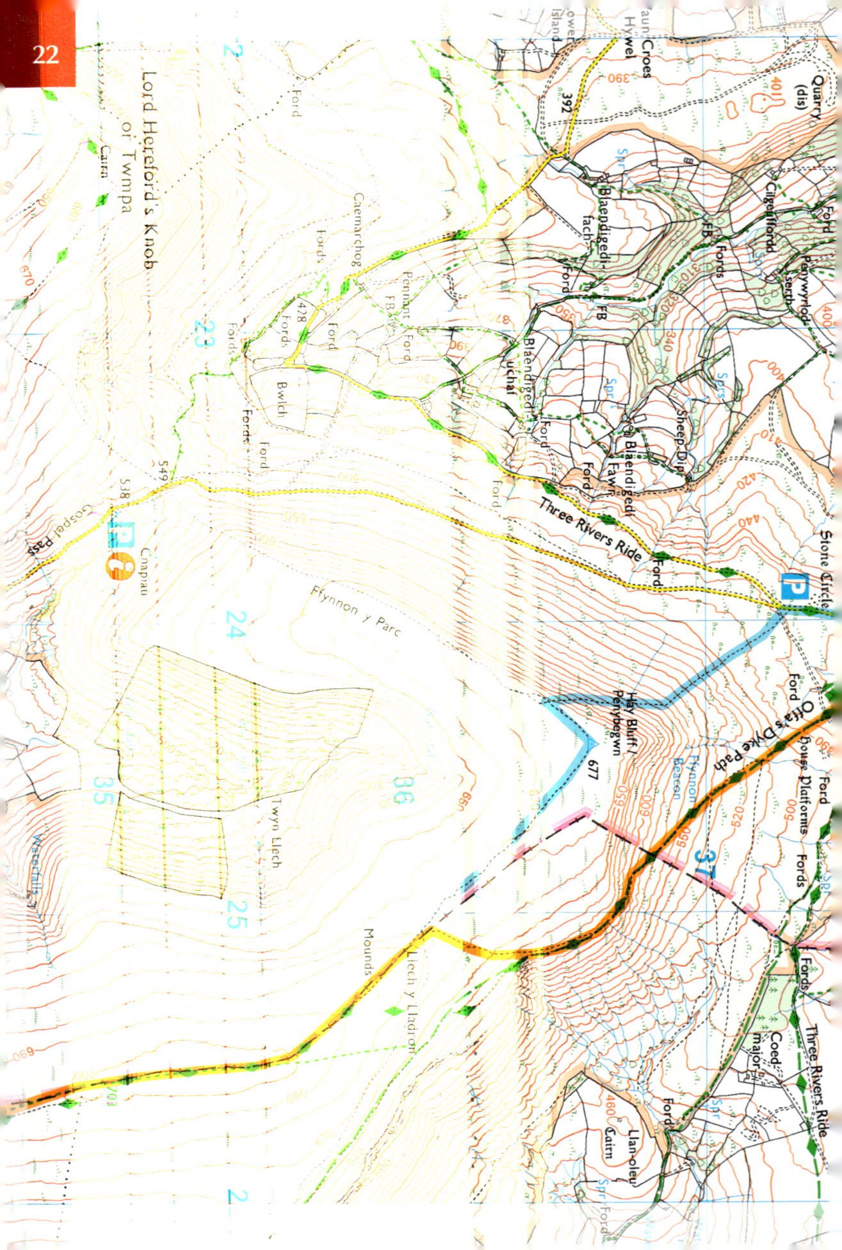
Lord Hereford's Knob or Twmpa
Cairn
Caemarchog
Fords
Pennant
Ford
FB
Bwlch
Gospel Pass
Chapiau
Ffynnon y Parc
Twyn Llech
Llech y Lladron
Mounds
Waterfalls
Hay Bluff / Penybegwn
Ffynnon Beacon
Offa's Dyke Path
House Platforms
Three Rivers Ride
Stone Circle
Sheep Dip
Blaendigedi Fawr
Blaendigedi Uchaf
Blaendigedi-fach
Cilgeuffordd
Penywyrlod
Quarry (dis)
Croes Hywel
Coed major
Llan-oleu
Cairn
Spr
Ford

Darren
Quarry (dis)
Wenallt
Allt Wood
Lower Wenallt
Wenallt-uchaf
Farside
Old House
Maes-coch
Cwmcoynant
Cattle Grid
Hill Farm
Quarry Ford
Cilonw
Penlan
Ty Allt
Waterfall
Spout
Neuadd-newydd
Penhenallt
Hen Allt Common
Cadwgan Farm
Cae'r bwla
Upper Danyforest
Llety-Evan Llwyd
Long Cairn
Pant-y-fithel
Wern Wood
Dan-y-capel
Quarries (dis)
Tack Wood
Twyn y Beddau
Cockalofty
Wern-Ddu
Lower Tack
New Forest
Esgyrn Brook
Pentre-Higgen
Ford
Craigau
The Birches
Upper
38
39
40

Hay-on-Wye to Kington

Start Butter Market, Hay-on-Wye (SO 228 424)

Finish Kington Museum (SO 295 566)

Distance 23km (14.5 miles)

Time 6–8hr

Hay-on-Wye to Pandy

Start Butter Market, Hay-on-Wye (SO 228 424)

Finish Lancaster Arms guest house, Pandy (SO 333 217)

Distance 26.5km (16.5 miles)

Time 7–9hr

Cwmithel
Cae'rneuadd Hill
Ty-mawr
Cwm-yr-eithin
Cae-Higgin
Pentwyn
Pen-Brilley
Waterfalls
Cwm yr Afr
Caeworthy Court
Llwyngwilliam
Wyndridge
Chapel Farm
Old House
Lower Bettws
Pant-y-cae
Ty-nesa
Penrhoel
Penycae
Old Penywrlodd
New Penywrlodd
Upper Bettws
Tump Farm
Bettws Dingle
Waterfall
Caballa Brook
The Banks
New Barn
Cwm
Cabalva Farm
MS
Bythel
Cwm-bwllfa
Crossway Farm
Crossfoot Farm
Standing Stone
New Plantation
Lower Wernypentre
Upper Wernypentre
Bronydd Wood
Little Gwernfythen
Gethin
Bronydd
Bronydd Farm
FB
Cwmbyddog
Gibbons Covert
Motte & Bailey
Court Evan Gwynne
Wet Covert
Moat
Offa's Dyke Path
Dismantled Railway
Lower House Farm
Pen-y-lan Wood
Penlan Farm
Clyro Brook
River Wye
Afon Gwy
Sch
Hotel
Mill (dis)
Pontvaen
A 438

Upper Lloyney
Blaencerde
Lower Blaencerde
Lloyney Wood
Llanyoyne Wood
Quarry (dis)
Offa's Dyke Path
Disgwylfa Hill
Baynham Hall
Newchurch
The Old Rectory
Great House
Sunnyside
Pen-y-Gwyddel
Llan-pica
Pontvane Farm
FB
Gilfach-yr-heol
Redborough Wood
Redborough
Little Wern
Little Mountain
Enclosure
Pit (dis)
Dolbedwin Wood
Dolbedwyn
Caeau
Red Lane
The Bush
Castle Farm
Resr
Crowther's Pool
Newgate
Cwmithel
Cwm-yr-eithin
Pen-twyn Settlement
Pentwyn
Penycastell
Spr
Sprs

Llan-Howell (dis)
Wern Farm
Foyce
Lane House
Gladestry
Sch
Yewtree Bank
Quarry (dis)
Broken Bank
The Camp
Penfaen
FB
Glanyrafon
Llan-yr-afon Wood
Cross
Llan-y-Felin
Upper Rabber
Rabber Dingle
Burnt House
Stone House
Quarry (dis)
Pen-twyn
Huntington Castle (remains of)
Lanerch-y-frain
Huntington
Upper House
Lower House
Huntington Court
Church Coppice
Wernol Brook
Fairfields
Lower Hengoed
Hengoed
Llanbella
Hill Gate
Shop Farm
Yewtree Farm
Penllan
Grove Farm
Resr
Green Lane Cottage
Hill Farm
Gorse Plantation
Upper New House
Cae-cwm
Blackfir Wood
Bank
Bungy's Head
Upper Hengoed
Turret Tump
The Dingle
Little Gwern-y-bwch
Middle Hengoed

Sunnybank
Granner Wood
Evenjobb Hill
Hanging Bank Cottage
Benbow Wood
Pettyfields Wood
Upper Radnor Wood
Knill
Offa's Dyke
Barland
Stocking
Offa's Dyke Path
Motte & Bailey
Hazel Point
Middler Wood
KNILL CP
Burfa
Burfa Farm
Burfa Bog Nature Reserve
Tumulus
Motte
Burfa Bank
Fort
White House
Knill Farm
Ditchyeld Bridge
Upper House Farm
Lower House Farm
FBs
Tan House Plantation
Knill
FB
Knill Bridge
Cross
Weir
Knill Court
Lower Harpton
Ford
Lower Harpton Farm
Croft Plantation
Watery Lane
The Turnpike
Herrock Cottage
Knill Garraway Wood
Knill Garraway
Herrock Hill
LOWER HARPTON CP
Offa's Dyke Path
Offa's Dyke
Rushock Hill
Holywell
Savages Wood

Bridge End
Whitton Bridge
Whitton Court
Little Gilfach
Gilfach Hill
Offa's Dyke
Gilfach
Impton Wood
Norton
Caravan Park
Litton Court
Lower Litton
B4356
Furrow Hill
PRESTE
Gilfach Wood
Green Wood
Ackhill House
Ackhill Farm
Iron Barn
Grove Bridge
Weir
Dolley Green
The Grove
Upper Dolley
Dolley Old Bridge (FB)
Dolley Farm
Yew Tree Farm
FB
Gumma
Sally Hall
Mound
Discoed
Lower House
Upper House
Quarry (dis)
Gumma Wood
The Warre
Rowley Farm
Tumulus
Cwmadee
Lower Rowley
Bwlch
Thorn
Upper Rowley
Timber Hill Wood
Pen Offa
Hilltop Plantation
Rowley Wood
North Wood
Cold Oak
Upper Dunn's Plantation
Chandlers
Dunn's Lane
Sunnybank

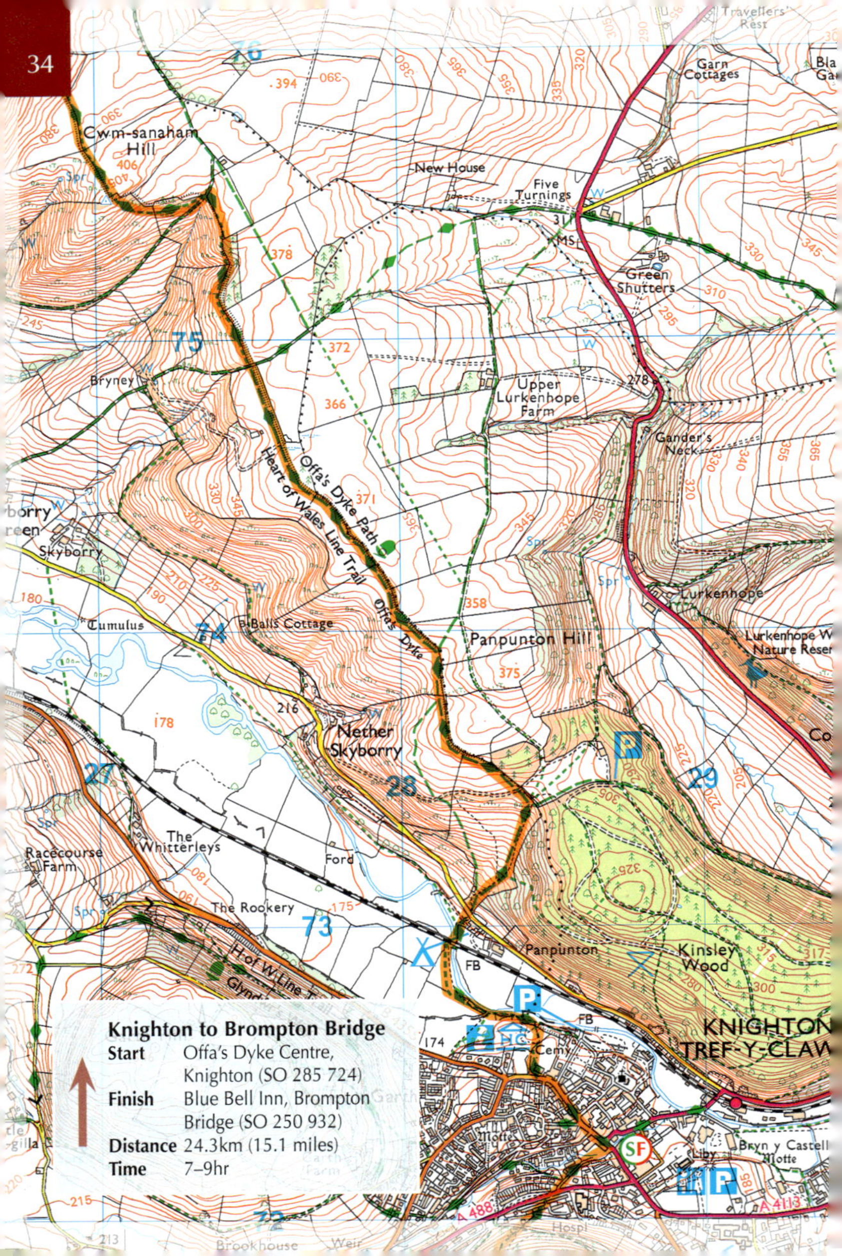

Knighton to Brompton Bridge

Start	Offa's Dyke Centre, Knighton (SO 285 724)
Finish	Blue Bell Inn, Brompton Bridge (SO 250 932)
Distance	24.3km (15.1 miles)
Time	7–9hr

Cefn Hepreas
WATERDINE CP
Jack Mytton Way
Offa's Dyke
Homestead
Cwm-Burholes
Offa's Dyke Path
Llandinshop
Little Selley
Lower Brook Cottage
Quarry (dis)
Llandinshop Wood
Garbett Hall
Black Hall
Ford
Waverhous Wood
Selley Hall
Upper Trebert
Selley Cross
Brynorgan
Llanfair Court
Jack Mytton Way
Lloyney
Graig
Lower Trebert
Selley Hall Cottage
Trebert Wood
The Lane House

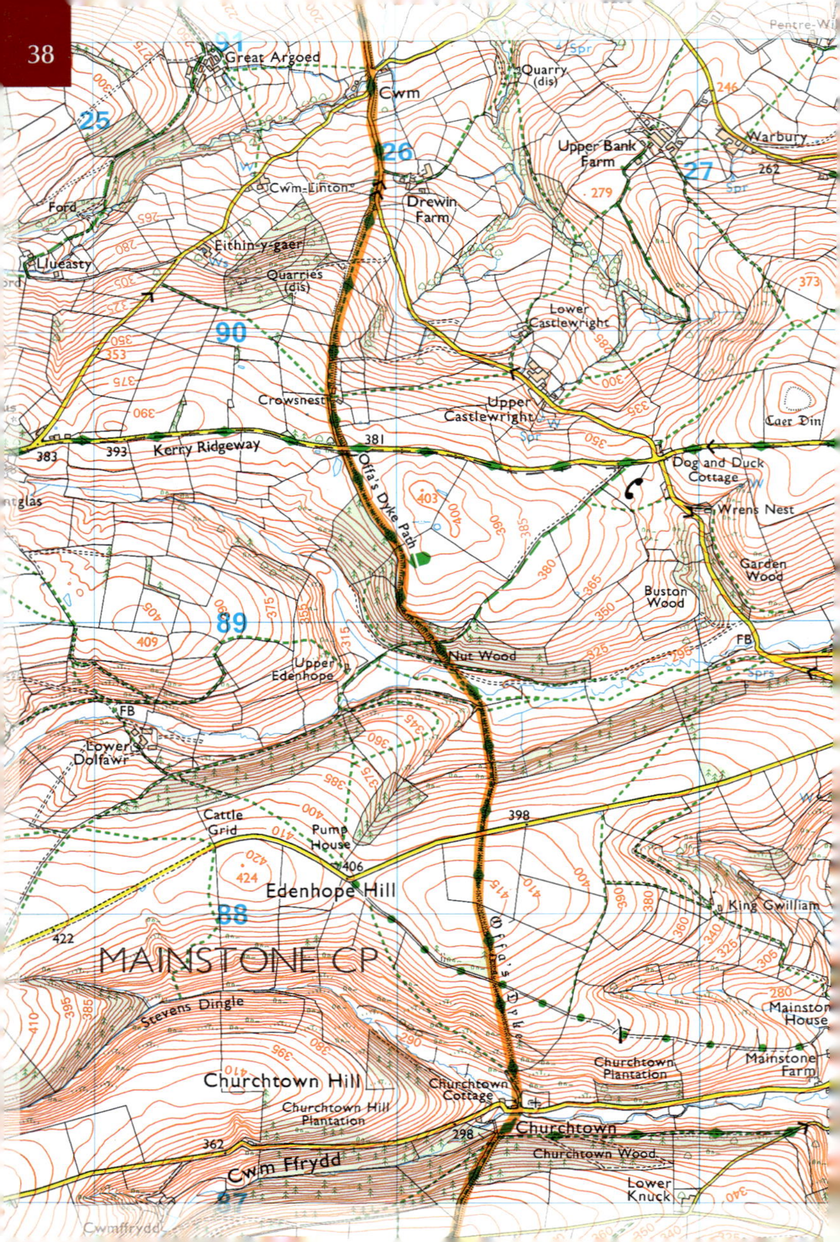
Great Argoed
Cwm
Quarry (dis)
Upper Bank Farm
Warbury
Cwm-Linton
Drewin Farm
Ford
Llueasty
Eithin-y-gaer
Quarries (dis)
Lower Castlewright
Upper Castlewright
Crowsnest
Caer Din
Kerry Ridgeway
Dog and Duck Cottage
Wrens Nest
Offa's Dyke Path
Garden Wood
Buston Wood
Upper Edenhope
Nut Wood
FB
Lower Dolfawr
Cattle Grid
Pump House
Edenhope Hill
King Gwilliam
MAINSTONE CP
Stevens Dingle
Mainstone House
Mainstone Farm
Churchtown Plantation
Churchtown Hill
Churchtown Cottage
Churchtown Hill Plantation
Churchtown
Churchtown Wood
Cwm Ffrydd
Lower Knuck
Offa's Dyke

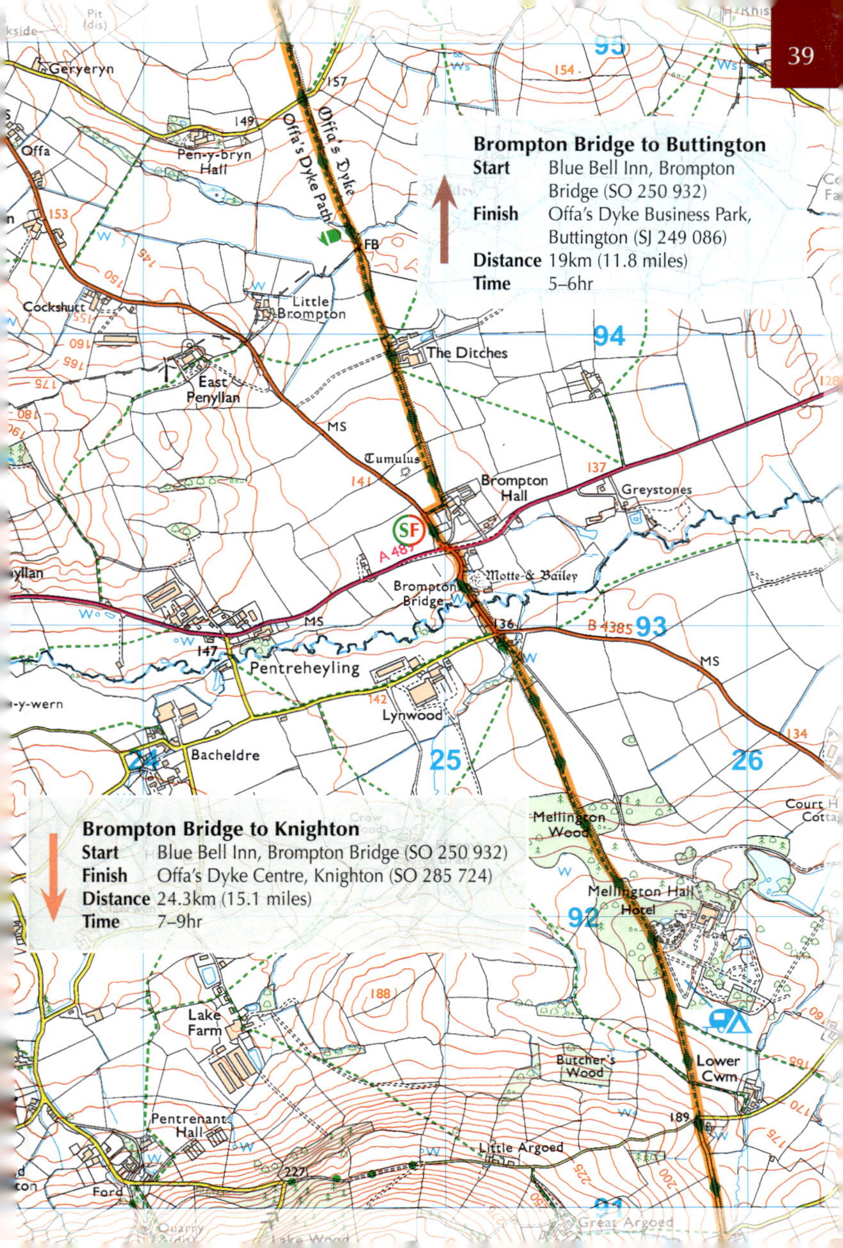

Brompton Bridge to Buttington

Start Blue Bell Inn, Brompton Bridge (SO 250 932)
Finish Offa's Dyke Business Park, Buttington (SJ 249 086)
Distance 19km (11.8 miles)
Time 5–6hr

Brompton Bridge to Knighton

Start Blue Bell Inn, Brompton Bridge (SO 250 932)
Finish Offa's Dyke Centre, Knighton (SO 285 724)
Distance 24.3km (15.1 miles)
Time 7–9hr

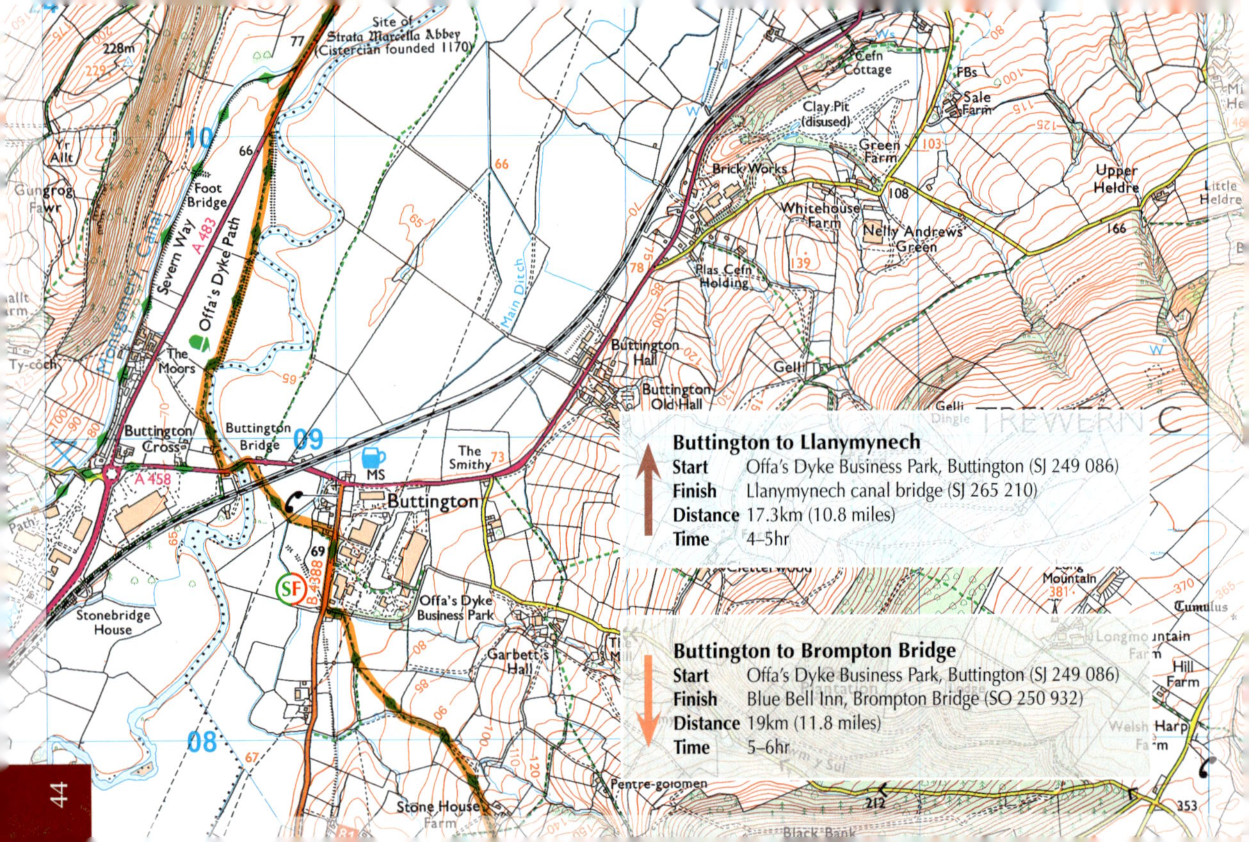

Buttington to Llanymynech

Start Offa's Dyke Business Park, Buttington (SJ 249 086)
Finish Llanymynech canal bridge (SJ 265 210)
Distance 17.3km (10.8 miles)
Time 4–5hr

Buttington to Brompton Bridge

Start Offa's Dyke Business Park, Buttington (SJ 249 086)
Finish Blue Bell Inn, Brompton Bridge (SO 250 932)
Distance 19km (11.8 miles)
Time 5–6hr

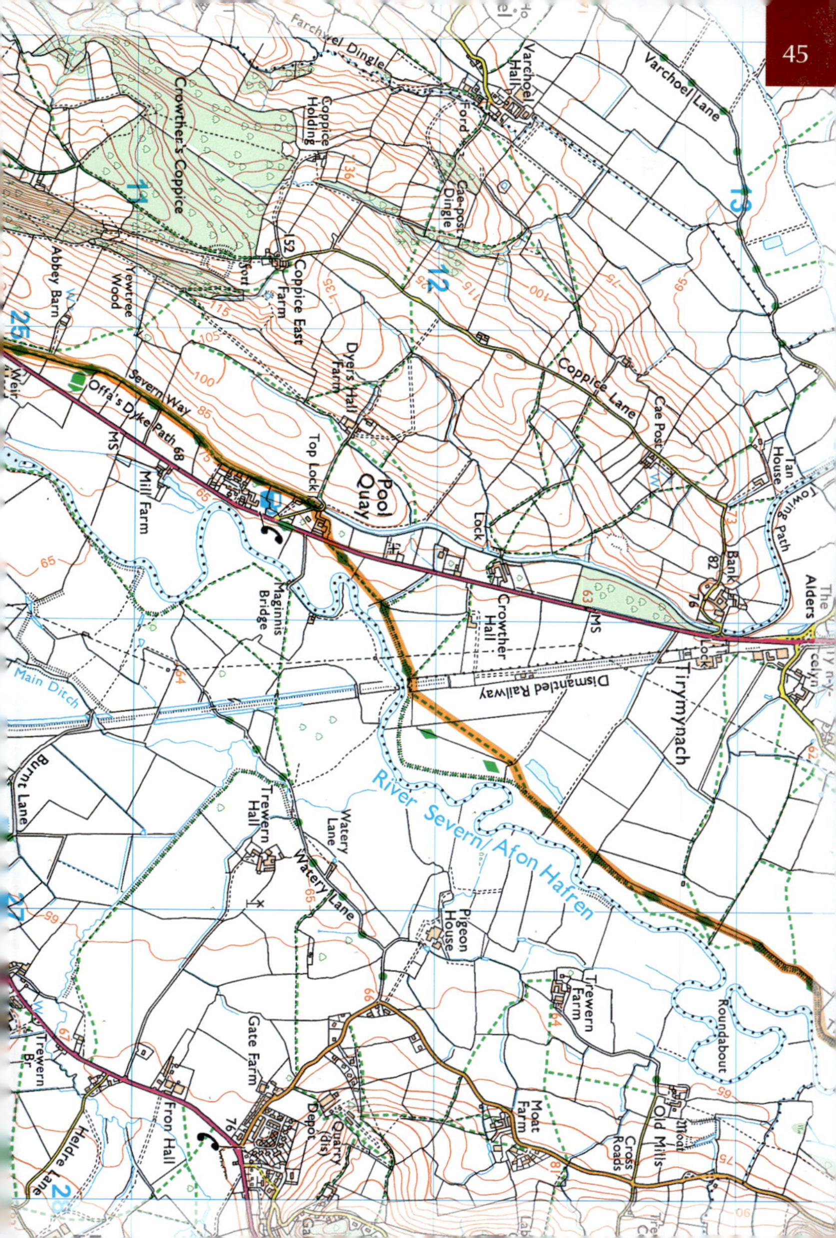

Farchwel Dingle
Varchoel Hall
Varchoel Lane
Ford
Crowther's Coppice
Coppice Holding
Cae-post Dingle
Abbey Barn
Yewtree Wood
Fort
Coppice East Farm
Coppice Lane
Dyers Hall Farm
Severn Way
Offa's Dyke Path
Weir
MS
Mill Farm
Top Lock
Pool Quay
Cae Post
Tan House
Towing Path
Lock
Crowther Hall
Bank
Alders
Maginnis Bridge
Main Ditch
Dismantled Railway
Tirymynach
Burnt Lane
Trewern Hall
Watery Lane
River Severn/ Afon Hafren
Pigeon House
Trewern Farm
Roundabout
Gate Farm
Trewern Br
Fron Hall
Heldre Lane
Depot
Quarry (dis)
Moat Farm
Cross Roads
Old Mills
Moat

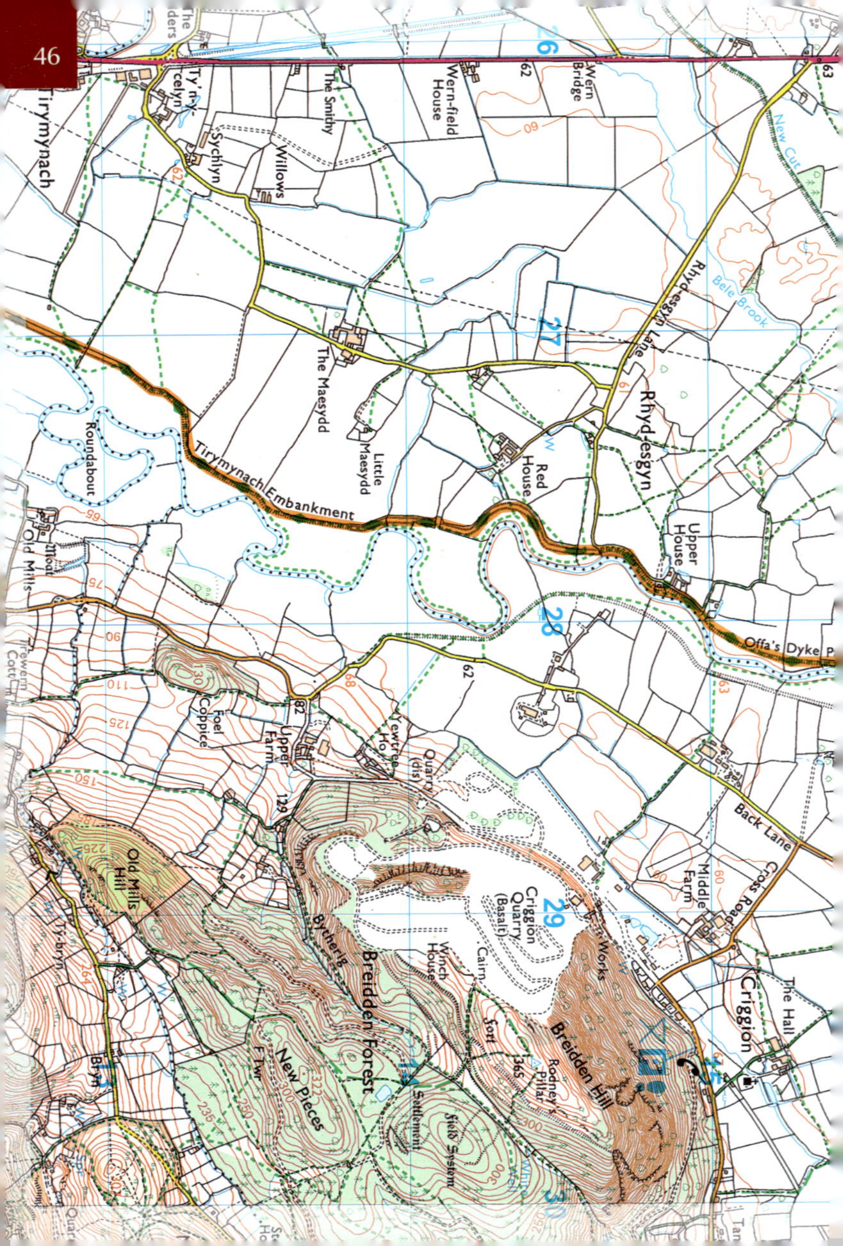
Tirymynach
Ty'n-y-celyn
Sychlyn
Willows
The Smithy
Wern-field House
Wern Bridge
New Cut
Bele Brook
Rhyd-esgyn Lane
Rhyd-esgyn
The Maesydd
Little Maesydd
Roundabout
Tirymynach Embankment
Red House
Upper House
Offa's Dyke P
Old Mills
Moat
Trewern Cott
Foel Coppice
Upper Farm
Yewtree Ho
Quarry (dis)
Back Lane
Cross Road
Middle Farm
Criggion Quarry (Basalt)
Works
Criggion
The Hall
Old Mills Hill
Bytherig
Breidden Forest
Winch House
Cairn
Fort
Rodney's Pillar
Breidden Hill
Ty-bryn
Bryn
New Pieces
F Twr
Settlement
Field System
White Well

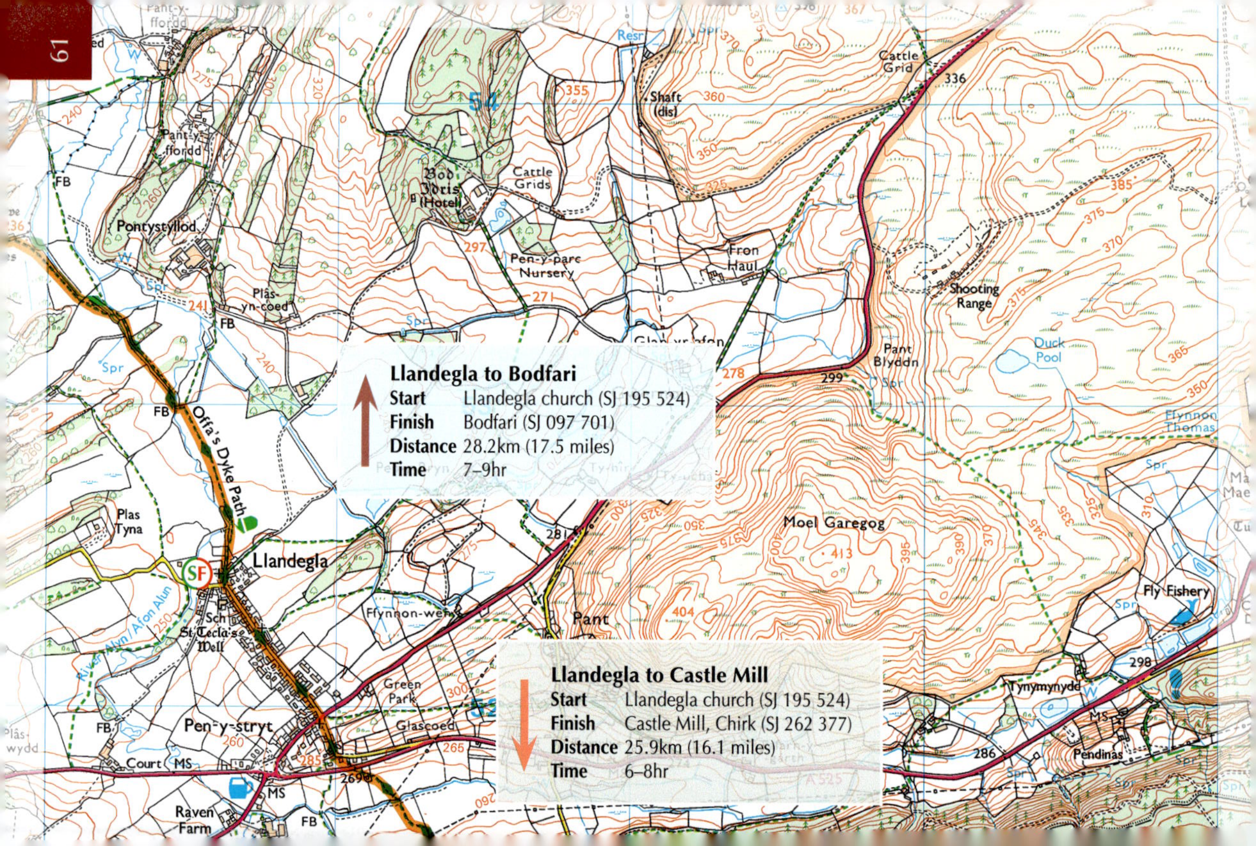

Llandegla to Bodfari

Start Llandegla church (SJ 195 524)
Finish Bodfari (SJ 097 701)
Distance 28.2km (17.5 miles)
Time 7–9hr

Llandegla to Castle Mill

Start Llandegla church (SJ 195 524)
Finish Castle Mill, Chirk (SJ 262 377)
Distance 25.9km (16.1 miles)
Time 6–8hr

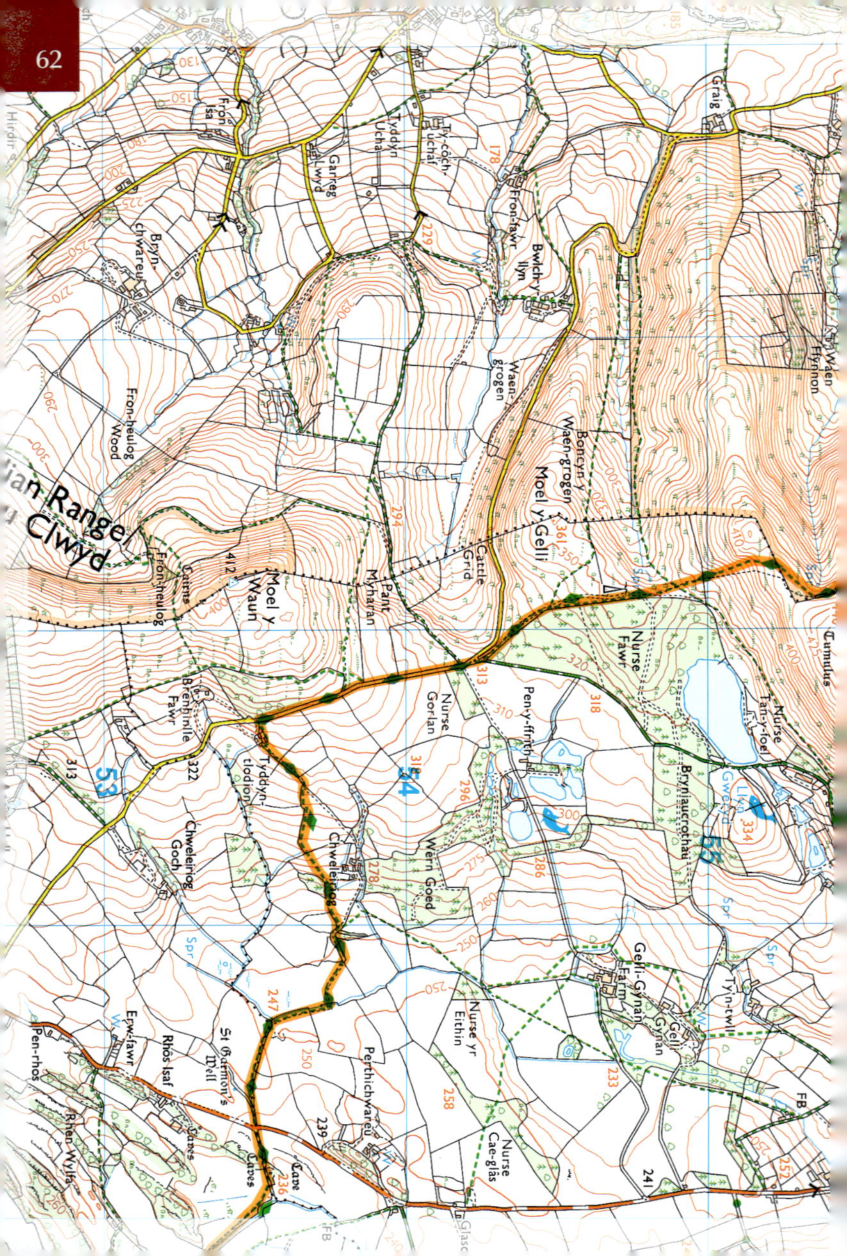
Clwyd
Moel y Waun
Moel y Gelli
Boncyn y Waen-grogen
Waen-grogen
Bwlch-y-llyn
Fron-fawr
Graig
Waen Ffynnon
Fron-heulog Wood
Fron-heulog
Bryn-chwareu
Fron Isa
Garreg Llwyd
Tyddyn Ucha
Ty-coch-uchaf
Pant Myharan
Cattle Grid
Brenhinlle Fawr
Tyddyn-tlodion
Chweleiriog Goch
Chweleiriog
Nurse Gorlan
Nurse Fawr
Nurse Tan-y-foel
Tumulus
Pen-y-ffrith
Bryniaucrothau
Llyn Gweryd
Wern Goed
Gelli-Gynan Farm
Gelli Gynan
Ty'n-twll
Nurse yr Eithin
Perthichwareu
Nurse Cae-glâs
St Garmon's Well
Rhos Isaf
Erw-fawr
Pen-rhos
Rhen Wylfa
Caves
Cave
53
54
55

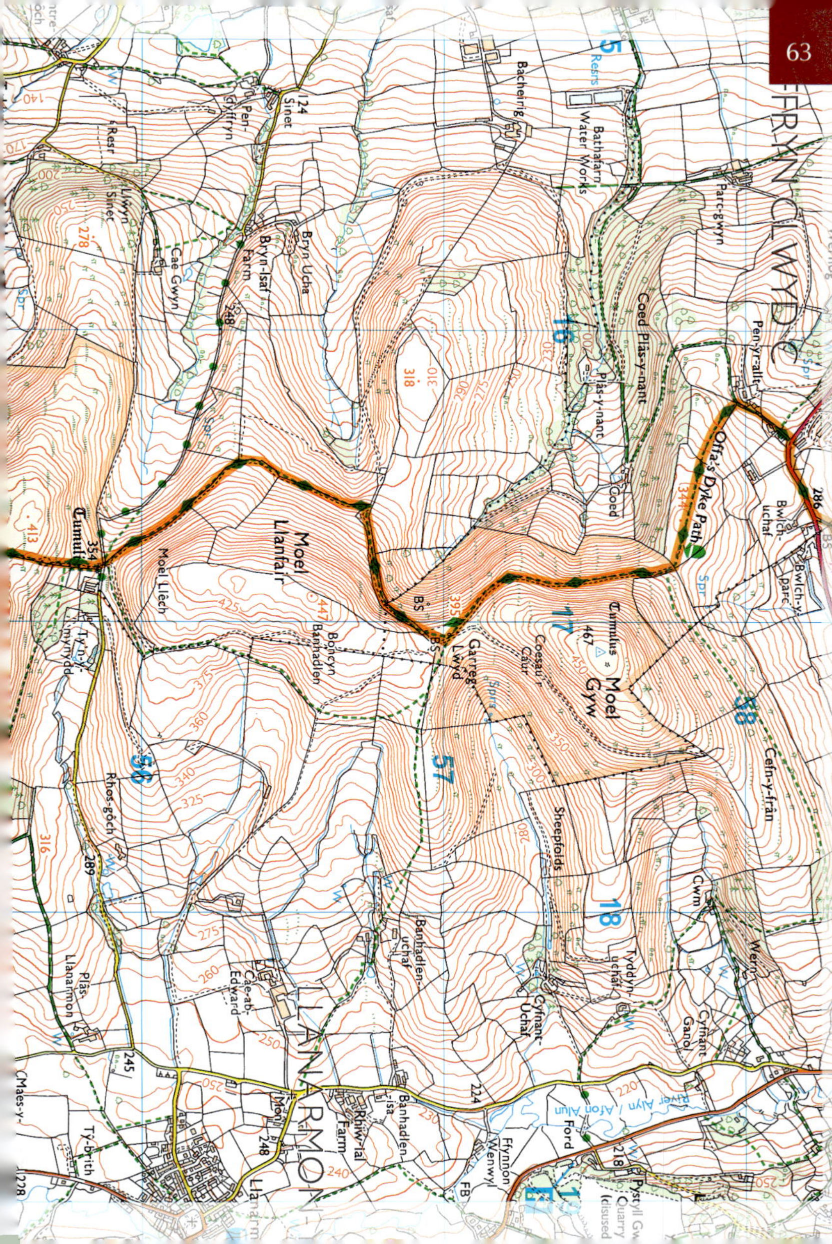
Moel Llanfair
Moel Gyw
Offa's Dyke Path
Coed Plâs-y-nant
Plâs-y-nant
Coed
Llanarmon
Bryn-Isaf Farm
Bryn Ucha
Cae Gwyn
Llwyn Sinet
Sinet
Pen-gyffryn
Resr
Bacheirig
Bathafarn Water Works
Resrs
Parc-gwyn
Pen-yr-allt
Bwlch-uchaf
Bwlch-y-parc
Tumuli
Tumulus
Moel Llêch
Ty'n-y-mynydd
Boncyn Banhadlen
Garreg Lwyd
Coesau Cŵn
Cefn-y-frân
Sheepfolds
Rhos-goch
Plâs-Llanarmon
Cae-ab-Edward
Rhiw'ial Farm
Banhadlen-isa
Banhadlen-uchaf
Cyfnant-Uchaf
Tyddyn-uchaf
Cyfnant Ganol
Cwm
Wern
Tŷ-brith
River Alyn / Afon Alun
Ford
Ffynnon Wenwyl
FB
Quarry (disused)
Spr

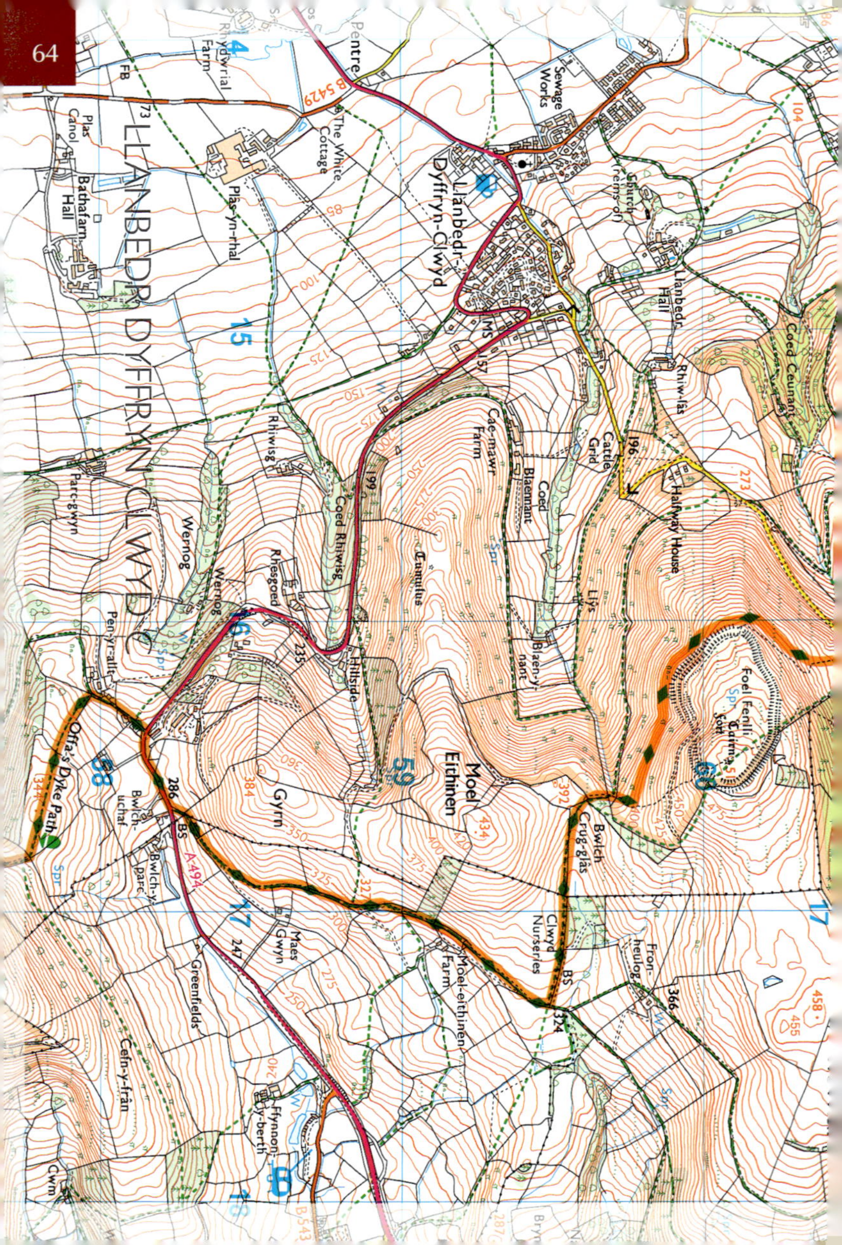
LLANBEDR DYFFRYN CLWYD
Llanbedr-Dyffryn-Clwyd
Pentre
B 5429
Rhydywrial Farm
Plas Canol
Bathafarn Hall
The White Cottage
Plas-yn-rhal
Sewage Works
Church (rems of)
Llanbedr Hall
Rhiw-fås
Coed Ceunant
Cattle Grid
Halfway House
Cae-mawr Farm
Coed Blaennant
Blaen-y-nant
Llys
Foel Fenlli
Fort
Cairns
Coed Rhiwisg
Rhiwisg
Rhesgoed
Tumulus
Hillside
Wernog
Parc-gwyn
Pen-yr-allt
Offa's Dyke Path
Bwlch-uchaf
Bwlch-y-parc
Gyrn
Moel Eithinen
Bwlch Crug-glas
Clwyd Nurseries
Fron-heulog
A 494
Maes Gwyn
Moel-eithinen Farm
Greenfields
Cefn-y-fran
Ffynnon-y-berth
Cwm
B543

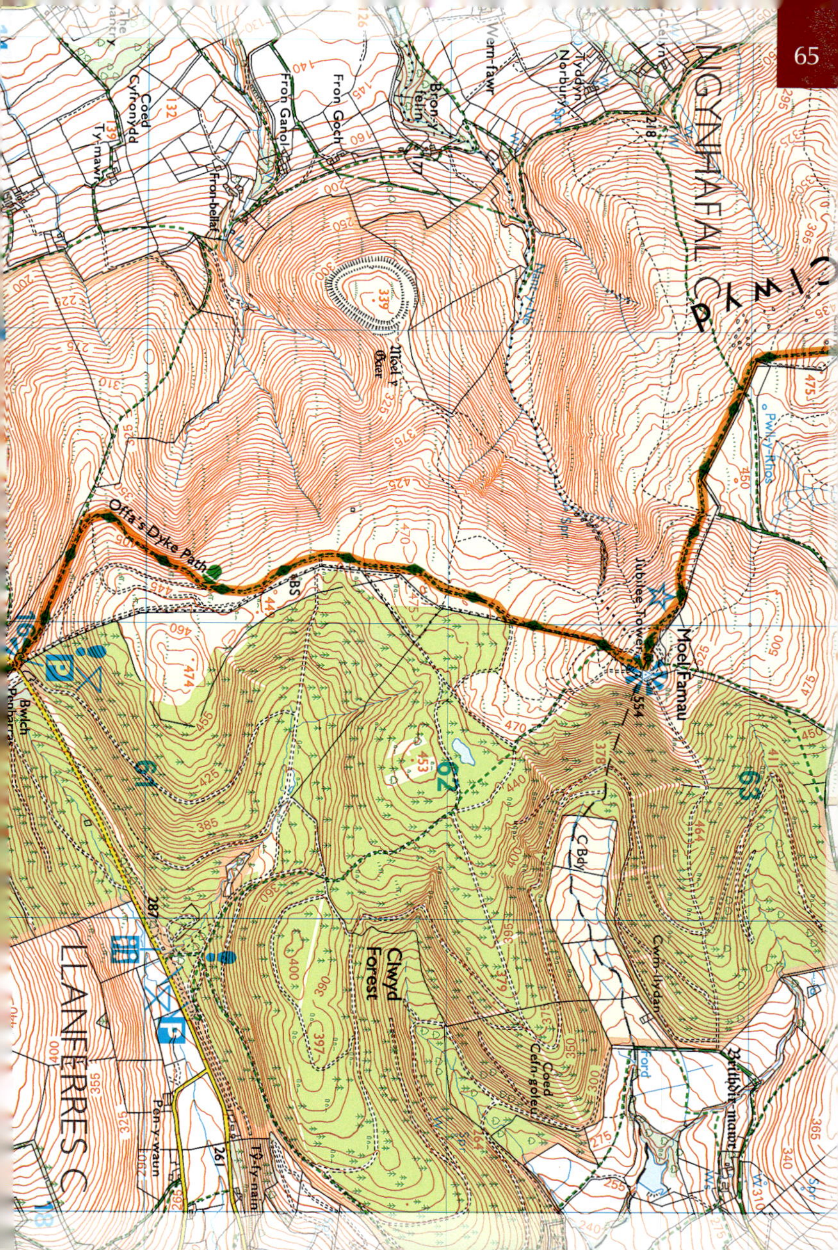
Offa's Dyke Path
Moel Famau
Jubilee Tower
Clwyd Forest
Coed Cefn-goleu
Cwm-llydan
Moel y Gaer
Fron Ganol
Fron Goch
Wern-fawr
Coed Cyfronydd
Ty-mawr
Fron-bellaf
Pen-y-waun
Pwll-y-Rhos
LLANFERRES
Ford

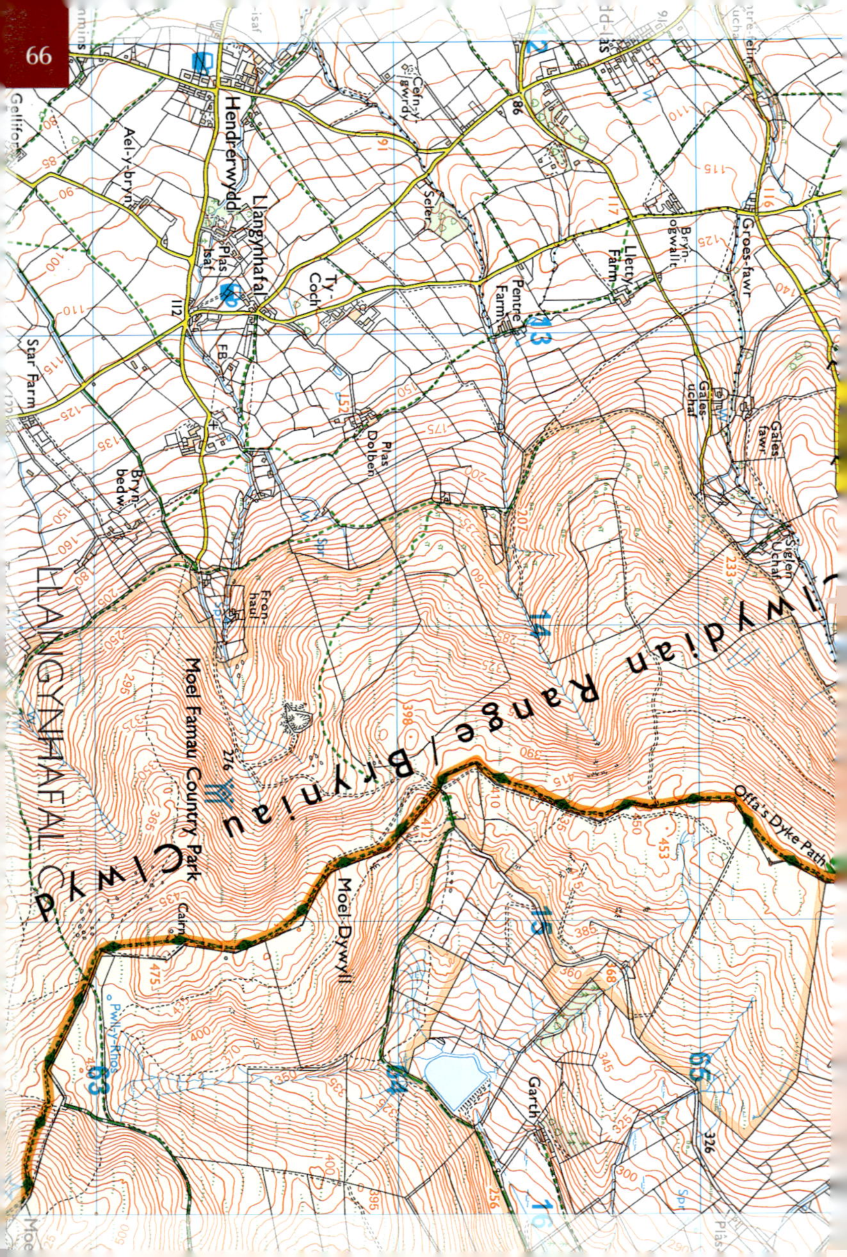
Hendrerwydd
Llangynhafal
Plas Isaf
Ael-y-bryn
Star Farm
Bryn-bedw
Ty-Coch
Seler
Pentre Farm
Llecty Farm
Groes-fawr
Gales uchaf
Gales fawr
Plas Dolben
Fron-haul
Moel Famau Country Park
Moel Dywyll
Offa's Dyke Path
Clwydian Range / Bryniau Clwyd
LLANGYNHAFAL CP
Pwll-y-Rhos
Garth

White House
Llangwyfan
Highfield Park
Rest
Vron Yw House
Pen Wyn
Fron-gelyn
Rhiwbebyll
Pen-y-bryn
Fron-dyffryn
Tan-y-bryn
Glyn Arthur
Penycloddiau fort
Mound
Boulder
Coed Pen-y-bryn
Shaft (dis)
Blaen-y-cwm
Pen-y-bryn
Levels (dis)
Moel Arthur fort
Cattle Grid
Sheepfold
Bryn-ffynnon
Moel Plas-yw
Moel Eyan
Plas-yw
Cattle Grid
Firwood Farm

Castell
Waen Goleugoed
Waen Farm
Corn-bwch
Fachwen Farm
The Meadows
Maes Gwyn
Llwyn Derw
Afon Bach
North Wales Pilgrim's Way
Glanrafon
Rhyd-y-Gwrta
Pant Ifan-goch
Hotel
Rhuallt
Plas Coch
Summer Hill Covert
Sychdyn
Ty Gwyn
Tynewydd
Summer Hill
Henafon Smithy
Ty-mawr
Pistyll
Bryn Gronw
Ty Mawr
Maen Efa
Garreg Fawr
Cildaugoed
Tremeirchion
Plesyn
St Beuno's College
Rhuallt Castle
Onen-Asaph
Res (cov)
Clwydian Range/ Bryniau Clwyd
Tumuli
Moel Maenefa
Brynffirion Farm
Mine (dis)
Cairn
Cae-gwyn
Penuchaf
Mynydd Bychan
Tumulus
Waen Hiiln
Bryngwyn Mawr
Earthwork
Pant Glas
Offa's Dyke Path
Glyn-uchaf
Coed Bron-fawr
Aelwyd-uchaf
C Bdy
Aelwyd-uchaf Belt
ROMAN (course of)

Marian Ffrith
Tyddyn-y-cyll
Ochr-y-marian
Plassau
Cumulus
The Flash
Pentre Cwm
Foel Fferm
Shaft (dis)
Cave
Plâs-onn
Tumulus
Marian-bach
Shaft (dis)
Marian Cwm
Church Wood
Tumulus
Cwn Road
Bryniau Isaf
Cwm
Tan-y-fforest
Bwlch
Tumuli
Pwllhalog
Pen-y-rhôs
Bryn Glas
Pen-y-rhos
C Bdy
CWM C
Ffynnon
Cil-haul
Springs
Tan-y-bryn
Penisa'r Waen
Hendre-fawr
Penisa'r Mynydd
Ty'n-y-caeau
Mynydd y Cwm
Coed Cwm
Tumuli
Coed Rhedyn-côch
Rhedyn Côch
Offa's Dyke Path
Ffrith Fawr
Bodlonfa
Coed yr Ynys
Ty Celyn
Coed Jenny-Morgan
Tynewydd
Waen-wen
Glan-llyn
Tumulus
Pant-y-dulath
Fron
Pen-y-mynydd
North Wales Pilgrim's Way
Airfield
Plas yn Cwm
Coed

Dyserth
DYSERTH
B5119
Bodrhyddan Gardens
Coed Holmach
Sewage Works
Penisa
Dyserth Hall
Hotel
Shaft (dis)
Graig Fawr
Bryniau
Bryn y-felin
Stamber Wen
Dyserth Castle (site of)
Pit (dis)
Nurseries
Tre-castell
Offa's Dyke Path
Caves
Shaft (dis)
Ty Newydd
Pandy Mill
Farm
Maes Hiraddug
Ochr Y-foel
Cave
Quarry (disused)
Pant-yr-hespin
Moel Hiraddug
Fort
Y Foel
Foel Fferm
Pentre Cwm
Hottia
Bryn Cnewyllyn
Morwylfa
Tyddyn-y-cyll
Tumulus
Marian-bach
Marian Ffrith
Cave
Plâs-onn
Ochr-y-marian
Plassau
Marian-Mawr
Marian Mill Farm
Henfryn Hall
Mia Hall
Gop Farm
Ffynnon Wen
Gop Hill
Gop Cave
Cairn
Erw Wen
Gloddiau Wood
Sewage Works
Tumulus
North Wales Pilgrim's Way
Pen-Y-Cefn-isaf
Glan Ffyddion
Pen y Cefn Uchaf
Bron Heulog
Tumulus
Terfyn
Pwllhalog

PRESTATYN
Meliden / Gallt Melyd
Gwaenysgor
TRELAWNYD AND GWAENYSGOR
Woodland Park
North Wales Path
Prestatyn Hillside Nature Reserve
Coed Yr Esgob
Plas Newydd Farm
Caravan Site
Llys Farm
Playing Field
Top Nant Farm
Top Nant Woods
The Dingle
Coed Bell
Tellia Farm
Bryn-llwyn
Pant y Coed
Home Farm
Home Wood
Stoney Wood
Acre Wood
St Elmo's Summer House
WT Station
New Plantation
Tumulus
Shafts (dis)
A547
B5120

Prestatyn to Bodfari

Start	Prestatyn seafront (SJ 060 837)
Finish	Bodfari (SJ 097 701)
Distance	20km (12.4 miles)
Time	5–6 hr

The descent from Cwm-sanaham Hill to Brynorgan, with the Dyke seen climbing Llanfair Hill in the background (Stage 6)

LEGEND OF SYMBOLS USED ON ORDNANCE SURVEY 1:25,000 (EXPLORER) MAPPING

ROADS AND PATHS — **Not necessarily rights of way**

M1 or A6(M)	Motorway
A 35	Dual carriageway
A30	Main road
B 3074	Secondary road
	Narrow road with passing places
	Road under construction
	Road generally more than 4 m wide
	Road generally less than 4 m wide
	Other road, drive or track, fenced and unfenced
	Gradient: steeper than 20% (1 in 5); 14% (1 in 7) to 20% (1 in 5)
Ferry	Ferry; Ferry P – passenger only
	Path

S Service Area

S Service Area

7 Junction Number

T1 Toll road junction

RAILWAYS

	Multiple track } standard gauge
	Single track } standard gauge
	Narrow gauge or Light rapid transit system (LRTS) and station
	Road over; road under; level crossing
	Cutting; tunnel; embankment
	Station, open to passengers; siding

PUBLIC RIGHTS OF WAY

	Footpath
	Bridleway
	Byway open to all traffic
	Restricted byway

The representation on this map of any other road, track or path is no evidence of the existence of a right of way

ARCHAEOLOGICAL AND HISTORICAL INFORMATION

✣	Site of antiquity
⚔ 1066	Site of battle (with date)
VILLA	Roman
Castle	Non-Roman
☆	Visible earthwork

Information provided by English Heritage for England and the Royal Commissions on the Ancient and Historical Monuments for Scotland and Wales

OTHER PUBLIC ACCESS

• • •	Other routes with public access	The exact nature of the rights on these routes and the existence of any restrictions may be checked with the local highway authority. Alignments are based on the best information available
◆ ◆ ◆	Recreational route	
◆ ◆ ◆	National Trail; Long Distance Route	
- - - -	Permissive footpath	Footpaths and bridleways along which landowners have permitted public use but which are not rights of way. The agreement may be withdrawn
— — —	Permissive bridleway	
• • •	Traffic-free cycle route	
1 1	National cycle network	route number – traffic free; on road

ACCESS LAND

DANGER AREA — Firing and test ranges in the area. Danger! Observe warning notices

MANAGED ACCESS — Access permitted within managed controls, for example, local byelaws. Visit **www.access.mod.uk** for information

England and Wales

Access land boundary and tint

Access land in wooded area

Access information point

Portrayal of access land on this map is intended as a guide to land which is normally available for access on foot, for example access land created under the Countryside and Rights of Way Act 2000, and land managed by the National Trust, Forestry Commission and Woodland Trust. Access for other activities may also exist. Some restrictions will apply; some land will be excluded from open access rights. The depiction of rights of access does not imply or express any warranty as to its accuracy or completeness. Observe local signs and follow the Countryside Code. Visit **www.countrysideaccess.gov.uk** for up-to-date information

BOUNDARIES

National

County (England)

Unitary Authority (UA), Metropolitan District (Met Dist), London Borough (LB) or District

(Scotland & Wales are solely Unitary Authorities)

Civil Parish (CP) (England) or Community (C) (Wales)

National Park boundary

VEGETATION

Limits of vegetation are defined by positioning of symbols

Coniferous trees

Non-coniferous trees

Coppice

Orchard

Scrub

Bracken, heath or rough grassland

Marsh, reeds or saltings

HEIGHTS AND NATURAL FEATURES

52 ·	Ground survey height	Surface heights are to the nearest metre above mean sea level. Where two heights are shown, the first height is to the base of the triangulation pillar and the second (in brackets) to the highest natural point of the hill
284 ·	Air survey height	

HEIGHTS AND NATURAL FEATURES (continued)

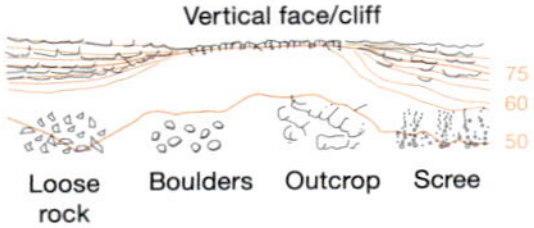

Contours are at 5 or 10 metre vertical intervals

- Water
- Mud
- Sand; sand and shingle

SELECTED TOURIST AND LEISURE INFORMATION

- Building of historic interest
- Cadw
- Heritage centre
- Camp site
- Caravan site
- Camping and caravan site
- Castle / fort
- Cathedral / Abbey
- Craft centre
- Country park
- Cycle trail
- Mountain bike trail
- Cycle hire
- English Heritage
- Fishing
- Forestry Commission Visitor centre
- Garden / arboretum
- Golf course or links
- Historic Scotland
- Information centre, all year
- Information centre, seasonal
- Horse riding
- Museum
- National Park Visitor Centre (park logo) e.g. Yorkshire Dales
- Nature reserve
- National Trust
- Other tourist feature
- Parking
- Park and ride, all year
- Park and ride, seasonal
- Picnic site
- Preserved railway
- PC Public Convenience
- Public house/s
- Recreation / leisure / sports centre
- Roman site (Hadrian's Wall only)
- Slipway
- Telephone, emergency
- Telephone, public
- Telephone, roadside assistance
- Theme / pleasure park
- Viewpoint
- Visitor centre
- Walks / trails
- World Heritage site / area
- Water activites
- Boat trips
- Boat hire

(For complete legend and symbols, see any OS Explorer map).

OFFA'S DYKE PATH

This trail map accompanies Mike Dunn's guidebook to walking Offa's Dyke Path National Trail, described from south to north, between Sedbury and Prestatyn. The guidebook features annotated 1:100,000 mapping alongside detailed step-by-step route description and lots of planning and other information about local history, geography and wildlife.

Penrhos Farm and Skirrid Fawr from below The Grange (Stage 2)